Ant Hill Odyssey

Not So Comfortable as It Looks

WILLIAM M. MANN

*A*nt *H*ill
*O*dyssey

With Illustrations and Maps

AN ATLANTIC MONTHLY PRESS BOOK
LITTLE, BROWN AND COMPANY · BOSTON
1948

ATLANTIC—LITTLE, BROWN BOOKS
ARE PUBLISHED BY
LITTLE, BROWN AND COMPANY
IN ASSOCIATION WITH
THE ATLANTIC MONTHLY PRESS

*Printed simultaneously
in Canada by McClelland and Stewart Limited*

PRINTED IN THE UNITED STATES OF AMERICA

T O   L U C I L E

Go to the ant, thou sluggard;
consider her ways, and be wise . . .

Solomon, Proverbs VI. 6

Contents

Illustrations

Ant Hill Odyssey

CHAPTER I Runaway

W HEN I WAS FOURTEEN my mother thought a military school would be the thing for me, not because she wanted me to be a fighting man, but because she was sure that in addition to other things I ought to learn to keep my shoes shined. She made inquiries among various friends, one of whom was Preston H. Leslie who had been Governor of Kentucky and twice territorial Governor of Montana. He knew the right place — Staunton Military Academy, "an ideal home for manly boys, situated at an ideal altitude in the Blue Ridge Mountains of Virginia. Personal instruction and pure spring water." The Commandant, Captain William G. Kable, had been an advertising man for a drug company, and his letters made not going to his school the acme of disaster.

With a second-class railroad ticket and money in my pocket for food en route, the journey to Virginia was a great adventure. I knew little of that state except that a great-great-grandfather of mine had left there and gone to Kentucky. Thence the family had moved ever westward, generation by generation, through Missouri and Kansas to Montana. I was reversing the procedure in five days.

The land of the Dakotas was interesting because I had been thoroughly steeped in "Hiawatha," and as we rode among the hills that Hiawatha and Mudjekeewis had used as brickbats in their fight, I glued my nose to the window of the car and recited to myself as much of the poem as I knew. In Kentucky the haystacks, conical in shape instead of the good flat ones that we had in Montana, seemed queer.

✻ ✻ ✻

I had reached Montana the convenient way, by being born there. It did away with the long journey in a covered wagon which my parents had had to make from Missouri. By the time I came along in 1886 the Indians had stopped shooting in the region of Helena and no herds of buffalo held up caravans a half-day at a time. The year I was born, the Sioux Indians staged one of their last sizable fights, and it was in that year too that Hornaday shot buffalo to mount the group still featured prominently in the National Museum.

Helena had grown up around the site where two early prospectors, about to return East after failure to find any pay dirt, took a last chance and discovered one of the famous placer mines from which was taken many millions in gold. "Last Chance Gulch," as it was known, later became Helena's Main Street. But Helena in my day had all the attributes of a great city. In fact it was a great city on a small scale. Faith in the future was its keynote and monuments to that faith were the Broadwater Natatorium and the Broadwater Hotel. The Natatorium was then the largest enclosed swimming pool in the world. It was heated by a natural geyser, making it hot at one end and cool at the other. Toads thronged around an artificial fountain outside and I once collected a couple of handfuls of them. I wrapped them in my handkerchief, but my mother, who did not appreciate toads, dissuaded me from bringing them home.

My mother had been brought from Wales to the United States by her father, her mother having died when she was very little. They settled at first in Missouri, and then she went with a covered-wagon migration to the westward, as did so many people from this part of the States. She remembered the Welsh language all her life, though she would not teach it to me. She was a steadfast Baptist and read the Bible a great deal; sometimes, when a passage was not clear to her, she would refer to the Scriptures in Welsh.

She had a great fondness for her friends, as well as a deep compassion for others poorer than she. In later years, whenever she heard of families in poverty or need, she would inevitably send me that evening with jams, jellies, and other foods for the children. I used sometimes to tease her about "Mrs. Mann's soup kitchen" because there was scarcely a day when someone did not drop in.

The year of my father's death, 1893, was also the year of a great depression; banks failed, and my mother lost some of the small amount of money that my father had left. However, she owned two houses on Eighth Avenue, one of which she sold, and then we moved out of the other into smaller quarters, where the difference in rent helped us get along. When things were particularly hard, she received a check through the will of one of her aunts who had lived in the Welsh community at Dodgeville, Wisconsin.

My father was a harness maker, something of an inventor, and an amateur taxidermist. He was a tall, slender man with blue eyes and a long black beard, and he had a long-barreled, ten-bore shotgun. One of my first recollections is of a large horned owl which he had shot and mounted. His great delight was in hunting and fishing, and the first sound that I can remember was the *honk-honk* of geese in the back yard — Canadian geese and snow geese, kept there to be used as decoys.

My father died when I was seven, but I have memories of two hunting trips with him. The first time I was wrapped in a buffalo robe and I stayed in a pit from which the others banged away at wild geese. I can remember playing with the still warm bodies of those shot. The other trip was after antelope on the Yellowstone. I remember looking into pools of clear water and seeing large fish. I entertained myself by collecting toads that were hopping about on small rocks, and, upon seeing a brightly colored, banded water snake, was filled with a desire to have one and keep it as a pet. I was left in a cabin by myself during the actual hunting, but the men returned with a fine pronghorn, with one horn bent in a curious way. My father mounted it, and I still have it, an example of early taxidermy.

It was from the roof of Smith's fish store on Helena's Main Street that I watched the animals from other parts of the world as they went by in circus parades. There for the first time I saw an African elephant in chains marching. After seeing a number of these parades, I reported at home that I had made a discovery about circuses: "There is something more, something in a tent." When I was nine, somebody took me to a circus performance, and since then circuses have been an integral part of my life.

That was a memorable summer also because I went to Chicago to visit my half-sister, Lily, and her husband Charlie, of whom I was very fond. There was Grant Park with its beautiful flower gardens; and above all Lincoln Park. Lincoln Park and its zoo were beyond anything I had dreamed of. There were lions and tigers, seals and an elephant, and a great big policeman. He was nice to me; for some time in my boyhood daydreams I envisaged myself as a policeman in the Lincoln Park Zoo — where I could walk around wearing a big mustache, swing a club, spend all my time with the animals, and be nice to visiting children.

Next door to us in Helena lived Emma Huffer, the first socialist I ever knew. She explained to me that eventually all races would be quite the same, and this would be brought about by the Japanese. She also ate great quantities of granulated sugar on her lettuce, which never seemed right to me. The first year I saw the long parade of Gentry's Dog and Pony Show, Emma told me that the small boys clad in red jackets, leading the ponies, and spaced far apart to make the parade look longer, were really cannibals. I believed this for a whole year, and then found that these cannibals were simply fellows like me, and that even I, by going to the circus grounds, putting on red cap and jacket, and leading a pony for long miles through Helena on a hot August day, could afterward see the show — for nothing. Mrs. Tom Thumb came with the show one year — an elderly widow at the time, making up for her small size by a vindictive attitude toward us children who crowded around her as she got out of the royal coach in which she had ridden during the parade. She did, however, make a nice speech about herself and General Tom Thumb from the center ring during the performance.

Our local carriage painter was Montana Jack McCrimmon, who had been with Buffalo Bill both scouting and in the Wild West Show, and had finished his public career by riding, balanced on his shoulders, on a horse galloping around the hippodrome track of the Adam Forepaugh Circus. Montana Jack still wore his hair long and curly. One drawback to the enjoyment of hearing him talk and watching him paint was that his very elderly mother would insist that we drink cups of "imported English breakfast tea" — very strong and black and bitter. One of his regular jobs was to keep in repair the gaily painted wheels of Mr. Beinhorn's Northern Pacific Express wagon.

Late one spring, when I had been frittering away my time in the seventh grade, Mr. Beinhorn came to me with great news. He was quitting the express company, had leased a place in Orofino Gulch, and was to realize his lifelong dream of being a dairy farmer. I was to be his chief cowherd during the summer. It was going to be life in the great open spaces, full of adventure but with no responsibility, except for the herd.

Each morning I would accompany the cows out to the grazing ground; then there was nothing required of me until I brought them home in the evening. But there were animals to collect: chipmunks, an occasional woodchuck, once a pine squirrel and once a grouse, all slaughtered recklessly with the Flobert .22 that Mr. Beinhorn had given me.

I got hundreds of chipmunks, and had I known how to prepare specimens, to make my own flat skins and to preserve the skulls, my collection might well be worth while today. All I did then was make flat skins and pin them to the wall of my room. If I had used salt, alum, and arsenic, the room would not have smelled so stale, and Dermestes beetles would not have destroyed the skins.

7

The Beinhorns also kept ducks, which I was allowed to feed. One morning in the water pan was what seemed to me a miracle. There were two things in it: they were three-eighths of an inch long, they had enormous oars on each side, and they swam around and around. I took the water pan into my room to keep these treasures forever. They were not there when I looked in the pan the next morning, and it was years before I knew that they were "water boatmen" — bugs that live in the water but fly from place to place at night.

Somebody gave me a bird cage that had seen better days and I kept this to hold any captive I might get. When I heard about drowning out ground squirrels, I carried buckets and buckets of water and poured them down a hole. The little ground squirrel that I caught in this manner came out gasping, completely exhausted. I put him in the cage, in a warm place where he would soon dry out. He dried out, and simply spread the flimsy wire bars and left.

I had started that summer catching animals for pets — after reading, in the Helena Public Library, Dan Beard's *American Boy's Handy Book.* It told how to do everything that a boy was interested in. There were instructions on how to make traps, and I tried the "Figure 4" trap, which required only a box, two sticks, and a bit of whittling with one's pocketknife. The animal was to come in, nibble at the bait at the end of stick number 2, release the trap, and the box was to fall on him. But the animal always got out when I raised the box. Then I took a sheet of wet paper, put it over the top of a jar, and cut two slits in it crosswise. Mr. Beard's plan for the animal was that when the paper got dry and hard, you put some bait on the top, and a chipmunk would come, take the bait, and fall into the jar. My difficulty was that my jars were always too small and the chipmunk jumped out again.

Sunday Schools were a part of my life; during the two summers that I functioned as cowherd, I walked into Helena, three miles away, every Sunday morning. My parents were Baptists, but I liked the Presbyterian teacher, so for these two years I attended both classes, never missing a Sunday. I still have the prizes I received for perfect attendance — Captain Mayne Reid's *Afloat in the Forest*, and Dana's *Two Years Before the Mast*. Both of these books affected me very much. I wanted to go to sea, and used to climb telegraph poles, when nobody was looking, to accustom myself to the mast-climbing that I would have to do. One must go to sea in order to be shipwrecked and then go floating in a canoe through a forest. *Swiss Family Robinson* was also a favorite. Mother Robinson kept all sorts of gewgaws in a box which she called her "treasure chest," so I started one, and put into it all the worthless things that I could pick up, hoping that they would come in handy later on.

The hours that I was not in school, or tending to my newspaper route, were spent for the most part in the public library. When I was twelve I was allowed in the adult stacks, where I soon discovered Rider Haggard. His books were about Africa, and peopled by Umslopogas, the Zulu chieftain, the ape woman, dying Englishmen, and the hero, Allan Quatermain. Reading these would make anybody an Africophile. I resolved immediately to make Africa my life's work. The dying (or dead) Englishman in the stories always had in his room a well-thumbed copy of Epictetus or Spinoza, evidently necessary to African exploration, so I got out the works of Epictetus and read them without a great deal of understanding. Spinoza, too, I read, but being a devout Baptist and Presbyterian I gave him up because I felt that he might weaken my faith. The *Ingoldsby Legends* were also frequently mentioned by Haggard. I tried them, too, in order better to qualify myself, but could not make much out of them. I read Kipling's *Jungle Books*, and *Tom Sawyer* and *Huckleberry Finn*. There was also *Life on the Plains*, with a vivid frontispiece showing two men facing each other with long Bowie knives in their hands.

Perhaps best of all was *Toby Tyler, or Ten Weeks with the*

Circus, and its sequel, *Mr. Stubbs' Brother.* These were about a boy who ran away with the circus and gave me a knowledge of the circus which was most impressive to those who knew no more about it than I did.

Living in a land of daydreams, I was not quite sure what I wanted to do: join a circus, be a shipwrecked sailor, wander through Central Africa saying "thee" and "thou" to my dark companions, or swing by one hand on the bough of a tree and live among the animals, like Mowgli. I practised this latter on a horizontal bar, without any great success.

There were interesting characters along the road from Helena to Orofino, chiefly prospectors. The hills of Montana are dotted with holes, each a lost hope of the man who dug it to find pay dirt. One very old man with whom I often used to chat was placer mining. I asked him once if he was getting gold and he replied with a good German accent, "Oh, yes, blenty." I have often wondered how much gold was "blenty." There was another one on the other side of the road with whom I often stopped and talked. He had prospected all his life, but he would beam at me and say, "Kid, I'm going to strike it pretty soon." That winter he bought a barrel of gunpowder, sat on it and dropped a lighted match into it. The next summer I would walk by the place where he had lived, sometimes at night with the play of moonlight on his cabin, and think that I saw him. There was no fear in me, because he had been a good friend.

One of the well-known characters in Helena was Tommy Cruze. When I knew him, he was a wealthy man, the proprietor of one of our banks. Before that he had been a grubstake prospector. The method of grubstaking was this: Some merchant, or somebody with money, would outfit a man who would start out prospecting for gold. The grubstake consisted of a sack of flour, a side of bacon and a few cartridges for the prospector's .44. The understanding always was that if he struck it, the grubstaker would get 50–50 on the mine. Tommy Cruze had dug, investigated, and otherwise prospected a dozen, or perhaps a hundred, places without luck. He came back to his wealthy grubstaker, asked for another stake, and was told, "I can't do it, Tommy. Too often have I lost money on you." So Tommy went out by himself and struck a mine, later known as the Drum Lummond Mine. He sold it for a million dollars cash and a million in stock, and after that everything he did turned into money. He bought abandoned mines around Missoula, and they paid. He became one of our most prominent citizens. He married, and he sent his daughter to Paris to be educated. Although he was a devout Catholic, he was a great personal friend of our Reverend McNamee of the Baptist Church. One story is that he had donated $37,000 for a spire on the cathedral. Money was hard to get for the other spire, and the clergy approached Tommy on the subject. He resented it. The clergy tactlessly reminded him of his past sins, and he replied frankly, with an Irish brogue, "Rather than give you another damn cent I'll join Brother McNamee and go to hell with the Baptists!"

When I was twelve, Mr. Beinhorn moved to Stanchfield Lake in Prickly Pear Valley, and I entered a new world. There was a rambling frame house, a tremendous barn, and an ice shed. To me, the ice shed was the biggest building in the world (except Montana Wesleyan University, which was four stories high and built of brick). I planned to buy the shed later to turn it into a zoo. In the evenings I would draw my plans on pieces of wrapping paper. The polar bears were to be in the left corner, elephants in the center, and lions in the right corner.

In the meantime, behind the Beinhorns' home was an abandoned outhouse. The front and back were completely out, but a wooden seat with two holes was still there. A couple of placer pans set in these holes made wonderful aquaria. The lake and the adjoining stream were reeking with unknown creatures; little Johnny Darters lived well in my aquaria and so did tadpoles. The wonder of watching a tadpole slowly change and turn into a frog! Once when I had brought a field mouse into the zoo and was ministering to his needs, an awful thing happened. The field mouse gave a shriek of pain, and a long, thick worm appeared out of his head, just back of his ear, and then went in again. This was my first suspicion that nature is not always kind.

Early one September morning I was bringing the cows in for milking when something new to my experience showed up: a little black-and-white animal with a bushy tail trotted along not showing the slightest fear of me. It was my first skunk, and I followed it at a discreet distance, though not certain what it was. Other wild animals scurried away at my approach, and I spent some time in observing this one that paid no attention to me. In consequence, I was late bringing in the cows.

Mr. Beinhorn was angry, and gave me a berating that seriously hurt my feelings. I realized that bringing in a herd of dairy cattle late for milking was an unpardonable crime, and being such a criminal I must get away. So I walked out of the house, around the lake, down to the other end, and stayed hidden back of the dam until at last I saw the milk wagon speeding up the road toward Helena; then I went back to my room, took my Flobert, a few cartridges, and my twenty-five cents, and started down the valley. A flock of crows had gathered, probably to migrate; they were flying overhead and cawing violently, I kept on walking, with a fellow feeling toward the crows. I, too, was going somewhere.

At dusk I reached Marysville. Lunch on wild-rose hips had been neither tasty nor nutritious, so I was glad to see the lights of the mining camp. I wandered into the mess hall, was received without question, and invited to a meal of slabs of beef and plenty of potatoes. When I was asked where my home was, I told them it was way down the valley, and I had walked too far without realizing it. A bunk was given me for the night and after breakfast next morning I ostentatiously started back down the trail, but cut around the valley to a railroad track and proceeded along it.

Six cinnamon buns bought for a nickel at the local store made me feel well provisioned for the day, but there was still that terrible feeling that I had done something wrong — I had run away from home. However, now that I was on my way, I could keep walking on the railroad track which I had heard terminated in Seattle. There it would be easy to get a job as cabin boy on a boat for South Africa. Getting through the British lines would be quite simple for a small and not very conspicuous boy, and then, of course, after I had helped the Boers win their liberty I could come home and all would be forgiven.

The railroad track ran into a tunnel, so I took a trail over the mountains and again walked till dusk. The trail did not seem to be leading anywhere, and I sat on a log to rest, only to be startled by a sudden booming sound. A male grouse was only a few feet from where I sat. I shot it sitting (which one should not do), and resumed my walk, eventually coming to a clearing with two cabins, but no one in sight. I sat on the steps of one, and after a time the owner appeared, an elderly gray-bearded prospector who greeted me with, "Hi kid, what are you doing here?"

I explained that my family had moved into a ranch down in the valley; I had gone hunting but got lost. This explanation was satisfactory and after I had answered negatively his query, "You aren't lousy, are you?" dined with him on molasses and "dough-dodger bread" made of flour, water, and baking powder. I slept under a couple of quilts such as my people made at quilting parties in Kansas, and he told me they had been made for him at a quilting party in Iowa when he left for the West to prospect and make his pile.

In the morning we had the grouse for breakfast. We parted after I had invited him to drop in to the nonexistent ranch in the valley below so that I could repay him for his hospitality.

The railroad track showed up again in the middle of the morning and I followed it throughout the day. As night fell, no cabin was in sight; but beside the track, in one of the little level areas so common in that part of the state, was a wheat field, and there were wheat stacks, scratchy to sleep in and not very warm. Twice during the night I was shaken awake by trains passing close by. The coaches were lighted and looked warm and pleasant — early September can be chilly in Montana, especially when one is clad in a shirt, knee trousers, and a pair of shoes.

In the morning it warmed up again. I resolved to get a temporary job somewhere. That night I moved into another ranch house, telling the usual story of my family having just settled down the road and how I had walked too far to get back. There was no question of a welcome, food and a place to sleep; and no omission of my courteous invitation for them to drop in at our ranch. People were coming and going, settling and prospecting, and everyone believed my little lie.

Toward noon on the morning of the fourth day the track made a sharp turn to the west, that is, toward Seattle. There was a bridge across the river and I went over to see an Indian village, a half-dozen tepees of the Cree tribe who used to commute, as it were, between Canada and Montana. They made some sort of livelihood by selling mounted and polished cattle horns to the tourists when the trains came through. Coming back, I stopped in the railroad station to invest one of my two remaining dimes in a cup of coffee. There was a man standing there — I think he had had something to drink — and he remarked to me, "Hey, young fellow, the police are looking for you."

As a matter of fact, they were doing nothing of the sort. Beinhorn thought that I had gone home, and my mother, thinking I was safe on the ranch, did not know of my absence for five days. But the uncongenial remark of the stranger was most disturbing. I sensed the reform school threatening me unless something definite was done.

Beyond Garrison the railroad made another turn, and ahead was a clump of cottonwood trees. It occurred to me that in the future I might better sleep in the daytime and walk at night. I lay down comfortably beside a cottonwood log and tried to nap. I remembered a New Jersey evangelist whom I had once heard in Helena. He compared New Jersey and Montana by saying they both had an abundance of sin and big mosquitoes. The situation was rapidly becoming desperate, what with the police looking for me and the mosquitoes finding me. I just didn't like this part of the country, even though there was a beautiful river, the Hellgate, and more small streams than I had ever seen before. In the distance high mountains were heavily covered with pine. After all, the mountains were my country, and mountain people my people. I knew that nobody would look for me there; and if they did, they couldn't find me. So I started in that direction, meeting after an hour or two a cowboy who stopped to chat. When asked where this road went, he said, "It curves around a bit and will eventually take you to Helena." There was a road going left, in the opposite direction, and down it I went.

In a little valley with irrigated fields was a three-room log cabin, a barn, and, a bit below, a cow shed where a man with a bald head and a walrus mustache was busily digging post holes. I stopped and asked him, "Mister, do you want to hire a boy?"

He looked surprised, but there was a twinkle in his blue eyes as he asked where I came from; and out came a lie that I had to live up to from then on. *Toby Tyler, or Ten Weeks with the Circus* flashed to my mind. They hadn't treated Toby nicely; in fact, the ringmaster whipped him, which was why he had left. Putting myself completely in the part of Toby I told him I had run away from a circus.

"What were you doing with the circus?"

"An apprentice learning to ride, but they were mean to me so I left, and I'm trying to get to Seattle to find my uncle."

He said, "I don't know about hiring you, young fellow, but you can come up to the cabin with me and have supper and talk it over. What's your name?"

"Tyler," I said. Then, feeling that I might be going too far, added, "Billy. Billy Tyler."

After a supper of bacon, potatoes and dough-dodger and a night's rest, I was ready to go to work in that bachelor establishment, helping with breakfast, doing the dishes, and making myself far more useful than ever before. There was no suggestion that I leave immediately; some chores were set out, and before a week elapsed, I belonged.

Ed Chaple, my boss, was originally from Wisconsin. He had been a cowboy in Texas but eventually had secured this little ranch with irrigation rights on Warm Spring Creek that flowed through the valley. He had a small herd of cattle, and several excellent horses, among them a fine stallion named Pilot, who became the father of a numerous family, at a fee of ten dollars per fatherhood, and supplied ready cash for the ranch.

Ed went out on the range one day and returned with a pinto pony — not too tame and not too wild, because he threw me only a couple of times — so that I could ride to Garrison once a week and get the mail, which consisted exclusively of the San Francisco *Weekly Examiner*.

Then we would have an orgy of reading the weekly paper. This was not, however, all our library, because we had what was then called "the sheepherders' Bible" — the Montgomery Ward catalogue — and two real books. One was Lee's *History of Virginia* and the other was the first volume of Prescott's *Conquest of Mexico*, both of which were read and re-read in the long winter evenings. It was not until years later that I secured the second volume of Prescott and found out what had happened to Cortez after he had spent the night alone under the Tristenoche Tree.

There was a thrashing party at the Widow Houck's ranch, which like many small ones was harvested by an itinerant thrashing crew and a couple of extra hands recruited from an ever-passing line of men we called "hobos," who were really wandering workers. They came, each with a roll on his back wrapped in oilcloth, and they hired out for a day or two or by the week. They followed the seasons in different parts of the States and showed up to help at harvest time. Eventually we came to know many of them, and it was fascinating to hear their tales of Minnesota and North Dakota, or of the wonderful climate and opportunities west of the Rockies. Most of them were perhaps a bit rough, but they had been places and seen things and in general were quite acceptable humans.

Mrs. Houck was a grand provider — not that Ed wasn't, but his menu did not get much farther than bread, bacon, and potatoes, sometimes with a luscious dessert of stewed dried apricots. These apricots came in gunnysacks and were also good to chew on between meals. But at Mrs. Houck's there was pork, for they had just had a killing; cabbage; homemade pickles; pies, and strawberry jam made from the tiny wild strawberries that grew along the banks of the irrigation ditches. The whole thing was like a houseparty — except for the pitching of wheat shocks. Mrs. Houck drafted me into the kitchen and permitted me to rest by helping her with the dishes.

One evening, when a group of us were standing by the road, a horseman drew up with a greeting, "Hello Billy!" I recognized him as a boy from Helena, some years older than I. My heart went up, and then down again, because I thought my adventure might be over. He asked me how everybody was at home. I looked frightened. He evidently thought I looked sad, because he only said, "Too bad; I had not heard about it."

Wishing me good luck he rode away, never once calling me by my last name. Apparently he didn't go back to Helena or know what went on there, because never in the furor over my disappearance did he mention having seen me.

After our roundup, we settled down for the work of the winter, feeding the horses and cattle, mending harness, cooking, reading once a week when the mail came, cutting fence poles, repairing fences, and — the job I liked best of all — halter-breaking colts. This meant putting the halter onto them, gaining their confidence, and leading them slowly around and around the corral until one could simply put a rope loosely around their necks and they would follow anywhere.

One day Ed told me to run the ranch; he had a mysterious mission to make, and would not be back until the day after tomorrow. When he came back, he brought with him a pair of trousers (my first long ones), a pair of heavy shoes, a waist-length reefer, and a woolen neck muffler. He presented them with the highest praise I have ever had: "You ain't been such a bad ranch hand." I wore the clothes to the Widow Houck's Christmas party and Ed loaned me his watch chain to wear; he carried the watch himself.

Sometimes I would go down to the foot of the valley and help the Skinners about their place, and the reward would always be a pound of butter. Mrs. Skinner was large and friendly. Mr. Skinner was friendly, too, but slender with a bushy gray beard, one bad eye and a useless ear. He had got a drop of water in his ear while swimming; this resulted in terrific pain and when, by thumping his head and having his friends thump it, the drop of water was released, scalding hot, he was never able to hear again. I knew this story by heart because it was his favorite and sometimes there was little else to talk about. Mrs. Skinner could make marvelous flapjacks, which we ate with plenty of butter and syrup. It was a treat to eat there, and I always snapped at a chance of helping them in any of the things I was able to do.

In return for their kindness I told them tales of circus life. Once Mr. Skinner asked me, apropos of nothing, "Billy, how do you spell your last name?"

For a minute I could not remember it, but Mrs. Skinner said, "T-y-l-o-r or T-y-l-e-r?"

I made it the latter, but apprehensive of a temporary lapse of memory I carefully wrote my name on the inside of my hatband in case the subject should ever come up again.

Warm Spring Creek never freezes. Some five or six miles above us it came out from the mountain side, and flowed down a narrow meadow, water crystal-clear and teeming with small shiners.

Then it tumbled over a falls and went on down the valley into the Hellgate River. There were trout in it, not many, but enough so that on Sundays I would always get a mess of them, using Ed's Bristol steel rod and (unsportsmanlike) bait. An occasional rabbit would show up around the cabin, and farther up the valley were sometimes sage hens, probably the easiest of all game to shoot, because they seemed to have no fear of man and his guns.

One noon I came to the cabin with a mess of trout. Some men from the logging camp up the canyon had passed through on their way home from Garrison and had left Ed some newspapers. We had seen no papers all winter except the San Francisco *Weekly Examiner*, but here were several Montana papers, including the Butte *Weekly Miner*. He was reading this, with his feet on the stove and his corncob pipe in action, and as I was just making the cut in trout number two he suddenly swung around with, "Say, young fellow, ain't your name Willy Mann?"

This was so abrupt that even a hardened criminal like me lost his composure. I tried to bluff for a minute, and then Ed said that my mother had been terribly worried. That had never occurred to me, and I found myself blubbering.

"Stay here," said Ed. "I'm going to Garrison and let your mother know you're safe." And then he added sternly, "And you be here when I get back."

At that he saddled Belle, his favorite brown mare, and cantered off.

At Garrison he bought a penny postcard, wrote the news, and mailed it. When he came back to the ranch and told me what he had done, I assumed my mother would come and get me. I was ashamed chiefly at having been caught in my lie, much as I had been astonished at everyone's believing it. I asked Ed that night, "Did you really believe I traveled with the circus?"

He replied, "Yep; but I didn't believe you ever rode much."

In Helena, my mother heard the news before the postcard reached her. According to the custom of the day, it was read in the post office and the message was relayed to her immediately. The Northern Pacific Railroad furnished a special car for the occasion and she came to Garrison the next morning, where I met her. When I saw her I forgot all about Seattle and the Boer War, in fact about everything except her and Ed. Like most small boys, I had taken my mother for granted, and I did not realize the worry she had had for the previous five and a half months.

An alcoholic insane case in the local jail had confessed, on Christmas Day, that he had killed me. According to him, I had climbed on his logging wagon and he had hit me with a log and left me for the coyotes to eat. All sorts of other rumors had come in. Both the Presbyterian and Baptist ministers had prayed for me, right out in church. The police of the state, the Masons, and the Odd Fellows had all searched for me. It was only because the C-Bar Ranch was off the main road and we got none of the local papers that I remained so long undiscovered.

Ed and I kept up a steady correspondence, and when the school year was over, I embarked again for Garrison — this time with the full consent of my mother — with money for train fare, and a brand-new boy's-size ten-gallon hat.

Life on the ranch was better than it had ever been. There was no longer any fear of being discovered, and besides, summers in Montana are much nicer than winters. Each day was much like the other, except for strolling over sometimes to visit the Cree Indians — where I became good friends with one boy about my age, named Bear Belt. Occasionally he went fishing with me on shares: I caught the fish and he took 50 per cent. He appreciated this change in his diet of horse meat, gathered by the squaws, and entrails of cattle when any killing was being done on the ranches.

Bear Belt gave me a buckskin bag; when I left the ranch at the end of summer Ed popped something into it, and admonished me not to open it till I got home. When I did, out slid eight five-dollar gold pieces. My mother was astonished and said, "Did Ed give you all that?"

"No," I replied with great pride. "I earned it." It was my first salary.

One day in our front room appeared a portly gentleman with a beard. He was Professor Lyon, who had a boys' school in Spokane; my mother thought it might be a good thing for me to go there. A week or so later, I was on my way, with my mind full of recollections of Louisa M. Alcott's *Little Men*, to a boarding school not unlike the one I had read about. I had in my pocket a tin can with two little sucker fish brought from Warm Spring Creek. These lived all year in a tin basin in my room. During fly season I put flies in the water and watched the little suckers draw in the fly's abdomen, leaving the thorax, wings, and head floating; when there were no flies they ate bits of meat.

The school was in a rambling frame house on Arlington Heights, in what were then the suburbs of Spokane. Mrs. Lyon was a niece of Elias Howe, the inventor of the sewing machine, who some years before had died leaving her a sizable fortune. Her husband decided that they would go West and invest the money in land and forest near Lake Coeur d'Alene. But a depression was on; the Howe estate did not realize the sums that had been set down in the will; and there had been a codicil on the will which provided that in case these sums were not realized from the estate, the inheritance of the married members of the family should be taken from them and given to the unmarried. Thus the Lyons, left with very little, had opened a boys' boarding school.

Lyon had spent fifteen years studying in Belgium and he and his wife usually talked French together. There was another male teacher, and this position was always filled by someone as itinerant as the hobo laborers in Montana. Two or three of them came and went each year, so we had a variety of instructors and instruction. One had taken a course in botany and knew considerable about plants. One of them, a small-time preacher, had been in Brazil and he had once had a pet monkey and a parrot. Another — also a minister, a very long and lanky one — would not let me read the *Encyclopaedia Britannica* during study hours because, as he stated, I was getting pleasure out of it. I was indeed; for, by skipping here and there, I could read about Stanley, Livingstone, Mungo Park and the other African explorers, and by diligent daydreaming travel with them.

After breakfast, the day's work started by our listening to Professor Lyon read a book entitled *Good Morals and Gentle Manners.* When he finished it, he would start over again, so during my two years at the Lyon school I heard it read through three different times.

On Saturdays Professor Lyon would take all twenty of us exploring. One time we went to see a man near by who had invented a motor driven by water; by attaching this to the kitchen tap the gadgets that it ran would do all the kitchen work and some of the farm work. Moreover, he had stocked some pools on his place with trout which would come up and take crumbs out of one's fingers. Another time he took us to the oldest building in that part of the world: it was a blockhouse fully fifty years old.

Except that he was the most rabid anti-Catholic I have ever known, Lyon was broad-minded and a man of wide experience. He wanted us to grow up broad-minded, too, so each Sunday we would hand him a little chit: "Please give me ten cents for carfare, ten cents for church, and ten cents for candy." Then we would go *en masse* to church, a different one each Sunday. When a Hindu missionary came we went and heard about Buddhism. If we showed too much enthusiasm for one minister we would less frequently be allowed to go to his church, but in time we visited them all — except the Catholic. We were also taken to the theatre, chiefly to Bittner's Theatrical Company, a "10-20-30," where we would see melodramas ranging from *Human Hearts* and *The Plunger* to *Quo Vadis.*

In the spring there were excursions to the Lyons' place on Micah Bay on Lake Coeur d'Alene (before going we each had to sign a statement, *I will not try to walk on the log jams* — once one of his boys had done so, fallen between two logs and drowned). There were wonderful tree frogs at Micah Bay, and I brought back a dozen of them in a Mason jar half-filled with water with a comb inserted, for the frogs to climb on; one boy who had lived in Switzerland told me of having seen such an arrangement there.

In the school, the bell rang at nine o'clock, lights were out and complete silence was in order. My tree frogs did not know this, and that first evening when everything became quiet one of them ventured a sprightly *Prrink*. He tried it again and soon all of them were singing. Mr. Lyon heard the noise from below; came up clad in a white nightshirt, with a candle in his hand. At the sound of his footsteps, the frogs interrupted their song. Mr. Lyon asked several of the boys if they were making the noise. None of them was, so he went below, and the chorus was resumed. Up came Mr. Lyon; but before he went down again he paused for a moment at the head of the stairs, and the frogs were identified. It was decreed that I could keep them on the back porch. But they disappeared, one or two at a time; it was not till they were all gone that I learned that some of the smaller boys loved to see the ducks in the back yard chase them and swallow them.

Once, on a bridge looking over Spokane Falls, I saw a fisherman with a box of live crawfish for bait. I begged one from him and took it back to school; it was my only pet that winter. When left on the windowsill overnight, it became imbedded in ice, and of course I thought that was the end of it, but when the ice melted the crawfish thawed out and lived for months afterward.

One of my classmates had had a course in elementary entomology at another school and he gave me an ancient cyanide bottle and explained how to put beetles and other insects into it, kill them, and keep them as specimens indefinitely. He apparently had not progressed far in his study because he knew nothing of mounting them on pins. I invented a process of putting corks from small bottles in the bottom of a cigar box and sticking them with chewing gum; to these I fastened my insect specimens, also with chewing gum (later I used glue), and during the spring made a small but to me fascinating collection.

Lyon School did not take boys beyond the eighth grade, so after two years it was time to go elsewhere. At the end of the year Johnny Longmaid and I came back to Helena carrying with us a pair of young Belgian hares that Mrs. Lyon had given us jointly. I wangled Johnny's from him, but when I decided to go back to the C-Bar Ranch I turned both hares over to my friend Larue Smith. He was a sentimental chap and his mother later told me I should have given them to his brother Jay, who was more practical. According to her, Larue would play with them by the hour and read books to them, but never thought of feeding them. So they perished.

Just before I left Helena, Ed had showed up unannounced and spent a couple of days with us. He told me that he was thinking of selling the ranch and going to Canada to buy a bigger one. He wanted me to go with him, but when told about the military academy he decided it would be better for me to "get a bit more larnin' there." That was the last I ever saw of him. We corresponded from time to time, but four years later, when I was in Texas, a letter addressed to him at Kamloops, British Columbia, was returned to me marked "Addressee unknown." I was never able to find him again, but for a great many years kept hoping he would show up and say "How be ye, Billy?"

Thirty years later, letters started coming to me at Washington with the theme, "We are looking for one William M. Mann, of Helena, Montana, who apparently is entitled to a substantial inheritance." With the well-known story of the Spanish prisoner in mind I dumped these letters, one after another, in the wastepaper basket. One evening I happened to show one to my wife. She said it would do no harm to look into it, so I turned it over to a good friend in my bank. My correspondent was one of those who make a living by looking up lost heirs, and after considerable correspondence we found that Ed had died in 1926 in Los Angeles, and his will, now twenty-eight years old, written in lead pencil, bequeathed everything to William M. Mann, son of Anna Mann, of Helena, Montana. With some of the money I bought a watch, and never look at it without thinking of Ed, his kindness to me, and the splendid carefree days spent on the C-Bar Ranch.

CHAPTER II   Military School

Now as I sat looking out the train windows at the Kentucky haystacks, I remembered that my great-grandmother was said to have been born under a tree in Kentucky when her parents were running to Fort Cook from an Indian uprising. Tobacco fields were entirely new to me, as was the language of fellow passengers with whom I talked; at a station where a vendor was selling fried chicken at fifteen cents a piece, I held out a quarter and asked: "Two for two bits?" The reply was: "You can have them for that, but we call them quahtehs down heah."

The academy was one of the oldest in the South. It had been established by the father of the present Commandant shortly after the Civil War. The old gentleman, with his beard, his slouch hat, and courteous manners, was known to us as "Big Bill" to distinguish him from his son, "Little Bill." It was through Big Bill that I was transformed from "young feller" to "young gentleman."

The school had had some hard times and the physical properties were pretty well run down. There were only seventy-six cadets, but "Little Bill's" advertising methods were about to bear fruit, and during the next three years the enrollment grew to over three hundred, from all the States and Cuba.

The elder Captain Kable was a scholar of the old school. His standard of education was high. Our day's work was patterned for us, commencing with Reveille and continuing till Taps; formation at mealtime, drill in the afternoon, and an hour's study period in the evening before bedtime. Sunday morning there was church, and in the evening dress parade. Monday was a free day when we could go downtown and spend our weekly allowance.

We could make our own choice of church, the two most popular being the Presbyterian, where the girls from Mary Baldwin Seminary always went, and the Episcopalian, where we could see the girls from the Virginia Female Institute. But each had its drawbacks: the Presbyterian minister preached very long sermons, and at the Episcopal church there was too much standing up and sitting down.

We went from one church to another, always in groups with an officer. This included the Jewish synagogue and the Catholic church, but the Negro church was "out of bounds." I could not understand this because the only Negro I had ever known was George Lee, whose father was the best plasterer in Helena. I found that opinions were quite reversed between Virginia and Montana: in Virginia, the noble Red Man of the West was held in high esteem, while Negroes were not.

Staunton was a village, with a Main Street of one- or two-storied buildings. Ice-cream sodas cost a nickel whereas in Helena they had cost fifteen cents. For thirty cents we could buy a pint of ice cream and pick our flavor: the flavor was poured in and stirred around. Two of us used to buy ice cream, each choosing a different flavor, and then sit down together alternating tea-spoonfuls of the two kinds.

In the little park was a zoo of two cages, one holding a badger that would come out and snarl at us, the other a black bear which seemed very friendly. However, one day he bit one of our boys on the hand, as bears do.

Betsy Bell Mountain was covered with chestnut trees; Professor Lyon had often told us that in the East there were many things to eat in the forest — chestnuts and other nuts, and berries. Here I first became acquainted with the chestnut weevil that infests the nuts.

There were turtles in the streams (turtles are rare in Montana), and lizards running along the fence rails. Best of all, there were milk snakes and king snakes in the woods. Those made wonderful pets, but from time to time the Commandant reminded me that if I wanted to keep such things in my quarters I must keep those quarters very neat.

The most astounding things of all were the spring lizards, or salamanders. I had never seen them before, though we do have them (of other species) in Montana. They were in every spring and I was fascinated by their big gills. I brought any number of them back to my room, where they would live for a while; but they require cool, running water and that I could not furnish them.

Drill and military training became a serious part of my life. Many of my fellow cadets were destined for either West Point or Annapolis. I decided to go to Annapolis and become a Navy man — Navy men traveled all over the world, they visited strange countries and saw strange animals and birds in these countries. I have since found out that the Army man has a better chance, when stationed abroad, to do work in natural history. In fact, some of the finest early work in our own Southwest was done by Army officers.

The next year I stayed out of the academy and lived in Chicago with my sister, going to a school that Charlie had selected. This was the Lewis Institute, a technical school, in which I did not fit at all. But there were other things for me in Chicago, such as the Lincoln Park Zoo, where sometimes I was able to get in a word or two with Cy DeVry, the head animal keeper. In Jackson Park was the old Field Museum of Natural History. There was newspaper talk of a proposed expedition to Africa. Instead of writing a letter offering my services and inexperience, I went in person to the museum one Saturday morning, hoping to get a job there in my spare time and really learn something by working on specimens.

Hornaday started in Ward's Natural Science establishment in

Rochester, New York, a commercial establishment where one could rise from sweeping the floors to the sublimity of going on expeditions. I had read his *Two Years in the Jungle* and knew that one required practical experience, not book learning, to do such work. Other famous naturalists had started at Ward's, among them Carl Akeley, A. B. Baker of the National Zoological Park, and William Morton Wheeler, who became dean of the Graduate School of Science at Harvard.

The Museum, an old frame structure (afterwards stuccoed by Carl Akeley with his newly invented "cement gun") seemed gloomy and inhospitable. It took some time and all the nerve I could muster to climb a flight of stairs and knock at a door labeled Laboratory.

The head of the Zoology Department at that time was Daniel Giraud Elliot, a bearded savant with many large and learned volumes to his credit. I had seen some of these in the John Crerar Library in downtown Chicago. Dr. Elliot was not in and the door was opened by a slight, pleasant, dark-haired man. His name was William J. Gerhard, and meeting him was the most fortunate episode of my youth as well as the beginning of a great friendship that has never diminished.

When I asked for a job he looked a little perplexed, and wanted to know what my idea of a job would be. I told him I wanted to work with specimens and learn something of their preparation and handling. He explained that they were taking on no new employees at the time, but if I liked he would teach me how to mount insects.

Before going into entomology, Gerhard had worked in a secondhand bookstore in Philadelphia which specialized in scientific books. He acquired a distaste for the business because, he said, when a scientist died, all he ever left his widow was a library on which he had spent all his surplus cash throughout his lifetime, and the books brought so little when sold. He then became a collector of insects and the most painstaking preparator that ever lived; so a wealthy lepidopterist in Philadelphia sent him on his one foreign trip, to the Andes to collect butterflies. Later on he came to the Field Museum, where he has spent half a century as curator, always helping young students in entomology. He directed my outside reading and got me to subscribe to an entomological journal, the contents of which I could not understand. But the fact of being a subscriber made me feel that I at last belonged to a scientific world.

The great Carl Akeley was in charge of taxidermy. In his laboratory I made my first birdskin, and later Ned Dearborn, the curator of birds, gave me further instruction in handling bird specimens. With Seth Meek I counted snake and lizard scales. This was during the dead of winter and it seemed forever until the weather broke and it became warm enough for me to go afield with a pair of tweezers and the cyanide jar that Gerhard had given me. Finally, on the edge of the Des Plaines River, a rotten log yielded a catch of one sowbug and eight beetles that were just coming-to after hibernating. Gerhard was kind though not impressed when I showed him this catch, and intimated that on some days I would get a hundred times as many specimens. Sure enough, when the weather got warmer, the heavens simply rained beetles, mostly June bugs, and giant water bugs, that fell to the ground under street lights. One of them, the Belostoma, attains a length of three inches and catches and eats fish as long as itself.

In the vacant lots of Chicago were (and still are) the most productive snake-hunting fields I have ever found; garter snakes and the little green grass snakes occurred under every bit of rubble and I gathered them by the hundreds because Meek at that time was building up a local collection and needed large series.

One evening on the way to a party I stopped to buy stamps at the corner drugstore and mail some letters, when I met two couples bound for the same party. We stopped to talk, and suddenly a voice from behind me bellowed, "Move on, move on."

I thought it was some friend being funny. I turned around with a grin and looked into the face of a policeman who had been having trouble with small gangs blocking the sidewalk. I did not know this and said something jokingly to him, whereupon he tapped me on the chest and I stumbled backward over a low fence and fell. Then I was furious, especially as the two girls were watching. Jumping up, I told the officer some things about himself. Then Harry Brown scratched a match and held it uncomfortably near the policeman's nose to see his number in order, Harry said, to have him discharged the next day, Harry having, or thinking he had, political pull. Whereupon the two policemen (another had come up at the sound of our argument) took the three of us to the Austin police station. Before locking us up, they made a routine search. Harry was an apprentice with the telephone company and had in his pocket a screw driver and a pair of pliers. These were suspected by the police to be burglar's tools, and were put in a large brown envelope and labeled. When my turn came, the policeman pulled out of my pocket a cyanide bottle. This, of course, is made with potassium cyanide, held in the bottom of the bottle with a bit of plaster of Paris, and used for killing insects. When he asked what it was, I told him, "Potassium cyanide."

"What is that?"

I answered truthfully: "The deadliest poison known."

He *h'mmed*, and pulled a second bottle out of another pocket. "More poison?"

"Yessir."

"Are you in the drug business?"

"No sir, the bug business."

He then informed me that I would soon find out that this was no place to be facetious.

We were permitted to telephone, one at a time, to our families; object, bail. My sister and brother-in-law were at a banquet at the University of Chicago on the other side of town; I could not get them. Harry got his father, who hurried over and bailed us out. The trial was next morning. We were charged with obstructing the sidewalk and interfering with the police in the discharge of their official duties. My brother-in-law had hurriedly got a lawyer, but after hearing our story and that of the police, the judge — who naturally resented Harry's statement that he had political pull — decided, "There has been some indiscretion both on the part of the defendants and on the part of the officers," and we were released.

My examination papers at the end of the year showed that I had devoted too little time to the Lewis Institute. Chemistry turned out all right, as did English History, but I failed in Mathematics, German, and Latin, and my disappointed family made plans to send me back to Staunton in the fall.

Early in the spring, I had seen in a show magazine a call to all employees of Ringling Brothers Circus to report to Baraboo, Wisconsin. Why not spend my summer vacation with the circus, working with animals, earning some money, and incidentally seeing the country? I wrote to the boss animal man and received an immediate reply, "Come to Baraboo the tenth of March to join the show." I had promised never to run away again and I wanted to go with full permission. With this letter in my hand I approached my sister. She looked upon the circus as an iniquitous institution, probably because the performers wore tights, but I explained that I would be busy with the animals. Weakening a little, she said, "If you will write to one of the owners and he says it is a good thing for you, I will pass the information on to your mother."

The letterhead contained pictures of the five brothers in a row. One of them looked very much like my brother Charlie; his name was Charles, too, so I wrote him, giving age, experience and my ambition to become an animal man. His answer, short and to the point, was: "Advise a boy of your age to choose some other line of occupation as more desirable in every respect."

I still have this, and circus fans look at the old Ringling letter-head enviously. Later, when I became acquainted with Mr. John, the last survivor of the brothers, I told him about it, and it became a favorite story of his.

Instead of traveling with the circus, I spent the summer in Kansas, and it proved to be nothing less than a collecting spree. From the station at Wathena I walked to my uncle's farm along the railroad track; on each side the weeds were teeming with interesting and to me new forms of life. The whole summer was spent collecting insects and live reptiles — to the great discomfort of various uncles, aunts, and cousins. At night I could read about them in a volume that the United States National Museum had sent: Cope's *Crocodilians, Lizards and Snakes of North America*. It was my bible at that time, and I even tried to memorize the families and genera it listed, giving the book to Cousin Lulu, who was a favorite contemporary, to hear my lesson.

Returning to Staunton, I worked harder at my studies than before, because I had found that Latin was essential in understanding the names of animals. Moreover many of the writings on zoology were in French and German.

In company with my roommate, William Matthew Galt Mish, of Washington, District of Columbia, I resumed my pilgrimages into the country — Christian Creek, about three miles away, being a favorite collecting place. He and I had a joint collection of snakes kept in a box with a glass front, purchased for a few cents from a grocery store. With a tree in it, and a pan of water, it made an excellent vivarium. One day on Christian Creek we turned over a log and found a snake underneath which had evidently been attached to the lower surface because it fell out on its back. Thinking it a milk snake, I picked it up, put it in the palm of my hand, and found that I was holding a copperhead, the first that I had ever seen. Naturally it was a moment of great pride, so putting its head between my thumb and index finger I opened its mouth with my entomological tweezers and carefully explained the fangs, the poison glands — in fact, told Mish all about it. At the conclusion of the discourse, the snake wriggled around and bit me squarely on the finger.

When a venomous snake bites, the first thing to do is to place a tourniquet between the bite and the heart; next, some incisions should be made to enable the poison to flow out with the blood. This can be helped by sucking the wound. With one of the rubber bands that we used to close the paper bags in which we carried home live specimens, we made a tourniquet; with a dullish knife we got the poison and practically all the blood out of my finger. The article I had read had said nothing about letting blood back, so we started for Staunton. Stopping at a farmhouse, we asked for a drink of whisky, which at that time was also highly recommended. It was illegal to give liquor to a cadet in uniform, and the woman hesitated, but when I offered to show her the copperhead in the paper bag she hurriedly poured about a third of a tumbler full of the first whisky that I had ever tasted — and the last for more than a decade. I swallowed it, did considerable coughing, and then the two of us started again for Staunton, I stepping very high and feeling buoyant and Mish wondering out loud if I could make it there alive.

Dr. Gibson, our school doctor, was not in his office and we waited ten or fifteen minutes till he got there. He asked how long the rubber band had been on my finger, and when I told him he made a few remarks about my complete lack of intelligence and sent me to barracks to bed. The finger remained numb for weeks. Next day I had a terrific headache, due probably to the whisky, but I asked Mish to bring Cope's manual to me. Turning to page 1138, I read a sentence that I will never forget: "It (the copperhead) is a dangerous snake, and causes serious injury and frequently death by its bite."

I was confined to the hill the following Monday on account of missing roll call the evening of the snake bite. The Commandant insisted that I had been guilty of contributory negligence by handling the damn thing.

In late fall, some time after midnight, a cadet on duty noticed a blaze in the barracks. In a short time the building was a mass of flame. It collapsed completely and by morning was nothing but a heap of smoldering coals. No one was hurt and most of the cadets' effects were saved, my sole loss being a plaster cast of Barry's lion. At Assembly in the morning Captain Kable, who had had a hard night and had seen the fruits of his first half-dozen years of hard and intelligent work at the Academy completely destroyed, gave us a pep talk. The school was to go on but it was decided to declare a six-weeks' furlough until things could be organized. Boys who wanted to stay in Staunton would be cared for, others were permitted to go home. Montana was a long way to go, so I wrote to the zoo in Washington, explaining the situation and asking for a job. To my great surprise I received a letter immediately, offering me a position as laborer at a dollar a day. I took the next train, and reported at the zoo office.

Dressed in cadet uniform except for a pair of loud and un-military socks, I was a source of some interest to the office force. They sent me to the lion house to report to Mr. Blackburne, the head keeper. He told me they were going to put me to work on animals, and called for Jake, who took me in hand and gave me my first lesson in cleaning a cage. It held a large spotted hyena, and Jake told me if the animal approached the front of the cage to rap the bars with the brush handle and that would send it back. This worked all right, but in the next cage were some rhesus monkeys. One of them grabbed a sponge from my hand and, when I got too close to the bars, struck at me, knocking my glasses to the floor; when I stooped to get them he caught me by the hair. Mr. Blackburne stood at a distance muttering something about God.

I was not immediately fired, as I expected to be, but Mr. Blackburne, who had been watching me, explained the ethics of cleaning an animal's cage.

"Remember," he said, "the cage is the animal's home. If you start working the scraper in the middle he doesn't know which side to run to. So you start at one end, and the animal learns that when you get to the middle of the cage he can step over to the clean part and not be annoyed. Animals do not like scrapers."

I told Mr. Blackburne that I wanted to become an animal man, and despite the fact that he was a great stickler for what he considered the proper way of doing things, and perhaps something of a martinet, he moved me from one building to another so that I got at least a bird's-eye view of how things were done in a zoo. Most of my time was spent in the antelope house, which was in the custody of an old English animal keeper, Jim Myers, who sometimes wore earrings, and heartily disliked Mr. Blackburne. Mr. Blackburne disliked him in return but each respected the other for his ability with animals.

While called the antelope house, this building contained a diverse collection: a Philippine deer that had been mascot on the battleship *Iowa;* a tame Brazilian tapir; and a fine Grevy's zebra, a present from King Menelik I of Abyssinia to President Theodore Roosevelt. There were rock kangaroos, a pair of dingoes, a baby jaguar, and, what I have never seen since, a mother Tasmanian wolf, or thylacine, with four cubs. This wolflike marsupial has become practically extinct, and as far as I know this group was the last to be exhibited in the United States.

Jim Anderson, who ran the aquarium, got me a room at his house, a short walk from the Park. Here I had bed, breakfast, and a lunch to take with me for noon, at two dollars and fifty cents a week.

Jim Myers had spent all of his life with animals and for a hobby bred canaries for the local market. As we worked together he would show me how to do things and sometimes explain the reasons for so doing. The proper way to give a lion or tiger his ration of meat is to toss it in the cage or pass it in on a long stick, because no matter how tame a big cat is he becomes excited at mealtime and may tear the keeper's hand. Myers impressed this on me by telling me about Captain Hobson of our Navy, whom he had heard lecture on his captivity in the hands of the Spaniards in Havana. Hobson had said, according to Jim, "Our food was t'rown at us just like wild animals." Therefore, said Jim, "You should always t'row the meat to the cats."

At first the work in the bird house consisted chiefly in washing bird pans and cleaning cuspidors — big brass ones placed in the aisles in the hope that the public would use them instead of the floor. Blackburne looked in one morning when I was busily but not enthusiastically cleaning these, and said, "You don't like to clean spittoons, do you?"

"No, sir," I replied.

Whereupon he took a handful of sand, scoured the cuspidor until it shone, washed it off, and said, "Whenever you do any sort of job, try to do it good. You like the animals, don't you, Billy?"

"Yes, sir."

"Well, just remember, you got to take the bitter with the sweet. As long as you live, and no matter what job you get, you'll always find there's some spittoon connected with it."

I had planned to work for a time in the zoo, and then take a week off to visit Washington before returning to Staunton. I did not disclose my whereabouts to fellow students in Washington who were vacationing, but roommate Mish found me and took me to his house on New Hampshire Avenue, where I stayed with his family till returning to school.

This was leading a double life. I rose early in the morning, much before the rest of the family because I had to be on the job; breakfasted alone at a perfectly appointed table, waited on by the servants of the house; then at the Park busied myself all day with scrapers, brushes, and brooms, cleaning and feeding my charges. At noon I joined the other men in the back of the aquarium to eat the lunch which had been packed for me at Mish's house, and was regularly twitted about the roast chicken or other fowl, molded salad in a paper cup, and dainty cream puffs that my lunchbox contained. After work in the evening I returned by streetcar to Dupont Circle and walked from there to the house, my clothes with such a zoo smell that every dog in the neighborhood became acquainted with me and accompanied me, sniffing, to the door. Mrs. Mish once commented to a friend, "Billy certainly has a way with animals. Every dog in the street knows and likes him already."

Mish and I wasted little time in the evenings. Many of them we spent at the theater. Joe Cawthorn was playing in *Mother Goose* at the National Theater, and at the old Lafayette (later the Belasco) were the four Cohans in a new musical play, *Running for Office*. At the Academy of Music there was a new melodrama each week. At the Columbia was George Ade's *Sultan of Sulu*. At seventeen Mish and I were most theater-minded, and I still remember these plays better than the ones I saw last year. We saw *Piff Paff Poof*, with Eddie Foy; *The Prince of Pilsen*; *Dr. Jekyll and Mr. Hyde*, and Chauncey Olcott in *Terence*.

A few days before returning to Staunton, I stopped work at the zoo. This enabled me to become acquainted with the National Museum and some of its curators. There I walked brazenly into the office of Dr. Leonhard Stejneger, the head curator of biology, and told him that I was interested in salamanders but was having difficulty in identifying them because it seemed impossible to work out their dentition. He brought several species out of alcohol bottles, and showed me how to slip a bit of putty in their mouths. When taken out it showed the position of the teeth.

R. G. Paine at that time was artist in the division of reptiles at the National Museum, and personally much interested in pythons which he would get when little, keep in his boarding-house until large, and then dispose of. He introduced me to some of his friends, among them Ed Schmid, and we spent occasional evenings working in Schmid's Emporium of Pets. Paine was a devout student of the big snakes. He is my friend to this day, but as often happens in government service, he was transferred – to the textile department of the Museum, at a higher salary, where he still is. However, he gets small pythons and raises them when he can.

Back at school for the final semester, I began to think about the future. Some of the boys were going to West Point or Annapolis, but for several years I had been wearing glasses, and knew that my nearsightedness would keep me from entering either branch of the service. There were a number of my classmates who wondered, as I did, what they would do to earn a living, and we used to discuss it seriously when we were not drilling or studying. Suds thought I ought to be a blacksmith, because a boyhood career of turning over logs and stones to see what was underneath them had developed my forearm muscles, as had my work on the horizontal bar, begun at Lyon's school and continued in the Staunton gymnasium. The muscular development might have helped, but I did not want to be a blacksmith. Mish volunteered to go into partnership with me and run a lemonade stand at the World's Fair in St. Louis. We knew how to make lemonade; and we had a marvelous slogan, which we practiced out of the corner of our mouths: "The little stand with the big glasses!" We wrote to the management of the fair and found that all the concessions had been sold. Then we heard talk about building a canal somewhere down in Panama. That sounded promising — high salaries, lots of adventure, perhaps a bit of collecting in the forest. We wrote to the commission in Washington for information on clerical jobs. Things got mixed up somewhere and we received long forms to fill in that would qualify us as steam-shovel foremen. Though I have since found out that in those days we might have filled out the forms and got the jobs without either of us knowing what a steam shovel was, we gave up the project. I wrote to the various commercial scientific companies whose catalogues were almost textbooks to me, but none of them wanted to engage a scientist who knew as little about science as I did.

Meanwhile spring passed. The frog chorus came on, as it always did at Staunton in the spring; millions of tree frogs called their loudest to make the night beautiful. Then we listened to valedictory talks, and finally, with a suitcase that contained a diploma, I set off with Dan Hoover for Chicago, he bound for Texas and I for Montana.

The railroad journey was broken for a day in Cincinnati. We rode up the funicular to the zoo, arriving there so late that the buildings were being closed. Our faces must have shown our disappointment, for a zoo employee approached us and asked in purest Cincinnati, "Iss it that you like the zoo?" We explained that we were just passing through and wanted to see the animals, so he took us from building to building until dark, telling us about the exhibits.

This was Sol Stephan, the grand old man of American zoos, superintendent of the second oldest one in the country. He had come there first in charge of an elephant that the zoo had bought from Carl Hagenbeck, the animal dealer in Hamburg. After he had delivered it, he was supposed to return to Germany, but no one could be found in Cincinnati who could handle the elephant, so he was persuaded to stay in charge. He did not realize that there would eventually be four generations of Stephans in the Cincinnati Zoo.

Before saying good-by in Chicago, I went with Dan to the office of the attorney of the Santa Fe Railroad. Dan's father was in the road's legal service, and he was entitled to a pass that would take him to Texas. The attorney beamed at us, and said to Dan, "Wouldn't your pal like to go to Texas with you?" I thereupon found myself with a round trip pass to Canadian, Texas, and promptly wired home that I was making a side trip before arriving in Montana.

CHAPTER III

Ranching

Dan Hoover's father had once run a grocery store in Texas, but after saving a few hundred dollars, he took a law course in Lebanon, Tennessee, and returned. Jobs as county attorney were easy to get those days, because the outlaws near by kept creating vacancies in the position. One time, after a court trial, Mr. Hoover was riding homeward when a group of four or five "bad men" came after him. He got into a deserted ranch house and prepared to fight it out with them, but as he looked out through a crack he saw another horseman, alone, coming down the trail. He was riding easily, holding the reins in his left hand and his right arm hanging by his side. When he saw the gangsters he rode up to them and asked, "What are you so-and-so's doing here?" using a word that in those days was a shooting one.

The reply was, "Nothing, Captain."

"Then get the hell out of here."

The lone horseman was a Texas Ranger, with a reputation for a quick draw and an accurate shot, and none of the gang cared to be the first one to reach for his own gun. The bad men rode away, the Captain joined Hoover on his ride into town, and Hoover resumed his law practice.

He had survived such adventures and was now attorney for the railroad. In those days, there was no government restriction on passes, and Mr. Hoover kept us supplied with unlimited transportation. We went to Hereford, where the Western Texas Cowboys' Association was having an annual fair, with bronco busting and — on the side — Molly Bailey's Circus, a famous show that never left the state but kept on the road the greater part of the year. It was said that Molly Bailey, irritated at the high rents charged the circus for showing in the various towns, bought a circus lot in almost all of the places she expected to show. This was done in the days of cheap real estate and she lost nothing by the procedure.

Dan, his younger brother Tom, and I went on to Pecos at the end of the line. It was a new type of collecting world for me. About a mile and a half from town we found great swarms of beautiful tiger beetles. At night they came in to the street lights and fell in numbers on the ground where they ran around and sometimes caught other insects. There were some delightful clear pools in the streams; in one we saw turtles, and collected them by stripping and diving into the water after them. When we got out to dry ourselves and dress again, we found that the breeze which had been blowing when we disrobed had suddenly died down. It was replaced by swarms of mosquitoes. Our retreat to Pecos savored of the burlesque, for we started out naked, stopping momentarily to put on a garment while we waved the others frantically in the air, and then ran on again. It took about a half mile before we finally were fully clothed.

After we returned to Canadian, Chambers's store had a sale. A promoter came to town and offered to rid the store of all the old stock of clothing and accessories on a percentage basis. Handbills were distributed all over the countryside announcing this stupendous sale and advertising for a hundred additional clerks — that is, in addition to the original Mr. Chambers and his one clerk. Actually six were put on, and I was one of them. Articles that had been in the storeroom for years were dug out, prices were marked down, and the store bustled. People actually did come from considerable distances and at the end of a week the sale was over, new stock was coming in, and I had money in my pocket. This was expended immediately upon a much-longed-for book — *The Vivarium*, by Gregory C. Bateman.

my order for the coral snake, but when the box arrived there was nothing in it but a bit of moss — the snake had got away. Nicholson sent me another. One spreading viper from Florida escaped the day after the expressman brought it to me.

When a snake will not eat naturally one opens its mouth and with the aid of a pair of forceps inserts a bit of meat into its throat. The little spreading vipers would swallow meat when it was placed in their mouths this way, but with other snakes I sometimes had to push it farther in and then gently massage it in the direction of the stomach.

Travel and collecting were foremost in my mind, and one morning Mr. Hoover made me a marvelous proposition. The Santa Fe Railroad was throwing open for sale a great deal of land in the Panhandle, and the firm of Hoover and Hare was to take charge. Would I be willing to travel about a bit and write short descriptions of various sections? Would I!

In a few days, old Judge Spiller, a man called Lete, and I were in a wagon with a chuckbox in one end, a tent and camping supplies. I carried a notebook, collecting material, and a volume of Shakespeare. When no ranch house was available, we camped, and alternated in cooking. Sometimes we camped in spots where wood was very scarce or completely absent, and we used for our campfire dried cow-manure cakes, "old dry" to us, which made a hot but short-burning fire. On dewy mornings it was necessary to mix some bacon with it to get it to burn. Judge Spiller used to say, as he rested his biscuit on a slab of it, "There ain't no harm in old dry." One week I would be bun chef, and the next week take care of the meat. One morning as we were leaving a ranch, the owner gave us an exceedingly large and tough-looking rooster for our dinner that night. Lete told me to barbecue it. This meant cleaning a fowl, wrapping it in brown paper soaked in water, and putting it on coals in a pit, then putting more coals on top of it, and covering it all with earth. When cooked overnight this way, it was delicious. But this was my week for being bun chef. I felt imposed upon, and stood up for my jurisdictional rights until both the Judge and Lete got nasty about it, and flatly demanded I barbecue the rooster. I dug the pit, made the fire, and placed the wet-packed bird in it. Next morning it looked wonderful. I fried some bacon for myself. At breakfast the Judge looked rather quizzically at what he was holding in his hand and said:

"Billy, you are supposed to be an anatomist; what part of the bird is this?"

I told him the truth — "guts" — and it quite spoiled his breakfast and Lete's. I had not bothered to clean the rooster.

This created a schism in our little party. Lete, knowing I was afraid of spiders, dropped one of the big, bright yellow, long-legged, orb-weaving varieties common along the creek's edge, down inside my shirt collar. The following evening when he was about to sleep in the tent, I asked him if he remembered that spider. In answer to his "Don't bother me," I opened a handkerchief and let drop on his blanket a small but buzzy rattlesnake. He threw the blanket off in one direction and tried to get out of the tent at the wrong end, which created considerable confusion. In reply to what they threatened to do to me, I informed them that I could find a bigger and better snake next time. During our meanderings I caught twenty-two rattlesnakes, but it was not necessary to drop any of them, as we declared a truce, and at the end of the trip parted good friends.

At some ranches, rations would be meager because supplies were short, but always we were given the best they had, and never was there any question of payment. To offer or accept it would have been completely un-Texan. The Judge told me the story of a friend of his, starting on a small ranch, who had built his house near a crossroads where so many people dropped in on him that his finances could no longer bear it. He took out a license and put up a sign: "Restaurant. Meals 25 cents." This made everything all right.

A rancher's wife asked me on one occasion if it were true that the damyankees were too lazy to bake fresh bread at each meal. She had heard, but could not believe it, that they made bread in loaves so that it would last for a week and could be eaten cold.

Ochiltree County appealed most strongly to me, particularly one section where there was a spring, and where rows of stones marked an old Indian site. Among the stones were not only beetles and lizards, but numerous bones. I took them for knucklebones of Indians, but the doctor at Ochiltree pronounced them prairie dog remains. This doctor was a student of law as well as of medicine, and traveled with us from time to time, though never for more than a day or two. He had once had an accident: mistaking a glass of formaldehyde for something else, he had drunk it and seriously damaged his insides, so he could not stand our camp cooking for long at a time.

The Judge had brought along a jug of what he called "100 proof." This was medicinal and only to be used in case of snakebite. It was my duty to catch at least one snake a day so that when sundown came the Judge and Lete could look at it and each have a protective drink. They warned me that any day I failed to show up with a snake I would be dunked in the next stream we came to. This was entirely reasonable, not like the injustice of the barbecued rooster affair. Besides, there were plenty of snakes and they were easy to catch, so I agreed. One day I had not done my duty. We were camped on the edge of the Washita River and I strolled down in the evening with a snake bag and a fishing rod. There were no snakes in sight, but I made a cast and caught a medium-sized bass. In camp later I opened him up and found a freshly swallowed water snake in his stomach. This saved the day.

Another afternoon I was catching bullfrogs for supper. A good way to catch bullfrogs is with a fishing rod and line and hook, the hook baited with a piece of bright red paper torn from the cover of one's notebook. This, waved gently and within striking distance of a frog, produces results. I had just pulled in the third one when I looked at the ground, and between my feet was a thirty-inch rattlesnake, probably on his way to drink from the pool. Being so close made me nervous, and I jumped aside and walloped him with the fishing rod. When he was quiet I finished frogging and, wrapping the snake up in a handkerchief, started back toward camp. Lete looked at me apprehensively and shouted, "Billy, what have you got in your hand?" The snake had not been dead after all, had wriggled loose, and six inches of him, the head end, were hanging down by my leg. My attention had been concentrated on the other hand in which I was carrying the frogs and the rod. This rattler had had two excellent chances to bite me and had availed himself of neither.

When our survey for the Santa Fe was finished, I went back to Canadian. There I started a heavy correspondence with one of the big animal-importing firms in New York City regarding the price of gnus. I thought that some way should be found in which I could buy Section 375 in Ochiltree County, and raise gnus for circuses. But after buying a couple of books, I had money neither for the ranch nor the livestock.

Then Mr. Hoover had a tiff with his partner on the Washita ranch. It ended by Hoover buying out the other man, and sending me out to the ranch until he could find a permanent foreman. In Canadian we picked up a couple of assistants — a sailor with a Scandinavian accent and a runaway boy from somewhere in the East who was, as he told me, starting on a "tower" of the world with the sailor.

There was another fellow on the ranch, a curious chap who did not like me because he had expected to be foreman. He had had a fiendish experience some years before in the Galveston flood, when all his family except himself had been wiped out. He had been found by a guard removing some sort of jewelry from the dead body of his sister, and sentenced to death for looting. He escaped by swimming out to sea and his descriptions of the way the sharks rubbed against him, and of the flood in general, may have been colored but they were graphic. He was physically a nervous wreck and would shake violently all the time that he was not drinking quadruple-strength coffee, which he made by the potful and drank black. He also had asthma so that at night when he lay down his breathing sounded like a pipe organ, loud and out of tune. We adjusted to this by letting him sleep in the one bedroom, out of hearing, while the three of us bunked in the ranch kitchen. We all worked together cooking and keeping house, feeding the stock and, as the weather became colder, riding the range and tailing "dogies." This consisted of finding cattle that had become stiff during the cold nights and were unable or unwilling to get up in the morning. With two of us lifting the forequarters, and another catching the tail, holding it over his shoulder and lifting, the animal was got on its feet, when usually it would stroll leisurely away and have something to eat. Sometimes instead it would calmly sit down again. On one occasion the others slipped, leaving me momentarily holding the weight of the steer on my right shoulder. This was not good for my back, and for years it was painful from time to time.

With ranch work there was little time for serious collecting, though I did find under a shock of Kaffir corn a pair of exquisite field mice, colored a rich brownish red above and white underneath, which made charming and interesting pets. In the short interval between supper and bed there was little to do, so we gossiped and bragged, but one evening I read aloud Kipling's "Ballad of East and West." I remember the neurotic from Galveston looking amazed and saying, "Is that poetry? I never liked poetry, but it *can* be good."

When the permanent foreman came out to the ranch, I went back to Canadian and then home to Helena. My live snakes I took

49

ANT HILL ODYSSEY

with me as pets; many of the pickled specimens still repose in various museums throughout the country. Gerhard got the hemipterous insects, Meek the lizards and the dead snakes.

With no plans for the future, I started as office boy in the firm of C. F. Ellis and Company, real estate brokers and insurance agents. The most enjoyable part of the job was looking after repairs to buildings and collecting rents. We managed the holdings of the Boston Realty Company, which included nearly all the buildings in Chinatown, where I became acquainted with Dr. Chung Mow and his apothecary shop. The formula for getting the rent was always the same.

"You wantee lent?"

"Yes."

"Mebbe you came Tuesaday."

Although it required two visits the rent was always forthcoming and in addition he sometimes gave me a specimen from his stock in trade, a lizard's skeleton or a tiger's tooth for my zoological collection, which now cluttered up all available space in my bedroom.

The Chinese Empire Reform Association occupied a clubhouse where meetings were continually held, and I assume that this, like thousands of similar organizations scattered throughout the United States, was fomenting the revolution that later turned China into a Republic. Another Chinese institution, Fanny Number Five, was nonpolitical. She was the last of a long series, all bearing, for bookkeeping purposes, the same name and a different number. She evidently had a credit account with most of her fellow countrymen in the town, and each rent day, when the handful of silver she produced was not equal to the rent, she would simply hail the first passer by, and after a discussion in Chinese he would count into her hand the money needed.

Each month I turned my earnings over to my mother. She put them away with the idea that someday I must go to college. Years later, when I was again receiving a salary, I sent her a check each month, but after her death I found that she had put them all into United States bonds and saved them for me. How she accomplished this with her very small income I do not know, but it saddened me, because each time I sent a check I had asked her in a lordly manner to go out and have a splurge.

My work occasioned lots of walking. A cyanide bottle was always in my pocket and many interesting things were put into it. The heat during the summer months in Helena can be extreme, and I found many insects lying dead on the walks. Among these was a tremendous fly, looking something like an ordinary housefly but twenty times as big. I had seen nothing like it before and when I showed my collection to friends, I reminded them of how large a fly walking across one's nose seems before one is quite awake, and I told them that I caught these before I woke up. Later I found it was a rare botfly (Cuterebra) which lays its eggs on live mammals. The maggot develops in the living tissue of its host till it emerges, burrows into the ground to pupate, and finally becomes an adult. It was perhaps one of these that had so excited and sickened me long before when a monstrous grub appeared momentarily in my pet field mouse.

The library was Mecca in the evenings. The librarian took me into a storeroom where there were piles of publications from the Smithsonian Institution, and allowed me to take out the ones in which I was interested. I discovered that the United States National Museum and the United States Department of Agriculture would send publications free to those requesting them, and that increased my letter writing.

I was given a copy of Leconte and Horn's *Classification of the Coleoptera of North America*, and commenced studying beetles in earnest. Some I identified myself; others I sent to specialists, with many of whom I now corresponded. While I was in Chicago and in Virginia my fellow beetle collectors to whom I wrote were courteous and helpful, but not very much interested in the specimens I sent them. Their interest increased when I sent them material from Texas and now from Montana, where not a great deal had been done in this field.

Professor Wickham of the University of Iowa wrote requesting more specimens of a little striped weevil that I had found by the dozens down near the Northern Pacific depot. He told me that it was exceedingly rare in collections, and made me feel as though I had accomplished something. It was curious to me at the time that these correspondents all seemed to appreciate tiny specimens rather than large ones, and I became interested in certain beetles that apparently were to be found only in ant nests. One, large, black, and heavily sculptured, was abundant in the nests of certain ants. The heavy sculpture reminded me of an Aztec idol, and when I turned over a rock there would often be masses of ants grouped about one of these beetles, as though in worship. Years later when I was studying these beetles systematically, I divided the genus into two sub-genera, one of which I named Myrmeceicon, "idol of the ants." The ants licked these beetles, which secreted a substance of which their hosts seemed to be passionately fond.

There was no monotony in collecting, because of the diverse aspects of the country. To the north of town stretched Prickly Pear Valley, named for its principal vegetation. Here were inhabitants of a distinctly arid region. To the west were Mount Helena and, beyond, Broadwater Canyon, dry hills and gullies; while to the east was flat prairie land dotted with huge nests of the Western mound-building ant (*Formica rufa*). Southward, I would zigzag up the flanks of Mount Ascension, cross the peak and on the other side find a sheltered mountain meadow, where in June the pearly-winged butterfly of high altitudes (Parnassius) swarmed. This had good exchange value to a New York firm that dealt in insects and in jewelry made from butterfly wings and gaudy beetles. In return for a few cigar boxes full of these butterflies, folded in paper triangles, Mr. Fulda would send me wonderful beetles from the East Indies and from Africa.

Beyond this glade were other hills and higher, and there was a spring — the water in it so cold that it hurt our teeth to drink it. Here we stopped to have lunch before we went slowly back down the mountainside, collecting as we went. My usual companion on these Sunday trips was elderly Fred Holroyd, originally an Englishman, but long a resident of the States, well-read, philosophical, and fond of long walks. Usually our lunch consisted of Bent's Cold Water Crackers, dried raisins, and a bar of chocolate — the last two nutritious, and the first taking so long to eat that one felt well-nourished. Once when he was unwrapping his lunch from a bit of newspaper, he muttered, "My, My!" and read to me a statement from the Department of Agriculture that we were going to have a billion-dollar surplus crop that year.

"A billion-dollar surplus in agriculture can cover up all the mistakes our politicians can make," he said. "Some year in the future we won't have that surplus, and then we will find out that we Americans are much like other people."

Fred's son, Hardy, then in his early teens, would sometimes come with us, and like most small boys on such trips would zig-zag back and forth, covering a great deal more mileage than we would. The ruins of the Big Indian Mine were here, the stamp mill and large sheds of various kinds, inhabited by hordes of pack rats that utilized these old buildings to shelter their enormous nests of twigs. There was an elevated runway that connected two of the buildings, rotten like the rest of the establishment, and one day when Fred and I were eating our lunch below it, some débris fell. Looking up we saw the boy hanging by one hand forty or fifty feet above a pile of loose rocks. He had slipped. His father, instead of shouting at him to be careful, simply raised his voice and suggested calmly that it was time for him to come down and join us at lunch, which Hardy did after much scrambling and loosening of débris.

We would sometimes return by a much longer but easier way

down the gully into Orofino Gulch. This way led through a grove of quaking aspens, and the edge of the trail was flaming with blossoms of Indian paintbrush. Here were silver-flaked fritillary butterflies, and once I found two males of *Argynnis leto*, one of the most beautiful of these, rich brown, red and yellow, sitting on the same thistle blossom. The female is comparatively plain, and quite abundant, but the capture of the two males was an event.

That year we had an unusually long, wet spring, and while I objected to its raining every Sunday, the collecting season lasted a month longer than usual. In the late summer and early autumn some of the insects disappeared and were replaced by different groups of beetles, flies, and wasps.

Insects abounded under the electric lights in town, and my collection grew so rapidly that materials for mounting and preserving became quite a problem until I found that some of the dealers in insect supplies would exchange insect pins and sheets of pressed cork for lining cigar boxes, for some of my specimens. My mother was perplexed by my collecting, as she did not see how it could lead to an income-producing job, but she was sympathetic with my activities and bought me, through Gerhard, an eight-power hand lens which increased exactly eight times my interest in the insect specimens. After collecting season was over, I had thousands of things to be mounted, studied and classified.

Correspondents increased, two of the most interesting being a father and son in France, one living in Rouen, interested in beetles, and the other in Caudebec-lès-Elbeuf, Seine Inférieure, and interested in bees and wasps. In return for my shipments, they sent me quantities of European and Algerian material, all neatly and correctly labeled. Once when one of their packages came to the post office, I found there was forty cents due to the United States Customs on a lot of dried beetles. I protested to the postmaster, who explained to me that this was a Republican government and tariff was a part of it. This seemed to me so unjust that I wrote to

Dr. L. O. Howard, then Chief of the Bureau of Entomology in Washington, who told me that he thought it was just as silly as I did, but law was law.

In spite of all these activities, I was discontented. I wanted to have more to do with the animal world. One day I wrote to Hornaday, dean of American zoological directors, telling him about my experience in the National Zoological Park, and asking for a job as animal keeper in the Bronx Zoo, so that I might learn more about animals. His answer was brief, and typical of him: "A keeper is too busy fighting dirt, disease, and disorder among his charges ever to learn anything about them. I would advise you to take up some other line of natural history."

CHAPTER IV　Special Agent and

Expert

I was disappointed with Hornaday's advice but turned toward college as a way toward natural history. My mother was ready to help with the expenses as much as she was able and I had saved several hundred dollars from my year in the insurance and renting business. My mother's idea was that I should become an educated man; my idea was to have clarified some of the difficulties concerned with the identification of the specimens that I was catching and mounting day by day. It seemed to me that a year in entomology under a teacher would give me a better understanding of labial palpi, trochanters, and scutelli. A heavy correspondence followed, chiefly in regard to college catalogues, some of which were confusing, but I did learn that Harvard University was not in New Haven, Connecticut, where I had written.

Then came a copy of the magazine, *The Canadian Entomologist*, and in it was an article entitled "The Hypopygium of the Tipulidae." I had to look up the words to see what they meant. The article had been written by Professor Rennie Wilbur Doane of the State College of Washington, and it seemed certain that anybody who could write an article with a title like that would be a good one to explain the things I wanted to know. His college, at Pullman, was the one I selected, though I did not tell my mother the exact reason for going there rather than to some place nearer home.

My collection of cigar boxes, lined with cork or peat moss and

56

containing row after row of insects, filled a large carrying case of the old-fashioned kind known as a "telescope." At Pullman I found that Professor Doane had left the faculty for Stanford University, but I deposited my collection in the care of Reuben Trumbull, whose name I had read in the catalogue, and whom I envied, as he had the title of laboratory assistant in the department of entomology. An agreeable fellow, he gave me instructions on how to register. In the office of the registrar, a shock awaited me; I applied for Entomology One and Zoology One in addition to the courses required for freshmen. The Registrar glanced in the catalogue and found, what I had read before, that Zoology One was a prerequisite for Entomology One, and he told me I had better run over and see the Professor of Entomology about it.

A. L. Melander, professor and head of the department — in fact, the whole department, except for Reuben — was sitting at his desk. He was a young man, of slight build but wiry, and he was already one of the leading authorities on certain families of flies. He merely glanced at me long enough to say:

"What do the catalogue and the Registrar say about it?"

When I told him, he had no more to say than a short "Well?"

I backed out of his office and walked around the science building, wondering what to do. It was now too late to go elsewhere, and besides I had spent all I could afford to get to Pullman. As I had planned only one year of college, chiefly for entomology, to be told that I would not be allowed to study entomology that year was more than a blow.

In the laboratory where I had left my "telescope," Melander was talking to Reuben, and both of them were looking at my collection. Melander asked, "Is this your stuff?" and then added, "Didn't you come to my office a while ago and ask if you could take Entomology at the same time as Zoology One?"

In reply to my "Yessir," he said, "You can go and tell the Registrar it will be all right."

Later I learned that Melander and his boyhood friend, Charles

Thomas Brues, had collected together when they were youngsters, and when they reported to Professor William Morton
Wheeler, then at the University of Chicago, to begin their college course, they had done just as I did and carried their collections with them to show him. At Pullman no other students had
registered for Entomology, so it was natural that the Professor
had not wanted to give the course for one, especially as part of
his time was occupied with a group of pre-college students in
agriculture, whose curriculum required a year in Systematic and
Economic Entomology. He was also State Entomologist, and doing a great deal of field and experimental work on the codling
moth and the San Jose scale, both of which were creating heavy
damage to fruit crops. Melander was a conscientious man, and
when he gave a course, he gave it; but years later, when he and
I were friends and fellow students for the degree of Doctor of
Science at Harvard, he told me that it had been tiresome to give
a formal lecture to only one student when that student yawned
and looked out of the window instead of at the blackboard on
which he had carefully drawn figures to illustrate his talk.

Besides Entomology, there was Zoology, under Professor Shaw,
himself an active field naturalist and collector, and a skillful taxidermist — in fact, his course in preparation of zoological specimens
consisted largely of collecting and making skins of birds and small
mammals. He was rather touchy about his favorite work, and
when I had made the mistake several times of referring to "stuf-
fing" an animal rather than "mounting" it, he informed me that
the next time I used the wrong term would do away with any
chance of getting "A" in the course. In Zoology it was wonderful to have a real microscope to look through. One could scratch
a bit of powder from an ordinary stick of chalk, and find that
it was composed of fossil single-celled animals (Globigerina),
which looked much like a circle with a dot in the middle, and
hence were easy to draw. We collected or raised a great deal of
our study material, slipper animalcule Paramecium from water

poured over dried grass, and Vorticella and other protozoa from near-by pools. Like most beginners in Zoology, we carefully drew pictures of air bubbles, thinking they were amoebae that had been described to us in a previous lecture.

My first roommate at Pullman was Don Gregorio Limon, a student of engineering, who had come from a larger university because Pullman was about the same size as his home, Orizaba, Mexico. He wanted, in addition to his engineering studies, to observe the running of an American town comparable in size to his own. Short and heavy, with a serious mien and most patriotic, he was good company. He draped a Mexican flag in one corner of our room and each night he would click his heels and salute it before retiring. We had the altercations usual to two students occupying the same room; the most serious of these was when he kept sitting in my Morris chair. I had paid eight dollars for this and was proud of it. Besides, it was comfortable to sit in, which the other dormitory chairs were not. One evening after repeated requests for him to clear out, I walloped him with a cake of soap and spoke to him more firmly. He did move to his own chair, but with the admonition, "Never again must you call me 'dammit.'"

Once a fellow student at our table, evidently with a peeve against all foreigners, upbraided Gregorio about being a Mexican. He kept silent and so did I. It gave me a great deal of satisfaction when I noticed a large green caterpillar on the upbraider's lettuce; even more when he folded it into a leaf and popped it into his mouth.

From Friday afternoon to the following Monday was collecting-time. For the first time in my life my friends did not look upon it as anything queer. Reuben Trumbull left Pullman to teach elsewhere two weeks after I arrived, and Melander asked me one evening if I would like to go on a trip with him. We went to Clarkston in southern Washington, in the Snake River canyon, where he initiated me into the art of running a spraying machine, using a sulphur-lime mixture to control the San Jose scale. This was work, but Melander was not above taking an hour or so off now and then and sweeping his insect net to catch the minute flies that were his special hobby. On the way back we stopped at Kendrick, Idaho, and spent the entire day rummaging around in the woods. There in an ant nest was a tiny beetle, new not only to me but to Melander, and as I found later when I sent some to Dr. Fall of Los Angeles, new also to science — my first blood on new species.

My list of correspondents grew. I sent material to specialists in various groups. They often returned some of the specimens with the correct names appended. Melander identified the more obscure flies for me. I became more and more interested in the minute beetles associated with ants. When I found that each of these often appeared only in the nest of one particular species of ant, I started writing to William Morton Wheeler of Harvard, the great authority on ants, and he named and returned some of my specimens. Then there was a wasp enthusiast in Colorado, S. A. Rohwer, some of whose papers were in our library. On receipt of one shipment, he wrote me that one of the wasps was new to science, and he was naming it *Oxybellus manni*. To say that I was excited is moderate. Though I got the letter late at night, I dashed down to Melander's house to tell him about it. He congratulated me with a twinkle in his eye, and said if I kept on working hard, perhaps similar honors would follow, and then he returned to the job he was doing — painting the bars of the crib of his baby son, Ivar, with quinine, to prevent the child from chewing them. (It didn't, by the way, but Ivar made terrible faces as he chewed.)

Melander made me part-time assistant, and took me with him on various field trips. He was busy with a new type of spraying nozzle. The codling moth, a terrific pest of apples, lays its egg in the calyx cup of the fruit. The larva bores into the fruit through the calyx cup and a tiny drop of lead arsenate deposited there, before the worm arrives, will kill it. Melander's idea was to use high-powered spraying machines and to shoot down rather than up, forcing the insecticide into the place where it does the most good. The ranchers had been using powder and spraying as often as five times a season, and were still losing a big proportion of their fruit, but Melander was showing them that one spraying with a curve on the end of the rod known as a "Melander crook" was better than the five ordinary sprayings. From time to time he visited farmers' organizations and lectured on the subject. Once in Walla Walla a man that had an orchard near Spokane was so impressed by these ideas that he jumped up and said, "Professor Melander, I'd give a hundred dollars to have my orchard sprayed that way." The following spring I got the job and collected one hundred much-needed dollars.

Some of the great fortunes made in apple orchards in Washington were possible because of Melander's experiments and the college raised his salary from $2200 to $2400 a year in recognition of his discoveries.

In the spring months the railroad companies provided transportation for little groups of college professors and their assistants. These "farmers' demonstration trains" consisted of a flat car from which lectures were given, a day coach where classes could be held in inclement weather, and — this was especially exciting to the students — a private car, usually that of the division superintendent. The meals were so good that I wondered why the college boys did not abandon entomology, botany, and other studies to become railroad superintendents.

We would pull into a station where the local farmers had gathered to meet us. On the flat car a tree would be raised by a pulley, and Professor Beattie, with a pair of pruning shears, would demonstrate the art of pruning an orchard. Then Melander would give his talk on spraying, and the two of us would demonstrate the Melander crook by starting a little spray pump and directing the spray downwards. The pump was run by a gasoline motor, and my job was to get it going by cranking it. I always forgot to push one little gadget that had to be pushed, and time after time Melander would stalk up proudly, touch it lightly, and the machine would start.

When we were not giving our show, Melander and I would rush to the other side of the tracks and do a hurried bit of collecting. At Ellensburg there was a nest of little red and black ants; the contents were duly collected and later on sent to Professor Wheeler with others for identification. He wrote me, "One species I am naming for you which is surprising." I was surprised myself, at the expression, but his stenographer had made a mistake, and it was really the ant that was surprising, because it belonged to a group in which the clypeus, the upper lip, is usually not notched, but in this species it was. Anyway it was my first namesake among the ants, *Formica manni.*

School holidays were even more delightful than schooldays themselves, because they were spent in long hikes. We would stroll till nightfall and then put up wherever we were. One of our camping and collecting areas was at Wawawai. To get there we walked some miles over the rolling Palouse country and then down a steep trail into Snake River canyon a thousand feet below, to find a different world as far as plants and animals were concerned. It corresponded to the Upper Sonoran region, with flora and fauna similar to those in parts of the great Southwest. Though the irrigated spots were veritable gardens, it was a desert country, and produced the fine fruit for which the state of Washington is famous. The walk back always seemed much longer, because we had to climb up the steep hill. During the many week ends in the two years that we collected at Wawawai I never once reached the dormitory on Sunday night in time for supper.

In Snake River canyon I found a new species of Cychrus, that long-legged, long-nosed beetle which feeds almost entirely on snails. It was thrilling to find, in ant nests, a tiny yellow beetle (Adranes) with short, thick antennae like two clubs, and a hollow in the middle of its back bordered by golden trichomes (modified hairs). The antennae are used by the ants as handles while carrying the beetles from place to place. As in many other beetle inhabitants of ant nests, there is an exudation from the trichomes, apparently in the form of a volatile oil, and Father Erich Wasmann, who devoted his life to a study of these beetles, compared the effect on the ant to that of a good cigar on a smoker.

After I secured specimens and brought them home, expenses started. Insect pins cost money, and so did containers. While checks came from home and also from my salary as entomological assistant, I sometimes did not have enough to buy these essential articles, but Melander solved the problem for me. He received a letter from a medical man in Algonquin, Illinois, Dr. William A. Nason, who had for years collected bees and wasps as a hobby, amassing such a quantity that he sold the whole collection to the University of Illinois. Without his collection he was lonely, so he had started a new one, and wrote to various universities to ask if any of the students would collect bees and wasps, not more than four of each kind, and priced at five cents each unnamed, and ten cents with their proper scientific names attached. With the aid of the college library and my own, which was growing steadily, I named everything to the best of my ability. Dr. Nason appeared satisfied and sent me checks. With them I bought insect pins, and thus my own collection grew.

That summer I had a real government job; the title was good: "Special Agent and Expert"; salary, fifty dollars a month. My chief was George Reeves, an employee of the United States Bureau of Entomology. The work was collecting and making observations on wheat fields, studying especially the parasites of the wheat aphis. These tiny black wasps laid eggs in the abdomens of the plant lice, and the larvae would eat out and destroy the lice, which became very dry, turned brown and swelled up a bit as the larvae grew. Eventually each larva would develop to the adult wasp stage, and would make a neat little door and emerge to carry on the work of its parents. When we were mounting and preparing specimens in the laboratory, Mrs. Reeves would read to us. She went through most of the humorous works of W. W. Jacobs, whose characters Sam Small, Ginger Dick, and Peter Russett are still favorites of mine. (Mind you, I was getting paid for this. It seems that always when I have most enjoyed myself, somebody has paid me good money for it, whereas the occasional bits of hard work I have done were gratuitous.)

The State College and the University of Washington decided the next summer to join forces at the Puget Sound Marine Biological Laboratory, and agreed that half of the six weeks should be spent at Friday Harbor on San Juan Island, where the University had an establishment, and the other three weeks on Orchus Island, the latter being favored by the entomological element in the group, who were anxious to explore a peat bog on top of Mount Constitution.

I joined the laboratory at Puget Sound as assistant, my job being to collect study specimens for the Zoology Department at Pullman, but with plenty of time to take several courses. Melander had invited some of his cronies, so there were Professor C. T. Brues and his wife Beirne, then of the Milwaukee Museum, and Professor J. M. Aldrich of the University of Idaho, both ardent entomologists. The University of Washington staff had also invited various friends. The University of Kansas was represented by C. E. McClung, and a couple of students. From Stanford came the ichthyologist E. C. Starks and Dr. Harold Heath. Dr. Bessey, the botanist and former professor of Beattie, came from Nebraska, and A. C. Haddon, the great anthropologist, from Cambridge, England, accompanied by his daughter Kathleen. The Brueses had their son along, a little boy named Austin, four or five years old. Austin had a parrot-like memory for names which he had heard his father use. His father would open a box of specimens, usually flies, and say, "Austin, what is this?" and Austin would say very seriously, "*Stomoxys calcitrans*" or

"*Musca domestica.*" "And what is this, Austin?" pointing to another fly, and Austin would say, "*Tabanus aurifer.*"

Professor Bessey, who knew nothing about insects, became interested in the precocity of the young naturalist. He asked Brues about it and Brues said, "Certainly, I will show you," and he opened a box of insects. "Now, Austin, can you tell Professor Bessey the name of this fly?" The child replied soberly, "Sodium bichloride."

I joined Professor Starks's class in the taxonomy of fishes, which, with collecting, took up most of the time. The officials had chartered a dredge, the *Gee Whiz*, with which we worked in rather deep water, sometimes so deep that the eyes of the fish brought up would be bugging out. When only students were aboard, the captain would go over a shrimp bed and bring up a small mountain of them. They were immediately steamed and piled on deck, and we ate them, leaving a trail of shells and legs in the wake of the boat.

There were quantities of chimaera, octopus, and other things new to me. I shall not forget the first time I saw salt water, or when I turned over a piece of driftwood and watched a dozen crabs scuttle away. Previously the only live crabs I had seen were some that Melander had brought to me from the West Coast. He had packed them in wet seaweed and they arrived in Pullman very active. With the help of the *Encyclopaedia Britannica* and materials from the chemistry department, we made some synthetic sea water, in which the crabs promptly died.

In the evenings around the campfire, lectures were given: McClung on cytology, Bessey on the evolution of the land flora, and A. C. Haddon on headhunters, black, white and brown, among whom he had lived in different countries. When Kathleen was little he had collected for her a great many "cat's cradles." Native peoples have developed these to an extraordinary extent, and she devoted one evening to demonstrating them. The most complicated one was a Borneo headhunter, in which, by a skillful arrangement and manipulation of the string a figure took the head from another figure and went rolling down the string pulling the head behind him.

A year previously Melander had purchased a binocular microscope which was just then being put on the market, and he and I were so impressed with it that he suggested I take it over to Moscow, Idaho, and show it to Professor Aldrich. Aldrich was on his way to a college football game, but delayed long enough to look at half a dozen flies through the lenses. One was a species of Diopsid that he had captured on skunk cabbage near Ithaca, New York. These Diopsids are characterized by having their eyes situated at the tip of stalks, sometimes long and complicated, sometimes thick; the one from Ithaca is the only species known in the United States, most of them being tropical. He had a whole series of them. I wanted one for my collection, but did not have the nerve to ask for it, and did not think I had anything worth exchanging for such a treasure. He showed me another fly (*Dolichopus hastatus*), a rare species of a family of slender green flies, this one characterized by a spear-shaped tip to the antennae. He explained that only three specimens had ever been found, each one on the top of widely separated mountains in Washington and Colorado. I ventured to ask — if I should ever find any of them, would he trade me a Diopsid for one? He said he would.

The summer that we were all at Orchus Island, Aldrich and I were sweeping our nets for insects in the swampy area on top of Mount Constitution. I noticed a half-handful of green Dolichopus, and looking at one with a hand lens, I saw the spearlike tip of the antennae. I ran to Aldrich with a loud shout of excitement. We then collected hundreds of this long-lost species and together in a few minutes took enough for all the museums in the world. But when I looked at the hundreds which he had taken I did not offer him one of mine for the Diopsid — which I never got.

It often happens that a species will be lost for a long time and then re-discovered. Perhaps it is known from only one or two specimens, and then suddenly the right collector will hit the right place at the right time, and it becomes a commonplace item. There was, for instance, a gigantic tiger beetle known from a few specimens from western Kansas. Professor Snow of the University of Kansas, an ardent collector, had visited this region several times with his student assistants, but he found exceedingly few of these beetles. One evening after sundown he found many of them coming out of the ground to do their hunting in the twilight. The species is crepuscular in habit; during the heat of the day and the black of the night it stays hidden in the earth and comes out only at the time when Snow and his contingent happened to be returning to camp for supper.

I had a similar experience later in the mountains of the State of Hidalgo in Mexico. By the electric lights at the Mina Guerrero, there were dozens of a large nocturnal moth that had been attracted by the light and were lying on the ground. When I turned them over to B. Preston Clark, the specialist in this group, he found that the type specimen, and the only one known up to that time, was a ragged one that had been captured in the tropical lowlands. This probably had been blown from the mountains down one of the big ravines or barrancas, at the proper time to be picked up by an entomologist, and I had accidentally stumbled upon its real home.

Then came a big day: Dr. David Starr Jordan, President of Stanford University, dropped in and talked to us about the biological laboratory at Penikese, where he had studied under Agassiz and been diverted from red algae to become the world's greatest authority on fishes. That settled it. Starks and the Stanford students had told me so much about Stanford (and Starks had offered me work in the Zoology Department), that I resolved to finish my education there. At the end of the season I hurried to Pullman, packed my collection, expressed it to Palo Alto, and then took my first ocean voyage, from Portland to San Francisco.

Starks and Heath were there to greet me and help me get settled. While the Zoology Department had offered me work, I was much more qualified at that time for Entomology; I met Dr. Vernon L. Kellogg, head of that department, and was immediately installed as assistant, with a salary of fifteen dollars a month. My duties were to act as curator of the insect collection.

The Cornell entomologists had developed the system of pinning each species of insect on a domino-like block of soft wood. This was called the "Comstock block." Instead of rearranging the insects themselves, the blocks could be rearranged. It was all right except that students kept jumbling the blocks. There were plenty of the classic Schmitt insect boxes in stock, so I revamped most of the collection into them. More recently the United States National Museum introduced a system which utilizes the good features of the Comstock block and does away with the objections to it. The insects are placed in little cardboard boxes set in a large wooden tray, each species having one or more of these compartments to itself. Then boxes can be shifted from time to time as the collection grows, and the arrangement is not disrupted as easily as that of the wooden blocks. The specimens, moreover, are caught in their own boxes if they happen to fall off their mounting.

Here at Stanford, in person, was Rennie Wilbur Doane, author of "The Hypopygium of the Tipulidae," a short-set man and most friendly. Doane had also written *Insects and Disease*, a forerunner of whole libraries that were to be written on this subject.

When Dr. Jordan had been selected as president of this new university, he had drawn assistants and colleagues from half a dozen colleges. The Entomology Department had first been a half-time work of Comstock, who came from Cornell; later, Kellogg, who was State Entomologist of Kansas, came as his as-

sistant. A brilliant and productive writer, he contributed much
to the study of entomology and to the fame of Stanford.
His book, *American Insects*, was practically a best seller. Heath
was young and active and had taken time to write a masterful
monograph on the solenogasters, describing the anatomy of these
marine worms, and he was a genius as a teacher. He made us
find things out for ourselves. There were no stated lectures; he
gave us the specimens and the microscopes; we would dissect and
draw. Occasionally he would go to a blackboard and announce
that he was going to perform. With quick chalk drawings he
would clarify questions that had been bothering us. Heath told
us that no one could pass the course without knowing how to find
Vorticella, a curious little animalcule that acts as though it were
attached to an elastic band; or without knowing how to fill a specimen bottle with alcohol without leaving any bubbles in it. The
first was difficult until we learned that these protozoa live in quiet
water with rotten twigs in it. The second was comparatively
easy, done by the simple scientific process of inserting a string
in the bottle and pulling it out alongside the cork.

Although smoking on the Quad was frowned upon at Stanford,
Heath used to lock himself in his laboratory to have a few surreptitious puffs from time to time; then he learned that the venti-
lator carried telltale fumes into the office of his superior professor
on the floor below. Being of an experimental turn of mind, Heath
found that a few drops of acetic acid judiciously placed in the ven-
tilator would counteract the tobacco smell. I had started smoking
cigars when with C. F. Ellis in Helena, and at Stanford I smoked
a pipe; but I had to be careful of my company when I lit it. Doane
was so susceptible to the effect of nicotine that when he went to a
faculty smoker he would come home and disrobe on the back
porch, taking none of the taint of the smoke into the house with
him. Dr. Gilbert, the head of the Department of Zoology and a
leading ichthyologist, also had an allergy toward tobacco, but I
did not know it. I had heard Dr. Jordan give his talk on "The

Ascent of the Matterhorn." On this excursion he had been accompanied by Dr. Gilbert, and Dr. Jordan used to tell of being caught in an avalanche, and of how "the light of the world went out" when he saw Gilbert overthrown and smashed by the avalanche of stones. It turned out that it was Gilbert's nose that had been smashed, and his sense of smell destroyed. I smoked contentedly when I was near Gilbert till Starks told me that ten years previously Gilbert had recovered his sense of smell and hated tobacco smoke as much as ever.

Corte Madeira Creek and the vast fields of the Stanford farm were favorite collecting grounds. New beasts, related to those I had known before, but quite different, turned up. The Histerid beetle living in ant colonies looked different. It proved to be a brand-new species, and the first one I ever described, naming it after Wheeler. The "idol of the ants" was represented by *Cremastochilus armatus*, twice as big as the ones I had previously known; it was not abundant but to be found by diligent searching.

For the balance of the year at Stanford, I took a course in the classification of fishes. This was compulsory for all majors in Zoology, naturally, since half the science faculty were fish experts. It was easy enough to key out the specimens as I had had much experience in this sort of work, and to keep me busy Starks put me at work on a collection of fishes recently received from Southern California. To my great surprise there were two new genera and also a species of fish that previously had been known from only one specimen from the vicinity of Cape Horn. These resulted in the publication, by Starks and Mann, of "New and Rare Fishes of Southern California," my first and last publication in ichthyology. The drawings were made by Mrs. Starks, who was professor of art in the university and especially skilled in fish drawings, having illustrated so many of her husband's papers.

Among fellow students, my closest companion was Bob Duffus, who was to become a distinguished writer in later years, and at that time was studying history. He knew nothing of entomology and cared less about it, but he liked to tramp, so we were together for what must have been hundreds of miles of walking.

Late in the season Starks came to me with the exciting news that the Carnegie Institution of Pittsburgh had given a grant of money for him and an assistant to live on San Clemente Island off Southern California and study the habits of fishes, and I was to be that assistant. As I had kept a number of fish in captivity I knew that they didn't have any "habits": they simply swallow a bit of food and spit it out and swallow it back again. But San Clemente Island would be a good place to catch beetles and reptiles in spare time. First there was to be a six weeks' course at Pacific Grove, then I was to join Starks at San Diego and go to the island for another six weeks.

Pacific Grove, in those days, was a quiet village, and a pleasant place in which to study, under Dr. McFarland, the comparative anatomy of the vertebrates. Duff and I camped together in a tent. He, being a mere historian, was spending the summer disguised as a janitor in order to have money for the next year in college. During spare time he took a course from me in entomology, no tuition being charged in this case, but at the end of the month I flunked him in an examination. In answer to the question, "Name one adaptation the grasshopper has for feeding," he put down "Its hind legs," and when I protested he maintained stolidly that the grasshopper's hind legs propel it in the direction of food.

As both of us were chronically short of funds we dined, as well as breakfasted and lunched, on rice pudding, which we took turns in cooking. He was much better at it than I, especially when we had currants to put in it. Occasionally we violated the game regulations and had abalone, which is too sweet for a shellfish, and tough unless eaten when too hot for comfort. We augmented our rice diet by going from time to time to a small restaurant which specialized in five-cent dishes. There was also a bakery near by, and we found out that the buns they made were considered fresh only the first day and that if we bought them when they were a day old we could get a dozen for a nickel.

While Duff was doing janitor work, I was investigating the private blood canals of the lampreys and the anatomy and classification of the Nudibranchia, on which Professor McFarland was a great authority. These occurred in abundance on a bell buoy, and I collected them until I was discouraged by having Bill Thompson, who had rowed me out, lose an oar and drift back to shore, leaving me sitting on the buoy with a bell tolling six inches above my ear. Bill picked up another oar and after some hours came back and rescued me, but I have never liked chimes since then.

Duff had secured a job for the latter part of the summer picking peaches in Banning. Until Starks invited me to go to San Clemente Island with him, I had planned to go with Duff, but afterward I was able to indulge in great superiority. The day before Duff left I received a postcard from Starks saying, "Be ready to leave for San Diego on the fourteenth." I promptly spent the remnant of my summer wealth on a large dinner for the two of us — three courses, including steak, for a quarter, and claret lemonade ten cents extra. Duff departed. The next day came another postcard: "Trip all off. Can't get permission to camp on the island."

The owner of the island had gone to Spain for a vacation, and while under ordinary circumstances we would have been welcome, the manager did not feel that he had any right to permit two foreigners to come there and research — whatever that was.

I had written home to the effect that the Carnegie Institution had endowed me for the summer, that I was a very consequential young man and did not want any more allowance; so now I was very much depressed financially, my only asset being a bicycle that had something the matter with the pedals and would jam every hundred feet or so.

Banning is near Los Angeles and Duff had gone there to spend a day or two with his fiancée before going on to his peach picking. I knew that if I could get there he would lend me enough money to go to Banning and would use his influence to get me a job picking peaches, too. Financially, Los Angeles was as far as Timbuctoo, but the head of the laboratory gave me a job replacing broken windowpanes, and I found a man who wanted to buy a bicycle. I let him try mine, and for the first time in several months it worked smoothly, clear around a village block. He handed me five dollars.

Hard work and rigid economy, after a few days, resulted in enough money to get me to Los Angeles. There was even a dime, enough for breakfast, when I arrived. Duff was in Pasadena, and after asking a policeman where it was, I started walking there. Then in the middle of the street I saw a large sign that looked just like a personal invitation to me. It read, "Free fare to Arizona." Every beetle collector wants to go to Arizona, because it is the home of the most beautiful beetles in all America, so I went in and asked for further information. The man told me that they wanted fifty Hungarians to go to Needles to work scrapers on the railroad. I told him I was Hungarian and liked nothing better than to work scrapers. My idea was to get to Needles, work long enough to pay for my passage, then write home for money and spend the rest of the summer collecting. The man was a bit dubious and asked to look at my hands; after years of turning over logs and stones in search of beetles, the calluses were impressive. He wanted to know why I wanted the job and I told him I was broke. He informed me that the next batch of men that were being shipped out were not going until Tuesday and asked if I wanted a job in the meantime. Thinking to strengthen my position with him I said I would take on any work, so he gave me a card and sent me to a restaurant as dishwasher.

I had been in a restaurant before, but never behind the scenes, so the day's work was something of a revelation to me. Moreover, I was not the chief dishwasher, I was the second. A hobo from New Jersey was my superior and he showed me how to wash dishes. One stood in front of a sink and the dishes were brought in by a waiter. The first thing to do was to remove the butter from the butterplates and put it in a crock, to be used later for things "à le beurre"; but this was the only food in the restaurant that was brought to the table a second time. This was July, and the climate, in combination with the steam and hot water, was "unusual."

From six to nine the work was hard, then there was a respite until the after-theater crowd. During this time a waiter spoke kindly to me. I shall always remember him as a superior and benevolent being. At midnight the manager came in and said, "Kid, you've done right well today; I don't know why we can't put you on regular." Then, to my chief and me, "You can go now when you've cleaned up the kitchen."

At one o'clock the kitchen was clean, I was given a dollar and a half and told to show up in the morning if I wanted any more work. During the day I had nibbled at a broiled lobster and several desserts, and one of the cooks had fried me two eggs, but I was too tired to eat them. I asked for some hard-boiled eggs, and just before the cook left he presented me with a half-dozen to put in my pocket to ward off hunger in the next few days. My chief asked where I was going to sleep, and as I had no plans he invited me to go along with him to the Salvation Army Home where he made his headquarters. We chatted on the way to the Home and he told me that he had run away from his New Jersey family, and that as soon as he had enough money to buy a new pair of kicks (by which he meant shoes) he planned to beat his way home again and surprise the old folks. He worked from eight in the morning until four. From four to six was time off, and from six to midnight he was in the restaurant again. When I asked what he did with his time off he said he usually went home and slept, so that practically all his waking hours were spent washing dishes. I was glad I was going to be a naturalist.

There was a choice in the Home of ten cents for a ward or fifteen cents for a room; I gave the extra nickel and had a room to myself.

In the morning I bought coffee and doughnuts. It looked as though I might start off for Needles and the scrapers the next day, so I thought I would visit some of the entomologists with whom I had corresponded and exchanged specimens. One of these was Dr. A. Fenyes, a Hungarian count who had been practising medicine in Egypt when he met and married an American woman who was visiting there. They came to Pasadena, where he settled down to devote the rest of his life to raising chrysanthemums and studying his group of beetles, a complicated family of rove beetles or staphylinidae, called Aleocharinae.

At his office I found that he kept short office hours, for as soon as I appeared, he put a sign on the door DOCTOR OUT and took me to his beautiful home on Orange Grove Avenue. I looked at his insect collection and his library, and finally, full of enthusiasm, told him I would get him some specimens from Arizona, explaining how this trip had fallen directly from above. He was not enthusiastic and said, "It sounds like foolishness to me. Now for a long time I have been trying to find a good collector who would go to the Huachuca Mountains to collect some Aleocharinae for me. Would you go?"

Every good naturalist wants to go to the Huachucas before he dies, and some of them believe that the next world for good naturalists will be not unlike this mountain range which lies close to the Mexican border and is now a forest reserve. Collectors had been there in preceding years, and each had brought out something new and wonderful. The sordid financial details were soon worked out: Dr. Fenyes was to pay my expenses and I was to have all the specimens secured except his Aleocharinae, on the collection of which I was expected to put in a fair part of my time. I spent the night at his house and the next morning I had the pleasant feeling of a book of travelers' checks in my coat pocket, as well as a ticket to Yuma, Arizona.

Then I looked up Duff, and we started off together on the train. He did not notice that the conductor had put a ticket of a different color in my hat band, and just before we got to Banning I told him what had happened. It was mean of me, and he looked distinctly lonesome as he got off the train. The summer was not bad for him, however, as he got a job as camp cook and profited more than he would have picking peaches.

Yuma was hot, but I found that you should not mention it, because the man you were talking to would buttonhole you in the sunny street and give you statistics on eleven towns in California that were hotter than Yuma. If you merely said you liked the town and stayed away from climatic subjects he would take you into the nearest store and buy you a glass of cold root beer. Lest you forgot the native hospitality and the genial climate, a large sign over the hotel proclaimed "Your room and board free every day the sun does not shine."

Collecting by the lights at night was unusually good, with insects new to me coming in clouds, and often just sitting still waiting for me to pick them up. After two days there I went to Tucson, and then took a branch railroad to Hereford, the nearest station to the Huachucas. I had heard that a butterfly collector, Carl Coolidge, was camping in Ramsey Canyon, a fifteen-mile walk from the station, and I started out to find him. First the way led across the plains, hot and arid, with little vegetation except cactus, and then up into the lower hills, covered with scrub oak, and on up the mountain to Bernie's Camp. This was among the hardwoods, and farther up was the evergreen territory. Coolidge welcomed me and asked me to share his tent.

He was collecting butterflies commercially for certain savants, amplifying his income by writing short and rather clever stories.

As we were interested in different kinds of insects, there was no rivalry between us, except that he had been there a month earlier and secured a number of specimens of a glorious and rare beetle, a large green one called *Plusiotis beyeri*. Coolidge did not like rattlesnakes and he had an order for some live ones from somebody in California. An exchange was easily arranged. For a half-dozen rattlers, which I caught and popped into a burlap bag, he gave me four of the beetles. I caught some rattlers also to be taken back to Stanford, among them the green Lepidus.

The rains came. With the downpour that opened up the season, there was a complete change in the appearance of the country. After two weeks Coolidge and I walked to Hereford to do some collecting on the plains, and the fifteen miles of flat, almost life-less road had turned into a veritable garden, with flowers blossoming everywhere and each supporting a family or more of desirable specimens. We got so many that it was difficult to care for them, and we sat up until late at night, sorting, drying and preserving our specimens.

Shortly after the rains commenced, there turned up under stones eleven specimens of a large slow-moving tiger beetle (*Amblichila baroni*), then known from only a few specimens. The larvae spend their time in the ground and the adults come up at mating time. Possibly they wander around at night looking for food, but all that I found were under stones. This was an exciting discovery. I wrote about it to various correspondents with whom I was exchanging beetles, and on my return to Stanford a month later found no less than four packages of exchange beetles, owed to me for a long time, waiting at the laboratory.

It was hard to leave the Huachucas, but Fenyes desired also specimens from the San Francisco Mountains of northern Arizona. At Flagstaff I made inquiries and found that a ranch family, the Hochderfers, who lived just below San Francisco Peak, sometimes took in paying guests. Leaving my collection at the hotel in Flagstaff, and equipped only with a knapsack of collecting material and implements, I walked to the ranch. This was eighteen miles, and of course I had to turn over logs and stones along the road to see what was underneath them. The sun was setting when I reached the ranch house and asked Mrs. Hochderfer if I might stay there a few days. Her reply, "Is it you like buttermilk? Because if you don't you can't stay," was staggering, but I suddenly developed an insatiable appetite for buttermilk and told her so. Then she explained that she had had one guest who did not like it, and never again could such a person stay there. This was logical, because besides bacon and fried potatoes, buttermilk was the mainstay of her menu.

Among the aspens on the flanks of San Francisco Mountain there turned up a dozen or so specimens of a purple beetle (*Cychrus roeschki*). This had been described from a single specimen, which had been destroyed by fire at the Academy of Science in San Francisco, so we had the name and description of the beetle but none in collections. These beetles were living under rotten logs on the ground, a site that unfortunately was also the favorite of yellow jackets, and I was stung so many times that after I had collected a dozen I felt that I had my share of beetles as well as stings.

This was the last expedition I ever made without buying a return-trip ticket when I started. Back in Flagstaff, my funds consisted of just enough to send an S O S telegram to Dr. Fenyes, who responded immediately. The return trip was broken at Prescott to spend a night collecting at the electric lights, where a rare type of rhinoceros beetle was supposed to be abundant. It was not; so when the train came through at three in the morning I climbed aboard, got in an upper berth, and slept later than anyone else in the car. When I did get up, every eye in the car was looking in my direction. They had seen such a dirty pair of high-laced boots protruding through the curtains that they watched curiously to see what followed the boots. I must have been a grimy passenger for a Pullman; a week's hiking in the hills concentrating on the collecting of specimens rather than on personal adornment gives one a rough appearance, so much so that when at Pasadena I chartered a one-horse wagon driven by a colored man and told him the Fenyes address, he looked sidewise at me and asked, "Mister, do you want to go to the front door or the back?"

I went to the front door, and when Mrs. Fenyes opened it she took one look and said, "This must be the young man from Arizona!"

Mrs. Fenyes's stepdaughter and granddaughter, both named Leonora, had just returned from India; there was a big tigerskin on the floor and the younger Leonora complained to me that all the time they were in India they had not seen a single riot, although there had been riots always just ahead of them or just after they had left a place. It had been a great disappointment to her. Dr. Fenyes, however, was not disappointed in my work as I handed him eight hundred specimens of his favorite beetles.

At Stanford in my senior year, my salary as entomological assistant was raised to twenty-five dollars a month, but the new position took more time than I was able to spend away from studies, so I hired Lee Dice, now at the University of Michigan, as my assistant at ten dollars a month and we worked together on the collection.

That year I spent many week ends in San Francisco with members of the Pacific Coast Entomological Society, a rare group of collectors and taxonomists. Dr. Blaisdell was Professor of Anatomy at the Medical School, but he had devoted eight years of his life to writing a monograph on that tremendously difficult group of beetles, the Eleodini. E. C. Van Dyke, a practising physician, was one of our leading beetle students. Carl Fuchs specialized in very tiny beetles. There were a postman, who was an ardent lepidopterist, and Nunnemacher, a gardener, whose hobby was the lady beetles, and whose papers on them were entitled "Studies amongst the Coccinnellidae." One could imagine him sitting amongst them and studying. There was an elderly bearded German who introduced himself to me by saying, "I drink, I smoke, I snuff." Usually Van Dyke and I would have dinner together; when funds were plentiful we would eat either at the Poodle Dog or the Bismarck; when funds were more limited we would go to Jules's, where for seventy-five cents one could have a good French dinner, beginning with steamed mussels, and accompanied by a bottle of either Riesling or zinfandel. After dinner we would work on beetles until time to sleep, and I was always free to use a spare cot in his office.

At the university, in addition to the customary courses, my work on the insect collection was equivalent to a course in classification. I collected constantly and could do some of this officially, because Kellogg was interested in genetics. Dr. McCracken was also busy with silkworms, studying heredity, and both Jordan and Kellogg were writing on evolution, a subject that had always been close to Jordan since his days with Agassiz. Agassiz had been a great opponent of Darwin's theory, so much so that Darwin had referred to him as "my ablest opponent and the most courteous," but he was such a teacher, encouraging his students to think for themselves, that nearly all of them became believers in and students of evolution. Jordan would tell, when he lectured on his early training, how after one of Agassiz's talks against Darwin, one student stood up in class, Agassiz having left the room, and said: "I have been reading the works of this man Darwin and I believe him," whereupon the majority of the class admitted they had been doing the same thing and with the same result.

Kellogg was much interested in the supposed change of coloration of a little spotted beetle occurring in swarms on flowers near the Stanford Museum. In a number of these the spots had coalesced into short stripes. He wondered if this beetle, a species of Diabrotica, was changing its pattern, and one of my jobs was to collect these beetles by the thousands and pin them so they could be assorted and tabulated. Collecting them was good fun, but the mathematics of genetics was too much for me, and Kellogg once told me he was afraid I was going to become a "mere" collector. Alarmed at this I talked with Gilbert, who said, "At one time to be a prominent zoologist you had to be a German-made morphologist; then you were nothing if you were not a physiologist; now genetics is the vogue. If you want to be an outstanding scientist, just absorb a smattering of everything and be prepared to jump at the subject most popular at the moment. But if you like your bugs and beasts, as you seem to, go ahead as you are and do what you like."

Then he quoted Jordan: "Success is doing what you like to do and making a living out of it."

To those of us who were going to be professional entomologists, the most important visiting lecturer was Dr. L. O. Howard, then Chief of the United States Bureau of Entomology. Short, stout, bald on top and with a bearded chin, he had, in addition to his scientific attainments, a keen sense of humor and a rare aptitude as an impromptu speaker. Asked to speak to our class, he leaned against the doorjamb and discussed entomology and entomologists in an entertaining and enlightening way. Besides his own research, he had read everything and knew everybody in the field. He was to be my chief for nearly ten years, though at that time I had no idea that I would ever join the government forces.

One day, when I was in the fish laboratory, Starks betrayed a confidence. There was to be a Stanford Expedition to Brazil, headed by Dr. John C. Branner, Professor of Geology; Starks was going with him to do fish work, Heath was going for reptiles and invertebrates, and also going was an old friend of his, Dr. Fred Baker of San Diego, a collector and student of land and sea snails. Starks told me about it, knowing I would not broadcast the information, for this expedition, like all proper ones, was not announced until the organization was complete. I thought the personnel inadequate, could not imagine an expedition to Brazil without an entomologist, and I wanted to go, too. For weeks afterward, every time I was alone with Starks, I would ask, "What's the chance?" The reply was always, "None."

As the situation got more desperate, I changed my line to "Professor Starks, isn't there a chance in a thousand?"

"No."

"One in a million?"

"No."

"One in a billion?"

"Well, I suppose even you have a chance in a billion of getting into heaven."

"Then will you ask Dr. Branner?"

After some hesitation, he said, "I will, if Heath will, too."

I rushed upstairs into Heath's laboratory, and there was a repetition of the conversation, except that Heath did not mention heaven, but he finally said, "I will if Starks will."

Later that afternoon, when I was looking through a microscope at Trichonympha, a protozoan that lives in the intestinal tract of termites and helps break up the food particles on which termites subsist, Starks came into the lab and murmured, "He says you can come."

I had to raise some money toward expenses, so I wrote here and there to moneyed collectors — they are not abundant, by the way. Dr. Ralph Chamberlin of the University of Utah sent me a check, for which he was to get millipedes, centipedes, and spiders. The Museum of Comparative Zoology at Harvard provided more money, so the affair was settled.

Then Wheeler, on a trip to the West Coast, spent a few days as guest of the Heaths. He accompanied me on collecting trips to all my favorite spots. At one point he mentioned, "Heath has told me that you want to come to Harvard and study with us." Of course I did, but in writing recently to my mother I had felt so grown-up as to inform her, "Never again need you send me a check." And I had heard about the expense of a Harvard education.

So I told Dr. Wheeler that I wanted to come, but after the Stanford expedition I was going to make a professional collecting trip. Dr. Fenyes had offered to send me around the world, following the equator as nearly as possible, with expenses paid plus a salary of fifty dollars a month. At the end of the year I could start at Harvard under Wheeler.

But Wheeler said, "It would be better to come directly after the Brazilian expedition. There will be plenty of time for you to travel later on, and now you are the proper age for study. A year out might get you out of the habit." Then he asked bluntly, "Isn't this the old financial question?"

I agreed that it was, and he then said, "You had better come direct to Boston from Brazil. Harvard will always take care of a student who will work."

CHAPTER V Armies of Ants

The members of the Stanford Expedition to Brazil came east by various routes and assembled in New York two days before sailing time. In addition to Dr. Branner, Dr. Fred Baker, Starks, Heath, and myself, there were three students, all majors in geology — Dr. Branner's son; Olaf Jenkins, and Earl Lieb. We met in a New York hotel, and sailed out of Brooklyn on the *Minas Geraes*, a three-thousand-ton Brazilian steamer, neat and well run. Until we got used to it, the manner of serving meals seemed queer. All the plates to be used in numerous courses were piled one on top of another, and as you finished one course that plate was removed, leaving a clean one underneath. On the plate next to the bottom was served a rich omelet that had been covered with sugar and then baked in the oven, and the final course was always cheese and guava paste.

There is no finer feeling than moving into a steamship stateroom and knowing that it is going to be your home for a long time. Dr. Branner had been making trips to Brazil since 1874 and the Brazilians would not believe that he was a real North American: few could speak such perfect Portuguese. He had written a grammar of the language, which we attempted to absorb on the way down, and we learned a little, with his help and that of some of our fellow passengers. There was a Peruvian school official from Iquitos, returning to his home by way of the Amazon rather than by crossing the Andes from the West Coast. It was he who passed me a dish of dried prunes, explaining: "Rare tropical fruit."

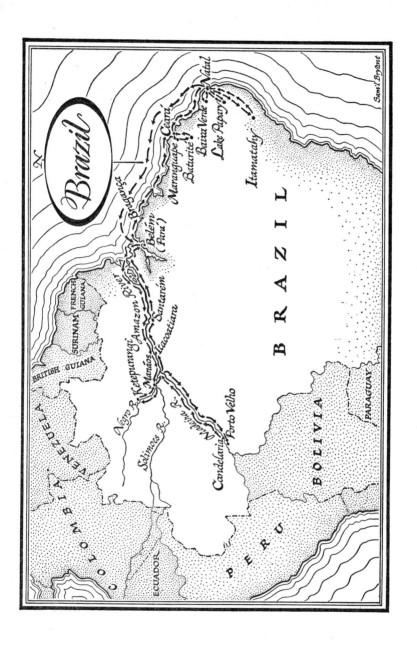

Brazil

BRITISH GUIANA
SURINAM
FRENCH GUIANA
VENEZUELA
COLOMBIA
ECUADOR
PERU
BOLIVIA
PARAGUAY
BRAZIL

Bragança
Belém (Pará)
Santarém
Itacoatiara
Manáos
Negro R.
Ketepurangi Amazon River
Solimoes R.
Madeira R.
Candelaria
Porto Velho
Maraguape
Baturité
Ceará
Barra Verde
Lake Papary
Natal
Itamataly

Sam'l Bryant

N

There was also a Chilean family of two sisters and three children, one a baby in arms, going to join the husband of one of them, an English mining engineer named Innis.

At the end of twelve days we saw ahead of us the sharp line of demarcation between the clear, blue Atlantic and the muddy water of the Amazon. As the boat entered the river, dark brown water and spray dashed up the sides and my Peruvian friend said to me, "Just like New York coffee." The river is four hundred miles wide at the mouth, so we sailed in it till dark, and woke up in the morning off Bragança, where I heard, for the first time, parrots and macaws screaming in the wild.

In Pará Heath and I went to the Museo Goeldi by streetcar, or *bonde*. When streetcars were first built in Brazil, bonds were sold to cover the cost, and since then the cars themselves have been known as *bondes*. Two cars together formed first and second class accommodations, and ignorant of the conventions of Brazil I stepped aboard the first one, clad in white duck trousers and a shirt; but that was not proper. Coats were absolutely *de rigeur* first class, and the conductor explained that I would have to ride second class. As the cars were tied together and exactly the same it made little difference. The next time I rode I was properly coated, and after handing the conductor my ticket, lit my pipe, to be informed, courteously though firmly, that pipes were not permitted first class, only cigars and cigarettes.

The beautiful zoological and botanical gardens of Pará contained also the museum of natural history and archaeology, with a large collection of pottery from the island of Marajó, representing a civilization completely gone and forgotten.

The zoo cages contained numbers of things I had never seen alive before: delicate monkeys from the Upper Amazon which ordinarily will not survive in other areas, and a manatee swimming in its cement pool, coming to the surface from time to time, and opening its nostrils to inhale. It was easy, there, to give it its natural food of water weed. There was one in the Amsterdam zoo twenty years later that had been in captivity more than a year — a record for this animal. The director of the zoo told me that it consumed 1700 guilders' (about seven hundred dollars') worth of lettuce a year. More recently, a couple of manatees were exhibited at a pier in Atlantic City. They had learned to eat boiled potatoes. They were also exhibited in the Aquarium in Chicago; but they died after a few months.

In a tank in a small aquarium was a specimen of the *piraracu*, giant catfish of the Amazon. I remembered this from a picture in my first geography book, where it was labeled "Giant Arapaima of the Amazon," and shown with an Indian holding a spear and sitting on the fish. It attains a length of eighteen feet and the meat, dried and smoked, is a common food on the Amazon. The *piraracu* scales can be more than an inch long and wide and are used by Brazilian women to file their fingernails. A ten-foot boa constrictor, instead of lying lethargically in its cage as in American zoos, here, in its native climate, charged visitors when they approached. The only non-Brazilian animal in the collection was a large chimpanzee which had been used by the English Dr. Thomas at Manaos in his studies on yellow fever.

More impressive than anything in the zoo were the ants stalking around — ones that had hitherto been wondrous rarities, things that I had only seen glued on tiny strips of cardboard on insect pins. There was a large one, half an inch long, slender and heavily armored with spines, walking slowly along the fences (*Cryptocerus atratus*). There were others smaller and even spinier (*Dolichoderus bispinosus*) that had made great carton nests three feet in length, and when these were prodded with my forceps the ants emerged in thousands and fell like rain to the ground, scattering in all directions, but chiefly in mine. They did not sting, but bit ferociously. Another ant, a yellow one with spines (*Daceton armigerum*), with a large heart-shaped head that at first glance looked as though it had been put on upside down, was just standing around on tree trunks. Before the day was over there were some dozens of different kinds of ants in my preserving bottles.

The museum and gardens were in charge of a German woman scientist, Dr. Amelia Schnetlage, an ardent collector and student of birds, specializing at that time on ant-thrushes, a group of small birds that follow the legionary ant to feed on the insects that they scare up, and sometimes on the ants themselves.

Heath and I could hardly wait for night and the wonderful collecting at the electric street lights. But it was an off night for insects. We saw a few cockroaches, and nothing more, and dejectedly returned to the ship.

We landed at Ceará May 6th and moved into a hotel where we waited twelve days for a smaller steamer to take us down to Natal. The first evening a young Brazilian doctor came in, asking for Dr. Branner, who was not there at the time. He had come to tell our party that two Italians had died twelve days before of yellow fever in an adjoining hotel, separated from us by a small garden with a cement pool in it. Heath and I looked into the pool and noticed quantities of unmistakable Aëdes larvae, the little mosquitoes that carry this disease. In the morning, in my mosquito net were six adults, all so fat there was no doubt I had been exposed at least six times. I hurried excitedly into the dining-room to tell Dr. Branner, who was breakfasting, but Lieb had got there first and was saying, "Eight mosquitoes in my net, all full of blood." The doctor was so sarcastic to him that I never mentioned the paltry six that I had found. Twelve days is the period of incubation of this fever and I admit that we did some thinking about it, and afterwards laughed it off because none of us had anything the matter with us. It was not a laughing matter, though; the Innis family, our Chilean friends of the steamer, moved into a mining camp and both women and two children died of yellow fever within a month of landing, leaving the father and the baby. We saw him later at Pará, on his way to take the baby back to England.

Ceará was an attractive town and near by were woods and a small river with numerous pools, where Starks hired all the youngsters of the village to collect fish. Part of the area was well-cultivated, with fields of cane and cotton. One man was building a fence, digging holes and putting in branches of trees, which often took root and grew, making a permanent fence. In digging these holes he found a couple of rare caecilians, burrowing wormlike batrachians, anomalous in being the only batrachians that have scales on them. These delighted Heath's heart.

The coast regions of Ceará are exceedingly arid. A breeze from the ocean tempered the heat, but when one got inland, out of this breeze, it was oppressive. We were there in the dry season. My first collecting was disappointing, a few beetles and little else during the heat of the day, but toward evening Heath and I strolled out to the vicinity of a stream and found some insect or other sitting on almost every leaf. They had known enough to avoid the midday heat, as we had not.

In New York we had purchased some ex-United States Army helmets, designed for the Philippines and then condemned by the army. They were so constructed that when we threw our heads back to look up, the back would hit us in the neck, and the helmet would fall off. At the end of the second day, five little native neighbors of ours were wearing white helmets and calling each other *ingenieros*, a name applied to foreigners because so many of them were engineers.

Mr. Williams, director of the railway, took us by train to the Baturité Mountains, where long ago a Father Schmitt had collected and sent specimens to Europe, so it was the type locality of a number of species. Lieb and I made a trip to the Maranguape Mountains, where the humid hillsides furnished a different variety of species. Naturally each of us collected as he could for the others, so I picked up some snakes for Heath. There was a black one that I picked up by the neck, and not having a bag to put it in, I asked Lieb to disrobe and lend me his BVD's to tie it in.

He demurred at first, but as the alternative was to hold the snake while I took off my underwear, he loaned me his.

In the evening we walked some miles to the railroad that took us back to Ceará, and part of the road was through a swamp where a chorus of giant toads (*Bufo marinus*) bleated "ha-ha" and "ho-ho" at each other and at us. This is one of the largest of the toads, occurs widely in tropical America, and has been distributed to other parts of the world, to destroy cane-boring beetles.

At Natal the governor had provided for us a house, thick-walled and high-ceilinged. The massive furniture was of Indian teak inlaid with ivory, teak being one of the few woods that is resistant to termites, the curse of all tropics. But in true Brazilian style there were hammock hooks in the bedrooms and we slept in hammocks alongside the elegant beds.

The town was mostly of mud houses, with a great deal of poverty, though I have no memory of anyone begging. A group of mixed Europeans, Spanish, Portuguese, and a few English, were drilling for oil. I said to Dr. Branner one day that the town would boom when they struck oil; but he replied, geologically and laconically, "No oil here" — and he was right.

Food was brought to us and here we became acquainted with *carne seca*, the dried meat of southern Brazil and the Argentine, a staple food on the East Coast, though supplemented with fish. The demand for fish was much greater than the supply and Starks would have to be up early on the beach where the fishing boats came in, to get a few specimens for his collection. So great was the demand for fish that a Grimsby trawler had actually been imported from England to help supply the local market. The boat was equipped with an otter trawl, and Starks made a couple of trips on it, but there was so much seaweed to wreck the net that very few fish were obtained. He fished in the tidal pools, and later in ponds and creeks in the interior.

At Lake Papary, about twenty-four miles south of Natal, the use of gill nets was prohibited, as that method of fishing was so destructive. However, the enthusiastic colonel in charge of enforcement suspended the law for a day, and a gill net was set out, enclosing a large area of water with many fish in it, which were then caught with cast nets or in the gill net itself. Starks returned elated with an enviable and interesting collection.

Heath and I collected in the near-by countryside the "large terrible ant" (*Dinoponera grandis*) known to the Brazilians as "*tocandero*" and, according to them, having a sting which brings on fever. I can well believe it, having been stung by one of its smaller relatives. It is a heavy-set creature an inch in length, one of the very largest of the ants. Heath and I often observed it walking about, usually singly, in the evenings or on cloudy days. Following one that was carrying an insect, we found its nest in a thicket. I dug out the nest, which extended along the under side of roots that formed protective roofs. The ants move slowly — which was lucky for us, because the colony was much more populous than I had imagined it would be, and my available vials of alcohol were soon filled. The ants kept coming and coming, in no haste, but with evident intent, and the two of us, who had been squatting among a tangle of branches and vines, got out with little dignity, but without being stung.

The railroad company gave us an excursion to Baixa Verde at the terminus of the little railway that ran out from Natal in a northwesterly direction. After a banquet in the railroad station, we had time for a short stroll near by. The country was arid, with much scrub and cacti, but little life in evidence. On the return trip there was an unfortunate accident. Our special train was running at an odd time, so a man asleep on the track did not expect it till it was on him. He was hurled through the air and instantly killed. All of us were sickened by the sight. Lieb shrieked out something in the direction of Dr. Branner, who told us most sternly that we had seen nothing at all. He wished to avoid having us taken as witnesses, who in those days were sometimes locked in the local jail till the trial was over.

What we had seen of Baixa Verde so interested Lieb and me that we returned a couple of days later. Lieb was especially anxious to look at some cuts in the rock along the railroad track. This time there was no table in the station, laden with food, nor were any of the officials there to welcome us. The village was tiny, and there was no hotel. The owner of a near-by house saw us as we stood on the station platform, remembered us as having been guests at the recent function, and took us into his home. We worked out from there for several days. On one hillside we found a number of hollow stumps of small trees that had been cut down. I hacked one open with my machete (known as *espada* in Brazil) and found a handful of the brilliantly colored beetles that are used so much as jewelry. These jewel beetles feed on morning-glories, and were estivating in the log during the dry season waiting for the vines to put out leaves again. They were in nearly every stump that I cut open, but where they did not occur, a wasps' nest did, adding to the interest of collecting. Under stones, with which the ground was strewn, were beetles, centipedes, and scorpions. I found no centipede as large as the one I had found in my shoe the morning after arriving at Natal. That one had taught us all the good tropical habit of thumping the heel of your shoe in the palm of your hand every morning to see what has taken refuge there during the night — a habit I am still apt to follow in Washington after returning from a trip to the tropics.

While I collected insects, a few lizards and land snails, Lieb made geological drawings of a cut near the railway. Our host was a prominent man locally, and one evening some cowboys, wearing broad-brimmed leather hats and leather trousers, came to visit him. Naturally, I exhibited my catch of small fry, and Lieb exhibited the drawings he had made. Later on, I heard loud and angry conversation outside, and though my knowledge of Portuguese was limited, I could make out the theme, "He is making maps. This is *our* country." Then I heard an itinerant jewelry salesman, also visiting the house that night, say something about "these North Americans" and calling our host's attention to the fact that he had a very beautiful daughter. To make it more melodramatic, the beautiful daughter came to me and told me in a low voice that an engine and a car were leaving the station in about half an hour. However, we decided to stay, and spent another night there, returning to Natal the following day.

From Natal, a group of us were guests of the railway that runs south. We were entertained at Itamatahy, near the village of Independencia in the state of Parahyba. This was the headquarters of two engineers on the railroad, Nye, an American, and Tessire, an Englishman. The country was hilly, with enough moisture to make abundant vegetation with numerous bamboo brakes; and collecting was so good, at least for Heath and me, that we wanted to stay longer, but naturally our large group could not impose on our hosts, whose house was small. Then came one of those breaks that one gets sometimes in travel: Heath and Nye got talking, uttered a few esoteric words, shook each other's hands, and disappeared into an adjoining room. Heath emerged with a broad grin and said, "He says the two of us can stay." They had discovered that they were fraternity brothers, so we stayed a week.

One night, awakened in my hammock by a prodigious itching, I turned on my light and found I was completely covered with bumps. As I wondered what tropical disorder I had picked up, I heard Heath mutter from his hammock, "Oh my, Oh my!" We compared notes, and decided that we both had a particularly severe case of hives. Most of the night we spent passing back and forth a small tube of analgesic balm, a little bit of which I would put on the bump that seemed to be itching most at the time and then wishing I had put it on the adjacent bump. We assumed that we had hives from the rich food we had been eating, but I have since thought that it might have been a case of "chiggers."

Back in Natal, I had my first case of malaria, shivering and quaking in my hammock, and obediently taking the three grains of quinine that Dr. Baker prescribed. A kindly, tall, bearded man in his sixties, he was a doctor of the old school and had had little experience with tropical medicine. Later on, upriver, when I got fever, a doctor accustomed to South American malaria made me take thirty grains instead of three.

After three months, Dr. Branner was taking his group back to Stanford, but Dr. Baker and I were in no hurry to return. There was a little money left in the expedition funds and I had read a book entitled *An Ill-fated Expedition to the Madeira-Mamoré*. This was an account of a former expedition to build a railroad around the great falls of the Madeira River. The attempt had been a complete failure but the book had described the magnificent forest. Knowing nothing except what I remembered of the book, I talked so hard to Dr. Baker, explaining that no one had ever collected in that region, and that most of his land snails would undoubtedly be new species, that he was persuaded. An American contracting firm was working again on the railroad project, which meant a place for us to stay and facilities for going about.

Dr. Branner turned over to us what funds were left. I was to take over the fish and reptile collecting in place of Starks and Heath.

Our week in Pará (now officially Belém) was not time wasted, because we collected every day and all day. First thing in the morning it was my duty to go to the market, where fishermen and country people would come from the Tapajós, the Tocantino, and other tributaries of the Amazon, beaching their boats at low tide on a muddy bank near the market and bringing their produce in for sale. This municipal market was in itself a museum of fish and other animal life, as well as of fruits and vegetables. I would go from stall to stall, selecting fish here and there for preservation, refreshing myself with great slices of ripe, juicy pineapple. Then we would go into the near-by suburb of Souza, where Alfred Russel Wallace had collected years before. Pará is said to have two seasons, six months of rain and six months of heavy rain. This was still the dry season, and we got only one shower a day, usually at two o'clock, so shortly before that we would stroll into the shelter of a cement strip that covered some water tanks, and there assort specimens till the rain was over, when a few moments of hot sunshine steamed up the entire world and insects became active again.

Our boat, the *Rhaetia* of the Hamburg-South American Line, arrived on its way from Germany to Manáos. It was a 6000-ton steamer, nearly twice as large as the one on which we had traveled from New York to Brazil, and exceedingly elegant.

We had been told to get up early the next morning to enjoy the voyage through the Narrows, where the steamer winds in narrow channels between islands. The branches of trees on the adjoining islands were almost close enough to scrape the boat as it stayed near shore to avoid the current at midstream. We saw a harpy eagle over the treetops, in quest of sloth or monkey, but little else in the forest except egrets and other birds.

Among the magazines in the ship's library was one that had a chapter of Conan Doyle's *Lost World*. Later I read the entire book, which impressed me as a delightful, imaginative tale, but on the river itself, looking out at the passing forest, it did not seem so improbable.

Four and a half days brought us to Manáos, and we put up at a comfortable hotel. We went in search of the United States Consul, who, we hoped, would introduce us to the railroad construction company, and help us get up the river. His office was in a large building and when we entered we met a dark-complexioned, heavy-set man and asked where the American Consul's office was. He indicated a room up the stairs, and then when I asked, diffidently, "Do you suppose he's busy?" he replied, "I hope so. He's working for me."

He was at that time merely a Vice Consul, and was employed

by the railroad construction company, to the head of which, Mr. May, we had been speaking.

We heard a great deal about yellow fever in Manáos, but the Vice Consul, who was keeping statistics, cheered us by telling us that in the previous year there had been quite as many deaths from tuberculosis as from yellow fever.

The next day we boarded a two-decker river steamer, the *Madeira-Mamoré* (known as the *Mad Mary* to railroad employees), as guests of the construction company, and headed for Porto Velho, head of navigation on the Madeira, some eight hundred miles away and headquarters of the company.

Each night we anchored and Captain Miranda would take some of his crew and a net about a hundred feet long and seine for fish off the shore. This was jam for me, because he let me accompany the party, and I had the fun of fishing as well as the pick of the catch for our collection. Once a six-or-seven-foot cayman was caught. In the excitement of having a big alligator-like creature thrashing around in the net, somebody kicked over the lantern, and the cayman had to be dispatched by the light of matches and the captain's revolver.

One evening we were fishing on a beach where a lot of logs and branches interfered with the seine. When we had come to anchor I had noticed a nice beach with no obstructions on the other side of the river, so I asked the captain why we did not fish over there. He replied, "Parantintin." I thought that was a Portuguese expression I did not understand, but next morning fellow passengers told me it was the name of a tribe of exceedingly dangerous Indians who had a habit of killing small groups of Europeans and dissolving into the forest when large ones came. The construction company had recruited engineers, draftsmen and laborers from every part of the world, including eight German storekeepers who got tired of the railroad, made a raft, broke their contract and floated down the river toward its mouth. Ignorantly they camped on a beach in Parantintin country and the next time the river boat passed, the passengers saw eight heads impaled on sticks on the beach.

Porto Velho was situated below the last falls of the Madeira near the native town of Candelaria, and contained a series of well-constructed screened houses for the staff. The railroad crowd was as heterogeneous as one could find: native Brazilians, Barbadians, and Jamaicans ("I's a British object, sir"). Some of them, when offered a tobacco pouch, would scoop most of the tobacco out, instead of just a pipeful, beam and exclaim, "God will bless you for that."

The medical department took care of us, and Baker and I moved into a house with Dr. Laidlaw, an English physician. Despite the fact that medical men had been recruited from the Panama Canal Zone and from various schools of tropical medicine, death from malaria and the concomitant black-water fever continued at a fearful rate. We were told that four thousand employees were already buried in the cemetery at Candelaria. Dr. Laidlaw immediately instilled such a respect for fever in me that I took ten grains of quinine a day and twenty on Sunday. The typical set-up on the dining table consisted of a bottle of Worcestershire sauce, a jar of pickled onions, and a large bottle of quinine in five-grain capsules, two of which were supposed to be taken with your first sip of coffee in the morning.

One doctor, a young graduate of Tufts Medical School, made his home in a heavily screened box car, and was almost unique in that he did not take quinine. Neither did he catch malaria, for he stayed protected when the mosquitoes were about. He believed, he said, in turning off the tap when it leaked instead of mopping water from the kitchen floor.

Food was good and abundant; medical care was the best that could be obtained, but still there was much sickness, including a number of cases of beriberi. It was not generally known in those days that this was a dietary disease, and as many who were sent downriver recovered when they reached the Amazon, they

97

thought that the fresh breeze on the river had cured them.

The road was being built on a cost-plus basis, and nothing was spared for the comfort and well-being of the employees. We had an icebox in our quarters and Dr. Laidlaw's unfailing greeting to me when I came in was, "There is a bottle for you cooling on a cake of ice." It was English ginger ale.

The railroad was built to connect the upper reaches of the Amazon tributaries with Porto Velho, head of navigation on the Madeira River, and to avoid shooting the tremendous rapids which each year took toll of many lives and many tons of rubber. It was built by American contract for the Brazilian government. The 266-kilometer railroad is said to have cost a life for each tie.

Brazil has been described as "one great ant nest" and observers have stated that there is not an inch in the forest that is not visited by ants in the course of a day. One of the most common was the kelep (*Ectatomma tuberculatum*), at one time introduced unsuccessfully into Texas to prey on the cotton boll weevil. Large and powerful as it is, it could not withstand attack by the smaller, local ants, and did not persist. There had been some exciting controversy on the subject of these ants by Dr. Cook of the United States Department of Agriculture, who advocated importing them, and Dr. Wheeler, who thought that they would be a failure, and each of them had indulged in print in some delightful acrimony against the other. We would see the keleps everywhere in the forest, on tree trunks or shrubs, moving slowly, and often carrying dead insects back to their nests.

In the evening would come columns of army ants, sometimes into the houses, to be fled from by the human inhabitants till they had completed exploring the quarters and marched away, carrying cockroaches and other insects. They would do a thorough job of housecleaning, though we did not appreciate it when we had to sit outside in the rain for half the night. They sting as well as bite, and travel in such tremendous hordes that they can be dangerous to large animals, including humans. In all, I found fifteen kinds of these army ants, from tiny species, some of which lived entirely underground, up to large ones nearly an inch in length, though in each colony there was much variation in size.

Eciton hamatum, one of the species, ranges from Mexico through Central America and over all of tropical America, and was abundant along the upper Rio Madeira. Armies, found in the woods almost every day, contained enormous numbers of individuals. The big-headed soldiers marched at intervals of from ten to twenty feet in the procession, conspicuous because of their large, light-colored heads and their mandibles, which, looking like old-fashioned ice tongs, were so long that the heads had to be held high to keep them off the ground.

The march of the army is rapid, and at times very definite in direction. Often it divides and sends some of its members up into the tallest trees, while others cross and recross the trails. If a grub, lizard or small snake is tossed near the column, it is instantly covered with the workers and stung to death.

Unlike some of the other species, *E. hamatum* marches in the daytime, especially on cloudy days, and the column travels beneath or over the leaves, over logs, and along the trails. Trunks of fallen trees are a favorite runway. Other species of ants seem to be the usual prey, for larvae and pupae of these made up the greater part of the booty carried by the workers. Several times I saw columns descending trees bringing larvae, pupae and even adults of an ant (*Dolichoderus lugens*) which secretes from the anal glands a large drop of yellow liquid to repel enemies.

In spite of its large size, and the number of individuals in a column, *E. hamatum* is timid in comparison with some of the others. When the column was disturbed by my picking up some of its individuals, those nearest would turn and run back, zigzagging from one ant to another, apparently missing none. An instantaneous antennal communication took place, the warned ant turned also, and instantly the whole army was retracing its steps as rapidly as it had come. In a few minutes, some would return, then more, and presently the army would resume its march. At other times, it followed a new path.

These columns were accompanied by guests or parasitic insects, some tubby Histerid beetles that looked ludicrous as they ran along in the file. Other beetles, a half-dozen species, resembled the ants in form and coloration. They had long legs, and moved so much in the same way as their hosts that it was difficult to make them out until my eyes became accustomed to discerning the differences.

There were long-legged wasps, wingless ones, the size of the smaller ants. These wasps are undoubtedly parasitic on the young of the ants and no one knows the reason they are permitted to live with them. Once I noticed one of these parasites stop running for a moment, whereupon one of the ants picked it up, held it underneath its abdomen in the same manner that it would carry one of its own young, and resumed the march.

Some of the Ecitons are subterranean and I found a colony of them that had come up to rest for the day under the carcass of a sheep. The gases engendered by the decomposition of the meat had evidently asphyxiated the entire colony, for there were piles and piles of dead ants.

The forest teemed with life, but during the heat of the day it was quiescent except in the deep shade. I used to sit on a log at the edge of a trail and look at things. Among the ants there would be hunting Ponerines, wandering about singly on the ground. Columns of the leaf-gathering, fungus-growing, big-headed ants of the genus Atta looked like a flowing line of leaves along the ground, as each ant carried its piece of leaf or flower to the deep, subterranean nest. Sometimes so many of these ants passed that they actually wore a path in the forest. When carrying brightly colored petals of flowers, they looked like some miniature holiday procession. But however romantic they appear to the observer, they are a pest to the planter, and there are instances in which they have defoliated and ruined overnight entire citrus orchards.

By digging out their nests I found large masses of the mycelium (fungus) on which they feed, attended by the very smallest of the ants that function as gardeners. Running in and out among these food masses was a tiny cockroach, Attaphila, a parasite which lives in the nests and shares the food. Pulling some loose bark from the log on which I was sitting, I found the nest of another species of a different mushroom-growing genus (Apterostigma). Tiny patches of fungus had been planted on a little pile of caterpillar droppings.

One of the most curious insects I have ever seen appeared on a low bush in a clearing near the camp. This membracid (*Combophora beski*), popularly known as "leaf hopper," had, attached to the pronotum (the first section of the thorax), a large, thin, shell-like structure, armed with spines, mottled in color, and actually larger than the rest of the insect. Among the Membracidae the pronotum varies a great deal in structure. It may resemble in miniature a Roman helmet, an anchor, or a pawn-broker's sign, and is often so large and awkward-looking that one would think it an actual hindrance to the insect. On the food plant it is not particularly noticeable, and may even be a good imitation of galls, seeds, fruit, and other things of a vegetable nature, and so be considered a protective adaptation. Numbers of them were on the leaves from which I was collecting ants, and, apparently disturbed by my forceps, they began to buzz and fly away.

I took two before they all disappeared, and then found that those I had picked up had flown also, after detaching themselves from the conspicuous pronotal development, and leaving only this for me to put in the collecting vial. Sometimes when a lizard is attacked it drops its tail off, and itself scurries to safety, the attacker grabbing the tail and the lizard eventually growing another one. But in the case of this leaf hopper the attacker gets nothing more than a hollow shell. Whether or not its owner reproduces another is not known.

Higher up on a branch was a stalactite-like paper nest of triangular-headed Aztecas. Disturbing the nest caused them to drop by the thousands, scurry around, run up blades of grass from the tips of which they could be lifted off in clusters and dropped into the collecting vial.

In the fork of a tree I found an ant garden, earth brought from the ground and held together in a ball by the roots of growing plants. As far as I know no entomologist has ever actually seen the ants (Dolichoderus) start one of these gardens, but we assume that the queen begins it with a small particle of earth, in which she plants a seed, and the colony, as it develops, builds up the nest gradually into the form in which we know it. These arboreal nests of fiber or carton or earth, each one with its own distinct form, were a source of never-ending wonder. One particularly interesting nest was in the fork of a recently felled tree at a height of what had been approximately forty feet. The nest was ovate in form, made of earth and about a foot in length and eight inches in diameter, held firmly together by the fine roots of a plant that ramified through it in all directions. When I dug into it, numbers of a tiny red ant emerged. While I was collecting some of these, I had a momentary glimpse of another ant, colored similarly but much larger and with longer legs. It came out of one chamber and immediately disappeared into another. Hoping to collect all phases of the ant, I brought a large empty quinine can containing a piece of cotton soaked in chloroform, broke the nest apart, and threw it into the tin. Numbers of the larger ant rushed out and my hand was severely stung before I realized that colonies of two different kinds of ant occupied the same nest. The large ones belonged to the genus Odontomachus, the "tick-ant" genus of the tropics. As they run along they hold their long mandibles spread apart at right angles to the head; these mandibles are provided with long tactile hairs and when they come in contact with anything the ant violently snaps them together, making a ticking sound, and sometimes throws itself backward.

There were all phases of both species of ant in my nest so it was evident that the two were living together. The tick-ant feeds chiefly on other insects, and it seemed strange to have it living with the smaller, more delicate ant. I returned on several occasions to what was left of the nest, and they had not moved out. A gentle tap on the surface with my forceps would bring out the little fellows. At a more serious blow the big ones would emerge.

This phenomenon of two species of ants living amicably together had been described before by Forel, the Swiss ant student, who had given it the name of "parabiosis." Odontomachus is normally a ground-inhabiting species, but here, high in the air, it had found the equivalent — that is, earth brought up by Dolichoderus. Both the ants were new to science, and the larger, more belligerent one I named after Mr. May, the head of the railroad company.

Baker elected to stay at Porto Velho, but I traveled around to a number of work camps. As guest of the railroad I was given letters of introduction and could travel on work trains and stay at the various construction camps. Some of these were only small clearings with the immense forest adjacent. Life at the camps was always comfortable, people were hospitable, and the continual felling of trees along the right-of-way made it possible for me to spend two months collecting in actual treetops, where live a large percentage of the forest creatures. I carried letters of introduction, but only once did I have to show them. One evening at Camp 28, Mr. Fry, the engineer in charge, appeared a bit disturbed and offish, and asked me to repeat my name. I did; he said, "Oh, you're the bug hunter!" and everything was all right. It appeared that somebody on his way to Bolivia had had a ruction with some of the railroad officials and word had gone ahead for none of the camps to show him any courtesy.

Fry and I became close friends and I spent a great deal of time at Camp 28. He was interested in insects, and was my companion on many forest jaunts. Sometimes the hospitality shown me became embarrassing. Once, toward evening, I stopped collecting near a train that was being loaded with dirt. When it was ready to go I hopped aboard, expecting to be taken to Camp 28, but the train started the other way. The conductor climbed aboard the car in which I was standing and I asked, "Aren't you going to 28?" He made a grimace; signaled to the engineer; the train stopped, and then began backing. The conductor told me it would have been better if I had told him where I wanted to go before they had her all loaded. I have had railroad passes since then, but never again has a loaded train backed two miles through the jungle to take me where I wanted to go.

The railroad employed native hunters to shoot for the camp messes, and with two of these, Antonio and Sebastiano, and a borrowed rifle, I crossed the river into Bolivia and camped with them in the forest. My hammock was hung between two trees, and a mosquito net placed over it. Night in the tropics comes in a hurry, and here it was announced by a wave of noise in the jungle. One insect would commence with a loud, piercing shriek (the men called it the "six o'clock bug"). Then other creatures that had been sleeping during the day would wake up and go noisily about their business. Noisiest of all were the howling monkeys, and for a short time there was bedlam in the air. Then it would all die out as quickly as it had started. When things were quiet I went to sleep, but was wakened by the crashing of an animal, or animals, through near-by treetops. I got out of the mosquito net, and sat on the edge of the hammock with my rifle in my hands. This annoyed Sebastiano, who was sleeping on the ground, and he said sleepily: "*As jupuras no faz mal.*" It was a troop of kinkajous that passed almost directly overhead — heavy-set, tawny-haired little animals that prowl around at night and jump from one tree to another. They are called "night monkeys" in

Brazil, but are not monkeys at all. I have had several as pets — gentle, quiet, sleeping all day and coming out in the evening — the ideal businessman's pet; but when full-grown they can be vicious.

In the morning the three of us separated. Game was abundant, but to get it required a knowledge of the forest such as only forest-bred people like Antonio possess. He and Sebastiano hunted day after day in the forest and returned usually with something — deer, occasionally tapir, many curassows (a game bird the size of a large rooster), and even macaws, which made a palatable soup though they were too tough to eat otherwise. Tinamou, on the other hand, was excellent. It looks, acts and tastes like quail but is actually related to the ostrich. The tamandua, the middle-sized anteater, we sometimes stewed and ate. When well-seasoned, it was good food, but tough.

Another time Antonio and I sat silently in sight of what he called a game trail, although I could distinguish nothing that looked remotely like a path through the jungle. I watched him think, apparently with the aid of his forefinger, which he would raise slowly in the air to indicate that perhaps something was coming. Finally it did. I had heard or seen nothing. He fired, and the first glimpse I got of the deer that he had shot was when it leaped and fell.

When the hunters went off looking for game, I stayed in sight of my hammock, for I had had one experience of being in the forest without a path. A five- or six-foot boa constrictor was crawling along a log. Wanting its skull for my collection I hurried after it with *espada* in hand. It outdistanced me into a thicket of spiny plants and disappeared, and then I spent the better part of an afternoon finding the trail I had just left. A Greek cook in one of the camps had seen a curassow fly over the clearing into the forest. Grabbing a shotgun he went after it, and was never seen again.

Most of the time at Camp 28 a mule carried me along the trails into the forest and gave me a sense of security, it being brighter at finding the way home than I was. Once in a little clearing that was swarming with gaudy specimens, I tied the mule to a cecropia tree. I untied it immediately, for flowing from the tree down the reins toward the mule was a stream of elongated yellow ants (*Pseudomyrma arbores-sancti*). My hands were covered with stings, which was not nearly so bad as if the ants had reached the mule who, I am sure, would not have waited for me. The tree is Triplaris, called *palosanto*, the "sacred tree," because the hollow stems and branches are always inhabited by active, stinging hordes of ants which keep away all who know. Dead Triplaris never contain ant colonies, but all live ones, even the smallest, do.

There were other things in the forest besides ants — big, metallically brilliant beetles, bees even more metallic and brilliant, wasps with dainty paper nests, each species with its own design; wasp-nests of mud and some that were simply holes in the ground; giant tree snails as big as a man's fist that made Dr. Baker's eyes bug out when I brought them back to him in Porto Velho; an occasional snake in or under a rotten log.

One evening in camp with the engineers we were having our usual after-dinner conversation when a native dashed in, shouting "*Jacare.*" Two of the engineers and I followed him to the river-bank, and there saw, floating in the water, a cayman perhaps ten feet long, clearly distinguishable in the bright moonlight. They agreed in a low tone to shoot together, when suddenly a cloud momentarily cut off the light. One of them said, "When the cloud passes I will count three, and we will shoot together to be sure of getting him." The cloud passed and the cayman again made a beautiful target. The engineer counted, "One, two —" but instead of "three" and a shot he swore in a loud voice and started slapping his ankles and stamping his feet. Hunter number two imitated him very well. What had happened was that while they were waiting for the proper time to fire, little black army ants in whose path they had stood, had had time to go above their shoetops and start stinging. Many ants were killed by whacking, but as far as we know the cayman is still there.

Burton, who was in charge of the warehouse at Porto Velho, was also interested in natural history, and spent many hours at night with me at the strong lights at the warehouse, picking up whatever was attracted there. Among the thousands of insects that came were huge scarab beetles, sometimes as large as one's fist, and with long horns on their heads, known locally to the railroad crew as "flying mud turtles." There were moths galore, and curiously, numbers of wasps, differing from most wasps in being nocturnal in habit. One of these made a nest about the size and shape of a pie plate. A large brightly colored tiger beetle that I had obtained earlier only by digging it out of holes it had made in the riverbank, came by the dozens.

After two months along the river, reveling in life that swarmed on every tree and branch, even on every leaf, on the ground, and under logs and stones, it was time to return. The "Mad Mary" took us to Manáos in four days instead of the eight it had taken to come upriver. We lazed on the upper deck, playing cards and caring for the young howling monkey that Burton had given me to take to the zoo in New York. We named it Guariba, the native name for this animal, and found it good company but tiresome because it wanted to spend most of its time clinging to us, not even getting off when it should have done so. One time Dr. Baker, in a clean white duck coat, had cajoled the little monkey into sitting on his shoulder. Monkeys cannot be housebroken, and I noticed an expression on its face that indicated something was going to happen. It did, and Baker beseeched me to take Guariba off his shoulder, because he had been bitten once before; when I recovered from my laughter I held out a hand, and the relieved baby climbed to my shoulder. If I left it tethered, it would raise a discord inconceivably loud for an animal of its size. Like most monkeys, it preferred to handle us, rather than to be handled, and was apt to bite if lifted up, though it would rapidly climb onto my hand and then onto my shoulder.

There was a delay of a week in Manáos till we could make arrangements to go downriver, and we were invited to a country place, called Ketepurangi, a short distance up the Rio Negro, the home of Don Antonio Autrun, a Cuban who years before had been cured of yellow fever by an American Army doctor. He had vowed to devote a certain part of his time in the future to nursing yellow fever patients, and had done so most successfully — and also profitably, we were told. He took us into his home. From the house a trail led to an open meadow covered with a cloverlike plant and teeming with bumble bees, carpenter bees, and the stingless bees that so abound in parts of tropical America. Some of these made a honey that was poisonous.

Across the meadow the trail entered the forest for about a quarter of a mile, and then suddenly stopped. I used to enjoy thinking that there was probably not another trail, except in the vicinity of Indian villages, between me and Venezuela. One day I heard something coming noisily in my direction through the dried leaves, and I stood silently to see what it was. A brilliant orange and black snake about six feet long crossed the trail a few feet away, and it dawned on me that I was seeing my first bushmaster, the largest poisonous snake in South America, attaining a length of eight feet or more. It is considered to be one of the few snakes that will attack man, but this one went into the woods and I went after it with my *espada*. It probably becomes aggressive only when man or another animal comes between it and its nest and frightens it; at any rate, although I stepped into a tangle of roots that trapped me for a minute, the snake did not come back, nor did I want it to as I struggled to free myself.

Don Antonio kept chickens, and he also had a pet peccary, a playful little pig that would nudge me gently while I was eating lunch, and when I did not immediately share with him would root in a determined manner. Dr. Branner had told me that one did not know what a domestic animal really was until one had lived in Brazil. One day at lunch we saw one of the hens fluttering along the ground as though badly wounded. Her chickens disappeared in the undergrowth as a large tegu lizard came on the scene. This habit of a mother feigning helplessness to attract a marauder away from her young is common among many wild birds, but this is the only time I ever saw it among domestic fowl.

We heard that a raft was being towed down the river from Itacoatiara to Santarém on the Tapajós to bring back railroad ties that were being cut for the company. To float down the Amazon on a raft sounded pleasant, so we left Manáos and got to Ita-coatiara on a launch, and moved onto a steamship hulk anchored there that served as office and storehouse of one of the railroad's commissaries. The wife of the manager had secured piles of branches on which were growing a collection of exquisite orchids. These attracted so many brilliant, metallic-green bees with ex-tremely long tongues (*Euglossa cordata*) that I made a good ento-mological collection even on a steamship.

In the village lived old man Stone, an American who had gone to California in the gold rush of '49, but in 1852 had come down the West Coast, crossed the Andes, gone down the Amazon and settled there. He had married a Brazilian woman and, with his sons, made the firm of Stone y Filhos, which produced cigarette tobacco, shredded and intensely strong. I spent hours with the old gentleman on the veranda of his house, drinking coffee to which had been added the beaten white of an egg, which was, he said, "much better than the canned milk you get." He kept in touch with the United States by subscribing to a couple of maga-zines. He had gone back once, and had been much impressed with the progress the country had made. This had been in 1876, to the Philadelphia Exposition. When I left he gave me a package of tobacco with instructions, "When you are up north and the snow is flying, and you are lonesome for Amazonas, just smoke this and think of old man Stone at Itacoatiara." The following year in Boston, on an unusually bleak and snowy day, I thought of this and put some in my pipe. It had become very dry and powdery, and after two puffs I saw black specks in the air and broke out in a cold perspiration.

The raft on which we traveled had a small cabin on it. We stayed in midstream to avail ourselves of the current, and the following morning were at Santarém. Looking overside we could see the bottom of the river, through the first clear water we had seen for months. Ashore in the village we met another American, David Riker. He was an old-timer there, his family having left the south after the American Civil War, so they would not have to live under Yankee domination. They had established the first rubber plantation, long before plants were taken to the Far East.

The river steamer took us on to Pará, where we waited a week for the ship that was to take us back to the States. To my menagerie of one howling monkey, Dr. Schnetlage added a four-foot boa constrictor and a kinkajou, the latter elegantly housed in a hardwood cage with neatly turned bars imbedded in the front footboard, which had taken the zoo carpenter three days to make. Dr. Schnetlage had told me to be on the lookout for a certain large scaly-tailed rat up the river. She thought there might be a new variety on the other side of the Madeira. A native had brought me a specimen one evening, which was duly skinned and dried flat. I turned it over to her, and she sent it to Dr. Old-field Thomas of the British Museum. He verified her suspicion and described it as a new subspecies.

At the Consulate was a stack of letters, and among them one from the Bursar at Harvard University, informing me that at the request of Professor William Morton Wheeler I had been appointed research assistant at a salary of thirty dollars a month. Naturally I was elated and bragged about it to Pickering, our good United States Consul there, who celebrated by giving me a pair of white duck trousers which covered more of me than the pair I had been wearing.

In New York I delivered the howling monkey to Ditmars at the Bronx Zoo, said good-by to Baker, and started off for Boston with the kinkajou and the boa, and a suitcase containing all the vials I had labeled with an X on the cork, indicating something rare or unusual. The bulk of the collection was shipped by express. I had with me also a long black-palm bow and a bunch of arrows obtained from the Carapuna Indians, which prompted a fellow tenant of the smoking car to ask me where I had been fishing.

CHAPTER VI   Presidential Passport

As soon as I arrived at Harvard, Dr. Wheeler took me into his home at Jamaica Plain. The Wheelers' house was a short walk from the Bussey Institution, then the Graduate School of Biology of Harvard, and formerly one of the first agricultural colleges in America.

Just then a disturbing letter came from Starks. According to him, they were starting a small zoo in San Diego, and Dr. Fred Baker had suggested that I be put in charge of it. As Starks said, "Now here is your chance to wear a top hat, chew an unlighted cigar, and point out the site of the proposed reptile house to wealthy visitors." Not feeling justified in leaving the work I had hardly started, I did not go, and it was nearly fifteen years later that I moved into a zoo for good.

The Bussey provided each student with a laboratory of his own, and I settled down to the pleasurable job of working on the Brazilian collection. The end of an expedition can be quite as exciting as the start of it. Material had to be distributed to those who had contributed funds; in New York, Baker and I had already expressed the can of reptiles and fishes to Stanford; the myriapods and spiders went to Dr. Chamberlin in Utah; and the bulk of the insects was turned over to the Agassiz Museum. The ants I was to work up myself, and I began mounting and labeling them. As I worked day after day, my profound ignorance of the ant kingdom became evident. Bottle after bottle that I had marked X for rarity contained common ants of the tropics. Large and showy ones were usually species that had been well known for years, but here and there was a rarity or a new species. Of the two hundred and twenty-three species determined, about forty were new to science.

There are about eight thousand different kinds of ants known, with more yet to be discovered. They are divided, according to structure, into five families, three of which have stings. This group of insects shows a development from the life of simple hunting savages to that of a complex organization which has often been compared to human civilization, with agriculturists, gardeners, millers, soldiers, slave makers, tailors, and carpenters. Some ants keep their own livestock — insects that function as pets, stimulants, or parasites. They have been featured, one way or another, in our earliest writings and are today being collected and studied all over the world, from the sub-Arctic region, where they occur sparingly, to the tropics, where they abound most.

In addition to our own laboratory work, most of us took courses at the University. I attended a series of lectures on the central nervous system, given by Dr. George Parker, who, as Wheeler said, had his lectures so letter-perfect and well organized that they passed through the students just like a dose of castor oil. An enjoyable course in botany was with Professor Fernald — we did some herbarium studies but also made many field trips. Fernald, interested chiefly in the flora of the Gaspé Peninsula, knew a great deal about the edible wild plants. When we visited a cranberry bog he would produce from a large knapsack a cup and some sugar and we would all have stewed cranberries. He said, and I believe it, that a man could live very well on the wild and usually ignored plants of New England. He grew pokeweed in the basement of his house, and had what he considered the equivalent of fresh asparagus on his table throughout the year.

Near the Bussey were big colonies of an eastern mound-building ant (*Formica exsectoides*), whose nests teemed with different kinds of inquilines. The little, oblong, reddish-brown Hetaerius beetle, which is covered with huge scales and bears little clusters of golden hair, had been rare in the Western states but occurred here by the dozens. We built artificial ant nests of glass and stocked them with small colonies so we could observe the habits of the ants and the beetles. When a beetle wanted food it would wave its two front legs to attract the ant which would come to it and feed it a drop from its own mouth. Once when the ants were shifting from one compartment in their nest, one which I had purposely let dry out, to another newly opened and dampened area, I saw one of the beetles crawl onto the rear of a working ant and ride along, not unlike the clown (for which Hetaerius is named) riding on the south end of a mule.

The Cambridge Entomological Club met one evening a month, usually in the library on the third floor of the Bussey building. In addition to the usual books, chairs and tables, the room contained a placard put there by Professor Wheeler, with a quatrain directed against careless borrowers of books.

I was made secretary of the society, the only political position I have ever filled, and also assistant editor of *Psyche*, the entomological magazine published by the club. Brues was editor. The duties of the assistant editor included putting each issue into envelopes and addressing them to the subscribers, and also helping raise funds to make up the deficit of publishing. This was the beginning of my real acquaintance with Tom Barbour, whom I had met before only on occasional visits to the Museum to see its director, Samuel Henshaw. Brues suggested I drop into Barbour's office and ask for a fifty-dollar donation. This is not easy to do even when one knows a person well, but I had heard so much about Barbour, his vast wealth and his great generosity, that I walked into his office without hesitation. He was sitting at his desk, a tremendous man, swarthy, with thick curly black hair. When I told him what I was there for, he turned and looked me straight in the face with a most pathetic expression; this changed into a ferocious glare as he said:

"Here I sit in my office, wondering where my next meal is coming from, and you, *you*, come in and ask me for fifty dollars!"

He used curse words in those days, and he punctuated this remark with several of them. Abashed, I was bowing my way out, when he roared, "Stop! Did you say fifty dollars? Wait a moment till I get my checkbook."

One of the members of the Cambridge Entomological Club was B. Preston Clark, a man of wealth and letters. He was deeply interested in hummingbird moths, of which he had the finest collection in the world with the exception of that owned by the great English collector, Baron Rothschild — and this he bought, later. He was the grandson of the statesman Charles Sumner, who, after the Civil War, had stood out against the annexation by the United States Government of the Negro Republic of Haiti, and his family had always been honorary consuls of the republic in Boston. Mr. Clark wanted specimens from Haiti; Samuel Henshaw wanted things from that region for the museum; Wheeler was making a study of the ants of the West Indies, and besides was always in favor of collecting trips either for his students or himself. It was decided, therefore, that I should spend the winter of 1912–1913 in the island. The only extensive entomological collecting that had ever been done there was by Père Sallé, who in the '40's and '50's had sent several shipments of the native fauna to Europe, where they had been described. Less than two dozen ants were known from there, and most of them distinctive and unusual forms which had been collected by Father Schmitt and sent to Forel in Switzerland. I called on Dr. Marshall Howe, a staff member of the Botanical Museum of New York who had worked on Haitian plants. He told me, among other things, that I would never be able to learn the language. Then I wrote to John B. Henderson, Jr., of the United States National Museum, who had done considerable collecting of mollusks there. He wrote me his opinion of political conditions in Haiti, but said nothing of the natural history.

One often has difficulty in securing accurate information about a country one plans to visit; however, provided with a passport issued by Clark, a round-trip ticket on the Royal Dutch West Indian Mail, vials and a supply of alcohol (which Mr. Henshaw had carefully poisoned to make it unfit for drinking), I went to New York. The steamship agent questioned the passport, and the clerk in the Haitian Consulate there flatly said it was no good and I must have a new one, price ten dollars. In those days it was necessary to have a special Haitian passport, although it was some years before it became necessary to carry American passports when traveling.

The *S.S. Prinz der Nederlanden* was a jewel, a small one, but the quarters were enormous and comfortable. Ensconced in the largest stateroom I had ever seen I tried to take a nap before the boat sailed, but could not because someone was continually opening and slamming the door, and I could hear, "One person only." After this had happened a dozen times I stepped out to see what the rumpus was about, and met an elderly, gray-haired Negro who proved to be the Consul. Madame Tancrède Auguste, wife of the President of Haiti, and her daughter were aboard ship, but the officials of the steamship line, rating science above politics, had given me the stateroom *de luxe*, and the Consul naturally wanted something done about it. He was affable, and when I told him how I had been treated at his Consulate, and showed him the passport issued in Boston, he explained that his clerk was new, and as the Boston passport was of a type not used for a decade or so his clerk had not recognized it. He proceeded to give me back my ten dollars. Naturally I turned over my luxurious quarters to the two ladies and moved into others, smaller but quite as nice. On landing at Port-au-Prince, I presented Clark's passport first — to try it out — to a guard who said something in a loud voice. Then others joined him. There was evidently disagreement about my entering the republic. An elderly man with a red rosette in his buttonhole appeared and asked if he could help me. I showed him the passport. He argued with the guard, the guard maintaining that there

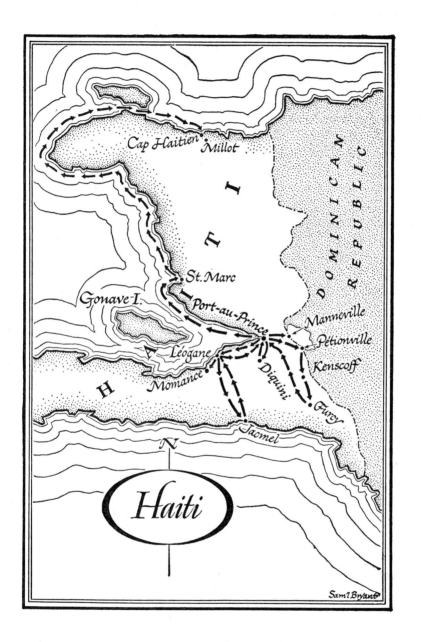

Cap Haitien · Millot

H A I T I

DOMINICAN REPUBLIC

Gonave I.

St. Marc

Port-au-Prince

Manneville

Petionville

Leogane

Momance

Diquini

Kenscoff

Fury

H A

Jacmel

N

Haiti

Sam? Bryant

was no consul in Boston, and the elderly man with the rosette telling him, "So little you know of the affairs of our republic! One was appointed there last month."

The American Legation was a few blocks away and I hurried there. A colored man with a goatee greeted me. In Brazil I had found that sometimes our consulates hired natives of the country as clerks, so I explained in my best French who I was and why I had come to Haiti. He looked perplexed but asked me in French if I knew any other language. I told him I had learned a little Portuguese and started talking that, when he interrupted to ask if I knew another language. I mentioned English and he said, "Then why don't you speak it? I was born and raised in Philadelphia." His name was Baptiste, he was in the diplomatic service, and he immediately introduced me to the other members of the Legation: the minister, Henry W. Furniss, Mr. Moore, and Mr. Furbush. They sent one of the messengers back to the dock with me where we cleared my stuff through the customs and brought it to the legation to be stored in the basement while I was traveling.

The Hotel Montagne, situated on a hill overlooking the city, furnished such a wonderful suite of rooms that my suspicions were aroused. The rooms were being held till the arrival of the new British minister, expected in a week or so. I inquired the price, was told it, and immediately moved to the American Hotel, run by Captain Gatchal and his wife, "Mother" Gatchal.

Captain Gatchal came from New Jersey, and was elderly, tall, slender, and a great devotee of Haitian rum, which he proclaimed the finest drink in the world. He should know. His breakfast, to which he hurried after a preliminary glass of straight rum, consisted of a shaddock, cut open at the top, seeded, and filled with rum. Shaddocks are a coarsely grained type of grapefruit, delicious in flavor and as large as a man's head. Then there was rum before lunch, before dinner, and afterwards.

One time, coming in from a collecting trip, I was showing my catch to a group of American railroad men. Among the things was a live Haitian boa, about five feet long. This is "the snake that crows like a cock," and enters into the voodoo ceremonies. None of my Haitian friends had ever seen the boa when it crowed, but several of them told me that they had heard it. I took the snake out of the cloth bag in which I kept it, and exhibited it to an admiring though distant group, then put it back in the bag and left it on the table.

The hotel bar opened to the right of the veranda. Captain Gatchal put his head out and greeted me, "Hey, feller," then hurriedly went back into the bar. He came out a moment or two later, looked me over and turned into the bar again. I expected more of a greeting from him when he came out the third time, but he just stood there looking at me and the bag. One of the railroad men called to him: "Captain, come and see the big snake Mann has brought in."

The Captain advanced slowly, I opened the bag, pulled the snake out and after he had a glimpse of it popped it back again and tied the bag's top. The Captain still stood there. Finally he said, "Was that snake in the bag the whole time?"

We said it had been, and he drew a deep breath. "*Well*," he said. "I came out on the porch to welcome you, but it looked to me like that bag was moving. I thought I had 'em. I went in and had another rum. When I came out, the bag was still moving, so I went in and had more."

When it was established that he did not "have 'em," he stood a round of drinks for the entire crowd, and he himself cheered up.

I thought that he was drinking too much, and when I became well acquainted with him and fond of him, I remonstrated once in a while. He won out in his arguments, however; and much later, when I was out of the country, I received a letter from the banker telling me of the Captain's latest adventure. He had had a disagreement with another man who also was an advocate of the native drink, and during the argument had received a .38-caliber bullet through one end of a lung. He had recovered. The banker showed him the letter before he sent it to me and the Captain had scrawled on the bottom, "Mann, this shows you what a liberal use of Haitian rum will do for a man's constitution."

Rum was everywhere and in any quantity. I remember passing a church when the congregation was leaving, and seeing a rum salesman dishing out his wares in very small tin cups to the thirsty faithful.

The American Hotel was headquarters for the small American contingent in Haiti, most of them employees of a railroad which was being built in the northern part of the island. With Madeira-Mamoré memories so fresh, I could talk railway construction with them, and Mr. Willoughby, the chief engineer, gave me a letter to the men in charge of his various construction camps.

Archbishop Conan also gave me a card of introduction to all the priests of his diocese, which brought me friendship, food, and lodging in many places.

At the bank I secured paper money, the bills fastened together like checks in a checkbook, to be torn off one by one as used. Tropical climates are hard on paper currency which tears easily, but the Haitian money could be made legal tender by fastening the parts together with unused postage stamps. In the interior I would see gourde bills, the value of which at the time was twenty-seven United States cents, that had been torn so often that the postage-stamp value was greater than that of the bill itself.

Years before there had been a fine silver currency, so much so that the gourde had a value of $1.18, but during the revolution and hard times it sank so low that financiers — or whatever you call them — bought up these coins at much less than their silver value and sold them, so that they are now quite rare collectors' items.

In the first few days, collecting in the near-by hills around the capital, I found a large proportion of the ants then known to the island, as well as a few new ones. Pétionville, or LeCoup, the summer resort of Port-au-Prince, was about three miles inland and at an elevation of fifteen hundred feet. There Madame Bajou maintained a boardinghouse. In addition to excellent French food, there was a cool swimming pool. The shady ravines and the hills sloping back of the town were good collecting grounds. Mr. Furniss had a summer cottage near by and we saw a lot of each other. Furniss owned the first automobile to arrive in Haiti. I forget the make, but it was made in Kokomo, Indiana, and the name *kokomobile* became the standard name for all automobiles. He was learning to drive, and took me with him the first time he rode to LeCoup. Something happened to the engine, which he patched up in about an hour, while I, knowing nothing of engines, collected along the roadside, securing a number of things new to me. He had spent eight years in Bahia, Brazil, and was a mixture of Negro and American Indian, and married to a German woman. A cultured man with a medical education, he was most helpful to me, arranging an audience with the President for the *"entomologiste américain."* When I was presented to His Excellency, he murmured to Furniss: *"Entomologiste?* Where is the bald head and the beard?"

In Haiti a passport was required for all foreigners to travel from town to town; sometimes there was considerable delay in obtaining this, or the visa of the local authorities. But President Tancrède Auguste presented me with one written by hand, giving to William M. Mann permission to visit all parts of Haiti for the purpose of collecting such specimens of insects as were necessary for his studies in entomology. This was a godsend, because it enabled me to proceed without interruption through the villages. Whenever I unfolded it and showed it to the local *chef de place,* it was greeted by an enthusiastic "Oh-oh!"

In many islands the fauna can be most uninteresting, in that it is like the coastal fauna of numerous other islands, but Haiti is different. Since more than half the species of ants on the island are strictly Haitian species, collecting even in the city was interesting. But of course it is the interior that appeals most; so after wandering in the near-by hills and getting some information and much misinformation about the back country, I left LeCoup early one morning for Furcy, a mission station a day's horseback ride inland. The trail went uphill most of the way, past the settlement of Kenscoff, through acres of vegetable gardens, because Haiti in addition to its abundant tropical fruits produces many temperate-climate vegetables — Indian corn, for instance, and some of the finest artichokes ever grown.

The *presbytère* at Furcy was at the far end of a long ridge, and as I rode toward it an ant walked across the trail, carrying its body high on its long legs, with the abdomen twisted underneath the rest of the body and pointing forward. I have told this story before and have been questioned as to how I could recognize an ant from horseback, but anybody can recognize a Macromischa. This was one of the long-lost types of Haiti. I dismounted, popped the ant into a bottle, and rode on.

Père Plombey welcomed me, and I moved into his galvanized iron house. Beamingly I showed him the ant in a vial of alcohol.

Before dinner I strolled in front of the house, where there were many shrubs of *Baccharis myrsinites*. On these shrubs were oval masses which I at first thought were wasp nests. They were constructed of finely shredded grass held together with carton, and were built around the branches of the plants. I tapped one very gingerly with my forceps and immediately the surface was covered with ants, again Macromischa. It proved later to be a new subspecies. The type specimen had been described by Auguste Forel from a couple that he had shaken out of a similar nest that Père Sallé had collected in 1850 in the heart of Santo Domingo. But here were enough for all the museums in the world; literally hundreds of nests were in the vicinity. When I returned with several vials of ants and showed them to Père Plombey with evident excitement, he tried very hard to look interested and murmured, half to himself (and I think, about me), "*C'est curieux, c'est curieux.*"

Furcy is a delightful place to visit. We looked down through pine forests into a deep canyon and a beautiful waterfall. Clouds would roll down, nearly filling the canyon, and then spurts of air from below would send them up like so many columns of white flame. The native buildings around the place were thatched huts and there was a great variety of agricultural produce, coffee and Indian corn, pine trees and banana plants. Dried ears of corn were hung in great clusters on pine trees, with a band of tin around the trunk as a protection against rats. The altitude is given variously by different authorities but the map that hung in the priest's home said it is 1730 meters.

Père Plombey became interested in the things that I collected, or that were brought in to me, and life with him was pleasant indeed. He had lived many years in Haiti and knew the people well. I asked him about voodoo, which one usually does not discuss with the natives, even though there are few moments, day or night, when the sound of drums cannot be heard. These, to be sure, do not always mean that voodoo ceremonies are taking place, but they gratify the natives' love of noisy rhythm. He told me that the most severe penance he imposed was for the practice of voodoo, but added, "Yet I suppose every member of my flock also practises the cult."

A combination of the two religions impresses me as quite convenient: Voodoo to placate the evil spirits in this world and Catholicism to take care of one in the next.

On my way back to Port-au-Prince I stopped again at the end of the ridge. There were many flat stones lying on the ground to the left of the road. I tethered the pony and started turning them over looking for ant nests and whatever else might be concealed there. Under the first stone was a Peripatus, the first live one I had ever seen and the first specimen ever recorded from Haiti. Peripatus has been described as "the nearest approach to the hypothetical ancestor of the arthropods" (insects, spiders, ticks, scorpions, and so forth). It looks like an elongated slug, bearing a pair of antennae on its head, and along each side is a row of short stubby legs. The skin is richly colored and velvety in texture, the eyes very small and apparently used only to detect light — from which it flees. It lives underground, sometimes in rotten wood, preying on small fry such as sowbugs and insects which are captured by the secretion of a sticky slime which gums up the victim. The slime is also used as a defense, and curiously it does not stick to the skin of Peripatus itself. The few species that exist are scattered throughout the world, in South Africa, New Zealand, the South Seas, the Malay Peninsula, and Sumatra.

There were more than sixty large flat stones in the vicinity and I turned over every one of them looking for more Peripatus without any luck. Stopping at the first native hut, I had them heat a little water in which to kill and relax the specimen just caught. Then I transferred it to a weak solution of alcohol, which I gradually strengthened, to harden and preserve it in its natural shape.

Three months later I returned to Furcy; throughout the time I was in Haiti I tried to revisit collecting grounds at intervals to see what changes the seasons had made in the fauna. I again turned over the stones — which I had replaced at the time of my first collecting, as every good entomologist does — but found no Peripatus. On the other side of the ridge were five pine logs on the ground. Under the first of these was a Peripatus — and of another species. Logs two, three, and four were barren, and the last one sheltered a wasps' nest, so my search was ended. These were the only two specimens of this interesting creature (both of them new to science) that I found during my stay, though later collectors have since found them in quantities.

In Pétionville I found one of my objectives, the long-lost ant, *Emeryella schmitti.* Until then it had been represented only by one broken specimen. This had been sent by Schmitt, the priest, to Forel. It was a new and unusual genus, and he named the genus after his old colleague, Emery, and the species after the priest. I had talked so much about this ant to my American friends in Port-au-Prince that it became popularly known as "Mary Ella Schmitt" and they were fond of greeting me on my return to town with the question, "Have you found her yet?"

Here she was, a single worker. I watched her for a time to see if she would go to her nest, but she kept wandering about, the way ants do, and finally I seized her and popped her into a bottle. She was easily recognized: nearly half an inch long, black in color, heavily sculptured on her thorax and with long black mandibles. I spent hours going over every inch of the area with everything but a fine-toothed comb, turning over every stone and log in the vicinity. But no more ants. After visiting several other parts of the island, I wrote jokingly to Wheeler that I believed the species was extinct and I had taken the sole survivor.

Months later, at Diquini, I was strolling through the woods in the evening just before dusk. Crossing the road in front of me was a millipede — a "thousand-legger" — which seemed to be moving in an unusual manner. It was, because it was dead and was being carried by a worker of Emeryella walking along underneath it. Standing still and following the ant with my eyes I saw it and the millipede disappear in a little hole beside a stone. Underneath the stone was the colony — half a hundred of them, workers, with their larvae and cocoons, and a little pile of dead millipedes on one side showing that this was really their natural food. Other workers, larvae, and pupae were in chambers deep in the earth, some six or seven inches below the surface.

To an entomologist there is as much thrill in discovering a "long-lost" species of ant as there is in finding a new one, and quite as much as there would be in capturing a baby gnu or giraffe — not so much exercise, however: Emeryella is a slow-moving, leisurely ant. It has a sting that could be severe; those I caught had no chance to use theirs. There was no queen in the nest, nor in another one that I found a few days later, so it may be assumed that some of the workers, usually infertile, function as egg-layers. But again, a future collector may turn up a conventional female of the species. Some curious males of a primitive ant, red in color and with light brown wings, were attracted to lights in the house of John B. Terres, the United States Consul. He collected them for me. As they belong to the same group as Emeryella, we assumed that they were the males of this species and described them as such.

South of Port-au-Prince and extending eastward is the Cul de Sac, an arid plain that was once under the ocean. A railroad crosses from Port-au-Prince to Manneville, on the west shore of a brackish lake, Etang Saumatre, sometimes called Lake Azuey, inhabited by descendants of various marine species. Part of the lake marks the boundary between Haiti and Santo Domingo.

At Manneville there was a Frenchman living with a Martinique lady named Fifi, and they took in paying guests — as did everyone in Haiti. After lunch the first day, I set out collecting. The country was hot and dry with typical desert vegetation, cactus, thorny bushes, and a few scattered cultivated tracts. The place is only slightly above sea level and I found what might have been expected: insects typical of dry regions, among them a harvesting ant (Pogonomyrmex) which collects and stores vegetable seeds in the same manner as its relatives in the western United States, and like them augments the grain with occasional bits of insect food. Some make mound nests, others live beneath stones. One species, beneath stones among the cactus, proved to be new (*P. saucius*), and it is indicative of my botanical knowledge that the cactus among which I collected day after day was described five years later by J. N. Rose as a new genus.

We were only a short distance from the frontier that separates Haiti from Santo Domingo, and Dr. Terres had insisted that I take a revolver with me. He was a devout friend of the Haitians, but suspicious of their neighbors. He loaned me a nickel-plated revolver with six chambers and I carried it in my knapsack as I had promised.

One of the curious cases of discontinuous distribution is that of a genus of stubby little scorpion that lives in Madagascar and in Haiti, and apparently nowhere else in the world. I had heard about these scorpions, and one morning, in a small draw about three miles from the Dominican frontier, I commenced finding them beneath stones. Excitedly turning over stones and picking up scorpions — with forceps — I paid no attention to an individual above me who addressed me in bad Spanish. Suddenly he picked up a large rock and hurled it at me. It landed a few feet away. I drew the revolver and fired in his general direction, whereupon he hurriedly ran away. When I returned to the house, I told the Frenchman and Fifi about it, and they could not understand it, telling me the natives were exceedingly friendly. Three months later when I returned to the locality, they told me what had happened, with broad grins on their faces. This native had seen me on my hands and knees arranging stones, perhaps making a new boundary line and stealing three miles of Haitian territory. He had later come to them and boasted of the service he had rendered his country by interrupting my frontier-fixing.

At another time I was shooting lizards with fine dust shot from my collecting pistol, .22-caliber smooth-bore, and as I stooped to turn over a rock, found myself surrounded by five Haitian soldiers on horseback, headed by the local general of the near-by town of Thomazau. He addressed me, again in Spanish, his knowledge of it apparently limited to the "*Onde va*" of my stone-throwing friend. On this occasion I presented my passport, which explained things; the soldiery dismounted, and took a great interest in "*les petites bêtes*" which I showed them in various vials of alcohol. They accompanied me back to the house, where Fifi set each of them up to a generous glass of rum, and we all parted, with many handshakes, as effusive friends.

There was a sequel to this. On my second trip to Manneville

my companion was Frank Rose, an English commission merchant whose office was in Havana. He had come from Santo Domingo on a coast boat, and was waiting in Port-au-Prince for a steamer to take him back to Cuba. We became acquainted in the hotel, and he decided to come with me for a couple of days to see the country-side and to observe how a naturalist behaved in the field. On his return to Port-au-Prince, the train stopped at Thomazau. The *général — my* general — had sent some of his soldiers to the train to look over any suspicious characters. Frank evidently seemed like one, because they took him off the train for questioning. He had no passport, but tried to explain by saying that he was a friend of the American who collected *"les petites bêtes."* This news was taken to headquarters, and the general, with a bottle of beer under one arm, hurried down to the train to apologize.

The best way to get from Port-au-Prince to St. Marc was by sea, and this was done in an open sailboat, the passengers sitting on the deck, and when it grew dark, sleeping there indiscriminately. They came aboard with quantities of food for the evening meal, *pois-riz* (beans and rice cooked together with a little oil), piles of bananas, mangoes, alligator pears, and loaves of the rather hard but excellent native bread.

The headquarters of the railroad company were in St. Marc, and the manager put me up in a dormitory. The merchants in the town had complained so bitterly to the general, who functioned as *chef de place*, about "the railroad Americans" who were visiting German and Dutch ships when they were in harbor and buying drinks there, instead of spending their money on warm beer or rum in the local bistros, that His Excellency had issued an order that no one could visit such ships without a permit, to be issued by him. I did not know about this, and the railroad boys did not care, so I accompanied them to a Dutch ship for dinner. After the meal there was a little serious drinking in the smoking room, and a nice time was being had by all when the general himself walked in. He called attention to his order, and in return some of the Americans called his attention to certain facts about himself which, whether true or not, were not complimentary to a man of his position and authority.

He strolled out on deck, leaned over the side, and ordered the boatmen who had rowed us out to the ship to return to the shore. They did, and I found myself on a ship due to leave within an hour for New York, without money, and with all of my collection and my other suit of clothes stored in the basement of the legation in Port-au-Prince. I addressed the general most courteously — three times — before he accepted the greeting. Then I asked him, "*Général*, as a matter of information, how under international law do you have authority over this Dutch ship?" He was glad to tell me about international law and stated, pointing: "While that anchor is down, this ship is a part of Haiti."

Never did a more beautiful idea occur to anyone. I remembered the passport in my pocket, and so I said, "But, *Général*, I have permission to be here."

"You have not. Those permits can be issued only in my office, and I have not signed one this week."

I showed him the presidential passport and pointed out the words, "*permission de visiter toutes parts d'Haiti.*"

He had a sense of humor, and after a couple of "Oh-oh" 's he smiled a huge smile and said, "You have permission and you can return to shore in my boat."

"But how about the boys in the smoking room?"

"Did you hear the way they addressed me?"

"Yes, I did, *Général*, but I think they were drunk. Were you ever drunk, *Général?*"

"Yes, yes, many times," he bragged.

"Well, there is no time to get drunk now before the boat goes, but wouldn't you join us for a few minutes?"

He followed me into the saloon. By this time some of the railroaders realized what had happened and were apprehensive themselves, so the general was invited to join us, and when the steamship whistle blew the signal for departure, we all returned in the now crowded official boat to shore.

Frequently for years afterwards I had a nightmare in which, while on an expedition, I found myself on board a homeward bound boat, having in some way left the entire collection ashore with nobody to care for it.

A half-day's walk from Cap Haitien is the Citadel of Christophe, his old fort, still in good condition. The cannons, hauled there by man power at the order of Christophe, were in place. There were also some four-pointed spikes, made so that no matter how they were thrown one of the sharp ends pointed outward. These had been used to throw in the trail, to interfere with the advance of barefooted enemies, and a hundred years later proved useful to the coach drivers in Port-au-Prince in their warfare against the newly arrived automobiles.

Christophe's tomb stands on a broad platform. There were ants, beautifully marked and new to me, running about on the mausoleum. They proved to be a remarkable new species, black in color with white stripes made of glistening scalelike hairs, and of course this species was named after the great king — *Camponotus christophei*. It is related to a species from St. Thomas, one which Forel described as *C. saussurei*, and called "the jewel of the Camponotus." Later at Pétionville I found a subspecies, which I named after President Auguste.

It was near Pétionville that one of Tom Barbour's prophecies came true. He had told me, when I started out, that there were in Jamaica two species of burrowing snakes, one in the north and one in the south. He thought this might be true of Haiti, although so far only one had been found, in the south. True enough I found another in the north. It was a new species, and Barbour named it after me, *Amphisbaena manni*.

Later on, in Port-au-Prince, Minister Furniss told me he had been talking with the Department of Agriculture. They were having trouble with a coffee disease in the high mountains north of Jacmel. Would I go, as guest of the government, see what I could find out about it, and make some recommendations? Naturally, I would, because the mountains north of Jacmel were not easy to get to and I was glad to be taken there. I journeyed by train down the peninsula to Léogane, where the *chef de place* provided me with a lame horse, a broken bridle, and a guide, and we started off across the peninsula. The ride between Léogane and Jacmel has been often described. Its chief characteristic is a winding stream which one crosses more than a hundred times in a day's ride. I did not do it on horseback, however, for the horse kept stumbling and falling; we spent the last half of the day walking, my guide leading the horse.

At Jacmel the local *général* greeted me and took me to his quarters, an old-time house, bare of furnishings but thoroughly clean. He was a friendly and intelligent mulatto. As he showed me to my room, which contained nothing but a mattress on the floor covered with a clean sheet, he said deprecatingly: "All I can offer you, my friend, is to share the simple quarters of a fighting man."

We had dinner together, and then, feeling military though tired, I slept.

In the morning there was a tremendous sound of drums; the local battalion was having its morning formation outside my room. It consisted of forty soldiers, some of whom carried their shoes in their hands; some, but not all, had rifles. The order to present arms came, and was fulfilled with military precision, but the captain got into an altercation with one of the privates who stood there holding his rifle in his left hand while he gesticulated with his right. I do not know what the argument was about, but the soldier finished it by giving a loud "Oh-oh," marching out of ranks, and disappearing.

The Jacmel *général* sent a courier into the interior to the coffee plantation for another *général* to come, meet me, and take me into his district. This was done by an eight-hour ride always uphill — on a pony that did not stumble.

The general's home was a two-room thatched hut, on a terrace cut out of the hillside. At night the three of us, general, guide, and myself, slept on the floor. When we had arranged ourselves in a neat row, the general's wife would come in and cover us with a quilt which I steadfastly believe was an heirloom. In the morning the general would say, "Monsieur, there is plenty of *salade*, but right now no bread." Fifteen centimes turned over to him secured a supply of the locally baked bread. The *salade* was dried Newfoundland codfish, shredded and mixed with black pepper, and was accompanied by cups of strong, locally grown coffee sweetened with brown sugar. For other meals there were beans and rice, chicken, plenty of mangoes and bananas, and the ubiquitous and delicious Haitian country soup; but each meal was preceded by a wistful request for fifteen centimes to buy the bread. Fifteen centimes was not a large amount, and I was amply repaid for the expense by hearing the general boast about me to some of his junior officers who came to call. "The *blanc*," he said, "cares nothing about money. I say to him, 'To have bread we must have fifteen centimes.' Always he says to me, '*Général*, here is fifteen centimes.' "

There were a larger terrace and a couple of huts some distance below us, and every night and all night we could hear the beating of drums. A voodoo fête was in progress. One evening the general, after absorbing a considerable quantity of rum (which I suspected had been purchased with change from the bread money), announced, "Tonight the *grande fête*. Tonight they eat the *petit bébé*."

That sounded exciting. By those who write about voodoo cannibalism, the victim is usually referred to as the *cabri sans cornes* (goat without horns), and they say that it is the kid of a goat. I blurted out to the general, "Could the *blanc*, a friend of the *général*, see the *grande fête*?"

He did not understand my French, but my guide interrupted with *"Pas pour vous,"* and said something to the general which implied that I did not want to see the ceremonies. My soldier guide looked at me very coldly.

Whether the general was spoofing me, or whether he was so drunk that he was willing to take his white friend to the ceremonies, I do not know; but I have no evidence, either from Jacmel or other parts of Haiti, that human children actually were used as victims. The white cock, yes. He is fed until he can hold no more; then, while the crowd sings a song with the refrain *"Il est replein, il est replein"* the *papa loi* (high priest) removes the tongue of the rooster, and with the bloody stump makes the sign of the cross on the foreheads of the devotees.

There was little money in the hills, but an abundance of food and hospitality. The general showed me his treasures, removing them one by one from a wooden chest: several clean sheets, some large wax candles, and a pair of flaming red trousers, which, when worn with light blue coats, were much in favor with the generals of the army. He showed the trousers to me regretfully, pointing to the seat, which was mostly nonexistent, and explaining: "You see, *blanc*, they are of service to me only when I am mounted."

His hut was commodious, comfortable, and clean, and in the yard was a pile of coffee, the one paying crop of this section. In fact, at this time the principal revenue of the government was derived from an export tax on Haitian coffee. It is of excellent quality, by the way, and greatly in demand in France. It grew in thickets in the canyons, and the disease which I was to look into was a well-known fungus that attacks the leaves. I brought specimens back to the States, where they were properly identified by the United States Department of Agriculture, and the information sent to the government of Haiti.

The day before I departed a large cockfight party was given. How these fighting cocks can devote their attention to annihilating each other when they are surrounded by a shouting, roaring and gesticulating horde is something I could never understand. Neither could I understand the rules and regulations of any of the fights, for though I bet small amounts on each combat, even if the cock on which I had bet killed the other I would lose by some technicality unknown to me.

One of the finest friends I had was General Geffrard, the son of one of the best presidents in the history of Haiti. He had an estate at Momance on the Léogane peninsula, where I visited him on several occasions. He was the most enthusiastic pro-American I have ever met outside of the States, and I think dangerously so for him. He had been to the States and visited in Buffalo, where he had acquired a roll-top desk and a formidable-looking mounted American eagle which was placed above it. We were talking once about the goatee which so many of his nationality wore, and he told me that he had taken it off in America. "But," said he, "with my goatee off I was just a 'damn nigger'; with it on — and by using my strongest French accent as I spoke English — I was 'a Haitian gentleman,' which was much more pleasant."

He spoke English remarkably well, which the local governor who came to dine with us one evening did not. There was some argument as to who should sit at Gef's right hand, and I explained to His Excellency that he, being the governor of the province, should have that place; but he benignly said, "When I am acting as governor, yes, but tonight I am here as a friend and not in my official — official — pomposity."

Anyway, his English was no worse than my French, and we all got along together.

After he had left I asked Gef why he had never gone into politics. He replied that it was too dangerous; then in a wave of excitement he jumped up and said, "Look, suppose I am in politics. I am in the Chambre des Députés, they are all assembled. I say, 'Look, this is the Constitution of Haiti —'" he grabbed a piece of paper, tore it into a thousand pieces, threw them into the air — " 'Now, members of the Chamber, let us send to the United States for a man to come and govern our country.' "

Years later, some did come, in Marine uniform; and Geffrard published a brochure, translated into English, full of pleasure and thankfulness for what our people had done there.

After seven months my finances consisted almost entirely of a return ticket to New York, so, with my specimens and a live parrot and one of the larger boas, I started home.

When I arrived in Boston, the parrot was put in a temporary cage in my laboratory at the Bussey, and for a long time maintained an un-Haitian quiet. The boa I turned over to Mr. Henshaw. He was glad to get it as a specimen, popped it into a large jar with a glass top, and poured some carbon disulphide on it to kill it mercifully. The parrot maintained its silence for some time and then one day, when I was at Cambridge attending a lecture, it opened up. My laboratory was opposite the lecture room where Dr. Wheeler was discoursing to a class. Professor Brues covered the cage with newspaper, shut the door and did everything possible to quiet the bird. But when I returned to the Bussey I found that orders had been issued to "get that damn thing out of here."

So, off it went to the Museum. Mr. Henshaw looked at it and said, "I think we will have to make a skin of it for the collection, as we have very few of this species." To make a skin means to kill the bird and then stuff it, but the parrot immediately began to moult. A good specimen must have good plumage, so Mr. Henshaw kept it in the Museum, pampering it, and becoming more or less fond of it, till one day it bit him and he got an infection from the bite. Eventually the new plumage came in, and the parrot was duly skinned and placed in a tray of specimens.

Skinning the bird reminded Mr. Henshaw of the boa which months ago he had put away in a corridor, forgetting to cover it with alcohol. He removed the glass top, and people in the surrounding laboratories fled from the horrendous stench. Never had there been such a smell even in a museum, and the curators in the Agassiz still talk of it.

One day Dr. Wheeler, with his red notebook in his hand (the book in which he kept notes on what research various students were to do and had written after my name "field work"), came to me and said, "There is a certain very distinguished gentleman interested in Sphingidae — "

Sphingidae are the hummingbird moths, and it was not hard to guess that the distinguished gentleman was B. Preston Clark, who had signed my passport to Haiti. He had connections in Mexico through the United States Smelting and Refining Company, and he wanted somebody to make a collecting trip to the State of Hidalgo. Little was known about the insects there, and my reply, of course, was "Yessir."

On the way to Havana, which was the ship's first stop, a kindly, elderly banker, who knew the country well, gave me considerable advice both about Cuba and about Mexico, and in particular warned me against a certain theater in Havana. Of course, after his warning, that was where I went. The show was a bit rough, as he had told me it would be, but as I sat in the front row, on the aisle, I could not help seeing my moral protector, and some of the other passengers, just across the aisle from me. Although we traveled together from there to Veracruz, he did not speak to me again.

At Progreso, Yucatán, the boat anchored in rather shallow water, in which we could see numbers of sharks slowly swimming about. The passengers leaned over the rail and made the obvious remark, "Wish I had a hook and line." By a strange coincidence the ship's barber showed up at that moment with a heavy handline carrying a large hook baited with a hunk of raw meat. The passengers mobbed him for it, and he grudgingly let one have it for a dollar. To the appeals of the others he muttered, "I might find some more," disappeared, showed up again with a handful of baited hooks on lines, which were passed out at the same price as the first one. The passengers fished, but the sharks did not take hold, and one after another the hooks and lines were disgustedly dropped on the deck to be retrieved by the ship's barber and sold in the same way on the next voyage.

After a short stop in Veracruz (where I saw an advertisement in English for a well-known Mexican beer, with the slogan, "The beer that made Milwaukee jealous") and a round of sight-seeing in Mexico City, I went to Pachuca by train, traveling over an arid plain. Carlos Van Law, manager of the mining company, said plans had been made for me to cross the mountains at Rio del Monte and move into the Hacienda de Velasco. Here was a beautiful garden, surrounded by a high stone wall, a comfortable house used by the mine officials as a week-end resort and occupied by the Van Laws' two children — Jesse, a four-year-old boy, and Billy, a six-year-old girl, their English governess, some servants and two guards, Jesus and Jarvis, six-foot Mexican ex-*rurales* who wore tremendous hats, gaudy jackets, clanking spurs and pearl-handled revolvers.

There was a room on the first floor with a door opening into the patio, with iron-barred windows and an open fireplace. This was assigned to me, and on the first week end it was christened "The Morgue" on account of the pickled and dried specimens I had already accumulated.

Elly, the governess, was young, blue-eyed, with a pink-and-white complexion and at least a temporary interest in my bugs. She liked to walk, the children liked to ride their ponies, and we spent the days in the near-by country, collecting, always accompanied by our two guards.

As I was looking especially for hummingbird moths I spent part of the nights at the Guerrero Mill and Cabrera Mine, in beautiful country, partly forested. The mill officials rigged up some extra large electric lights in front of a whitewashed building and at night the wall would be covered with insects, including a satisfactory variety of the things for which I had been sent.

Our day trips took us farther and farther, and once we made a camp for the six of us, in a pavilion at San Miguel. Funston, one of the mining officials, heard of our plans for the camp, and knowing the owner of a hacienda there, sent word by a messenger that we were coming. When we arrived we found that he had things a little mixed up. After greeting us, he said, "Now, your children can stay with my children; they are about the same age. Here is the room for you and the Señora." This was embarrassing, and the first thing that occurred to me was to explain that the Señora's lungs were in such bad shape that she had been forbidden to sleep indoors, but I had been told of his lovely pavilion on the edge of the lake, and we would all camp there if he permitted it. Accordingly, we installed ourselves in the pavilion, built a big fire, and cooked a hearty camp meal. Then as we sat around to digest it, we were surprised by two servants of the house carrying baskets from which they unpacked for us a tremendous quantity of food — barbecued mutton, beans, of course, and tortillas, none of them lacking the proper amount of pepper. The children could not enter into the deceit which we practised. We rolled them in blankets, and then Elly, the two guards and myself ate a second and heavier dinner than we had had before, under the pleased eyes of the two who had brought it to us. Jesus and Jarvis simply lay on the ground and snored all night, but Elly got acute indigestion, and I spent most of the night heating hot water for her to drink.

The plains around San Miguel were 7000 feet high, and the terrain rose gradually to about 9500 at Guerrero; of course the plant and animal life varied with the altitude. There were quantities of cactus, and among this, one evening, we came upon the exact time for catching Monolema, a beetle, the larvae of which live in cactus plants, boring through the inside and eating the fiber. It is a longicorn beetle, and its heavy elytra are fused together, so that both in color and form it resembles the Pinicate beetle so abundant in all arid tropics. It is usually black, but there was one in Hidalgo which was almost white.

The ants were the same genera found in the mountains of Montana, but as no specimens had ever been collected in the state of Hidalgo, practically everything proved to be a new species, and, curiously, most of them were much darker in color than the related forms in the north. This was also true of the ant-nest beetles that I found. What causes this melanism, I do not know, though later Wheeler suggested that it might be due to their protracted isolation and the high altitude in which they live. He also noticed that the wings of the female ants were longer than in related species from lower altitudes, probably because of the rarefied atmosphere.

This life was almost too good to last, and it didn't. One night, just when cards had been dealt, the telephone rang. Elly answered it, talked a moment or two, then returned and with the nonchalance that the English use to impress more excitable people, played out her hand before she said: "The message was from Funston. Bandits from Tulancingo are coming this way, but a company of *rurales* has been sent from Rio del Monte. Funston will be with them and he hopes they will get here before the others."

We took the two children down into the "Morgue," reached from the main part of the house by a spiral staircase. We left the lights burning in the rooms above, and, there being nothing else to do, waited in the dark. I unsteadily held the .25-caliber automatic and Elly lost her composure long enough to beg me to "save the last bullet for her."

As we waited, I remembered the time when as a youngster in Helena, I had been the leader of a band of sturdy outlaws. With Jesse James so recent, and the Cole Younger outfit too close to us to be romantic, we went farther afield for our ideal: our textbook in robbery was Howard Pyle's *The Merry Adventures of Robin Hood*. We read it and talked "thee" and "thou" to each other, and had combats with quarterstaves. A lath makes a very good quarterstaff and does not necessarily hurt. There was no Sherwood Forest, but there was a lovely robbers' cave that had been formed when a street was cut through to the north side of the High School, between Warren and Main Streets. This could hold all eight or ten of us while we made plans for our career, which was to be banditry. In summer we intended to go to Yellowstone Park, where we would rob the tourists and live off their picnic lunches; in winter we would go to Yosemite. Although we did not know Yosemite Park, we had read that the climate there was mild. Where we were to get the buskins and the longswords with gold-braided scabbards we never worked out, but we assumed that our parents and Mrs. Beinhorn would help a great deal in outfitting us.

One evening when we entered the cave for our meeting we found in the far end a great pile of purses and wallets. Searching them, we discovered that they contained quantities of streetcar tickets, worth ten cents each, and a few trout flies. There were address cards and other trivialities of no importance to seasoned bandits. As our society had no branches we could not imagine how this treasure had appeared.

At that time William Jennings Bryan was making a campaign tour through the West, and he had honored Helena by an address. He was accompanied, most unofficially, by pickpockets, who had looted the hip-pockets of our fellow citizens. They had taken from the wallets most articles of value, and seeing a hole by the side of the road had dumped the rest of the things there. Our parents, when we told them about it, reported the find to the police, and I felt very important when the sheriff interviewed me as the head of the bandits. He took away the wallets, but later returned to us the unclaimed articles. The streetcar tickets we sold to our parents. The trout flies we kept; they would be handy later on when we were actively engaged in our profession.

I don't know how long Elly and I waited there in the "Morgue" with the children, but suddenly there was a burst of shooting. The two groups had met each other outside the gate, and one of them could be heard hurrying away. We could not tell which side had won, and we waited some more. Then we heard the clanging of the gates. Mexican gates are always locked with an unnecessary amount of iron; I have never known one to open quietly. There was the sound of hoofs as somebody galloped from the gates to the house, and we could hear their side-arms and spurs clanking as they dismounted and entered the room above. Then there was conversation in undertones. After standing it in the "Morgue" as long as I could, I sneaked slowly up the stairs in my stocking feet, and cautiously put one eye around the corner into the lighted room, to be greeted by the pleasant sight of Jesus and Jarvis, and an officer of the *rurales*. Funston showed up a moment later carrying two rifles, one of which he handed to me with a very grave expression. But the fight was over. In the morning we saw two corpses just outside the gate, lying by the road with their big hats beside them. It had been a small fight, but it disturbed life at Velasco. The children and their governess could not stay there any more, so Elly dressed Billy and I dressed Jesse, putting his little trousers on the wrong way, so that he had great difficulty sitting down, on his ride across the mountains to Pachuca.

Before leaving Mexico I made a walking trip to El Chico, a mountain village a day's walk from the mill, taking with me an Indian guide. I was to stay at the priest's house there, but he had gone on a journey, so I put up at a tiny *fonda*. I bought my guide a liter mug of *pulque*, which I had ceased to drink myself after trying it once. It is made from the juice of the maguey plant — which looks like a cactus — fermented in goatskin receptacles with the hair on the inside. I do not know whether they are ever cleaned. The drink tastes like a mixture of sour milk and bad eggs. I prefer my sour milk from a cow, and — if I have to have them — my spoiled eggs from a chicken. But the guide downed his in two gulps, and then, when I threatened to wallop him if he had any more that evening, informed me, "No, señor; I do not like it."

Lolita, who ran the *fonda*, was a good cook but a slow one, and it was two hours before dinner was ready. She cheered me up by coming in at intervals and announcing, "One little minute more." Three young Mexican engineers with high laced boots showed up. They were regular boarders and she had, quite properly, postponed dinner until they came. When we sat down, one of them courteously passed me a large platter of peppers fried in batter, glancing slyly out of the corner of his eye at his companions. They helped themselves and then watched me devour mine. I reached for another in spite of the fire in my throat. During the evening they expressed wonder that a gringo could live in Mexico long enough to eat peppers like that, and yet speak such poor Spanish.

In Mexico City I found my Pullman roommate, Gregorio, working as a government engineer. He was a little chagrined about his home town's welcome after his return. In the customary after-dinner speech he had compared Pullman, Washington, to Orizaba, Mexico — their electric light and water supply, and the public schools. He should have stuck to coffee plantations and cherimoya trees, because his fellow citizens did not like the comparison and dubbed him *Yankado* or "Yankee-lover." He had left to become a government engineer in the city. We spent some time together, and he insisted that I visit his family at Orizaba on the way to Veracruz.

His father met me at the station and took me to "his home and mine." He was a grand, elderly Mexican, with great pride in his family of two sons — both of them away at the time — and eight daughters, some of whom I believe were adopted. We dined and supped at a long table, and between meals Señor Limon showed me the sights of the city.

The train from Mexico City to Veracruz passed through Orizaba at four o'clock in the morning, and I had to take it if I were to catch the boat for New York. The family invited me to stay with them till train time, but I did not want to keep them up, and decided to wait at the station. It was already so late that no porters could be found, and my luggage was heavy. Practically all my insect collection was in one big telescope suitcase. However, some of the girls helped me on the streetcar, and when we reached the station the conductor gave me a lift with the baggage. Everything was fine until twelve o'clock, when the stationmaster came to me and said: "We have to close the station, and my orders are that no one can stay here." To wait from midnight until four in the morning outside the station, on the edge of town, where there were always chances of "*bandidos*," was not pleasant, and I appealed to an army officer who was standing there. He asked me my nationality and I told him "*Americano.*"

"But what blood?"

I told him Welsh, German, English, and Irish; he decided that was a good mixture, called the stationmaster and gave him an order, whereupon they pulled loose two of the iron rails that separate seats in station benches, pointed out the place as my sleeping quarters, and left me to doze until train time. At four o'clock the station was open again, thronged with people even at that hour, and it was the stationmaster himself who carried some of my baggage onto the train and arranged a private seat for me by ordering the man who was occupying it to take another.

CHAPTER VII   Dates for Bait

In the course of my studies I went often to the Museum of Comparative Zoology, and in the spring of 1914 I ran into Outram Bangs, curator of birds, who grabbed me and said, "Just the man I was looking for. How would you like to go to Sardinia?"

That talked me into it. It appeared that Dr. John C. Phillips, also of the Museum, wanted to go there to hunt mouflon, the wild sheep that is considered an ancestor of some of our domestic sheep. He had expressed a desire to take a naturalist with him to collect the smaller fry — birds, mammals, reptiles and insects.

Wheeler gave his consent, and there was the usual getting together of vials, nets, scalpels, and other utensils, and the excitement of reading up on Sardinia. Then Phillips telephoned me: "Can't get permission to hunt in Sardinia. Would you just as soon go to Palestine?"

"Yessir."

Later he explained that there were bandits on the rampage in Sardinia at the time and the American ambassador in Rome, Thomas Nelson Page, had vetoed the trip for us. I did not see Phillips again, but he sent me a check and told me to meet him in Cairo, and to go to a firm there named Munari and Company, to look over lists of supplies and arrange for a two-months trip across the desert.

In Alexandria I was taken in hand by a dragoman, Mahomet Ali, who guided me to the Customs House. I wanted to send the trunks in bond to Suez, where we could take them out of Egypt without opening them. The native clerk told me I must open the trunks

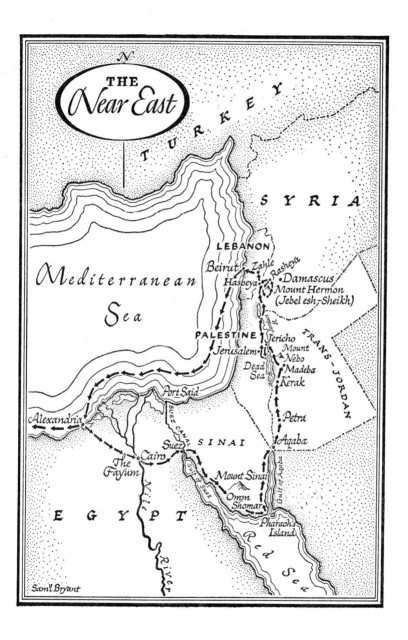

THE
Near East

N

T U R K E Y

S Y R I A

LEBANON

Mediterranean

Beirut
Hasbeya
Zahle
Rasheya
•Damascus
Mount Hermon
(Jebel esh-Sheikh)

Sea

PALESTINE
Jerusalem•
Jericho
Mount
Nebo
Madeba
Kerak
Dead
Sea

TRANS-JORDAN

Port Said

Petra

Alexandria
Suez Canal
SINAI
Aqaba

Suez
Cairo
The
Fayum

Mount Sinai
Omm
Shomar
Pharaoh's
Island

E G Y P T

Nile
River

Red
Sea

Sam'l Bryant

and pay duty on everything they contained. The duty, he said, would be returned to me when they opened the trunks again at Suez and compared the contents with the customs receipt. With a hundred mouse and rat traps, ammunition for all our firearms, which ranged from a .22-caliber shotgun for lizards and small birds to the heavy English three-barreled gun, two barrels for 12-gauge shells and one for .301-caliber bullets, with saltpeter and alum and arsenic for preparing bird and mammal skins, entomological vials and taxidermy tools, I was appalled at the thought of going through all this with a hostile clerk who spoke none too good English. I decided to have a good rest, and next morning get in touch with the head of the customs.

Having put my suitcase in the hotel, I walked up the street, getting angrier and angrier as I thought about the customs clerk. Thomas Cook and Sons had an office near by, and there was a young Englishman sitting on a stool behind a counter near the window.

I went in, to be greeted with, "What can I do for you, sir?"

I told him he could listen a few moments to what I thought of the so-and-so customs officials.

"But why don't you let Thomas Cook take care of it for you? Have you receipts for your baggage?"

I had. "The fee will be five shillings, and you will have to pay the express charges when you pick up your luggage again in Suez." That was a relief. Retrieving my hand baggage and such of the guns as could be taken down and put in a trunk, I took the evening train for Cairo.

At Shepheard's Hotel there was news from Phillips. He wrote from Athens that Mrs. Phillips was ill and he would be delayed a week or so. There was, however, a crowd of guides to meet me, some of them attracted by my guns. They left cards, and among them was that of EMBARAK HASSAN, SHIKARI (hunter). Phillips had had a guide by that name on the White Nile some years before, and the next morning Hassan established himself by identifying Phillips with, "And *his* name is Doctor Flips!" So instead of the usual and annoying dragoman, it was Hassan who guided me about the city, and kept the others off. He kept talking about hunting; I told him Phillips would be with us in a week, but he said we would have time to go to the Fayum and shoot foxes. I visited Munari and Company, who were to organize and provision our caravan for the two months' trip across the desert, and persuaded them to substitute quantities of canned roast beef, corned beef, and canned vegetables for the canned lobster, pâté de foie gras, and other delicacies usually provided for a three days' camp in the Fayum. Then I told Hassan to meet me at eight o'clock the following morning and we would go hunting.

And hunting we went — by streetcar to the citadel, where is situated the Well of Moses; then, hiring donkeys, we rode a couple of miles into the desert, with Hassan protesting that there was no hunting there, and moreover we had brought no guns. We dismissed the donkey boys, and I started looking for things — ants, of course, and beetles. Both were abundant, the former with their nests under stones. To my great delight, many of them were harboring the curious little ant-nest beetle, Thorictes, that supports itself by hanging on to the antennae of the ants and stealing food as one ant feeds another. There were also Tenebrionid beetles running around in the hot sun, black ones resembling those I had found in Mexico and Arizona, but of course quite different genera and many of them with long sharp spines.

Embarak Hassan soon caught the spirit of the thing, and would run these beetles down, putting them in the bottle of alcohol I had given him. He glanced about from time to time, and once when some people on donkeys passed near us, he stopped and sat down as though he were merely accompanying me. He was a well-known hunter and might have lost face had his fellow hunters been told of this expedition.

We wandered slowly back as we collected, finally reaching

the streetcar, and rode to the hotel. As he said good-by that evening he announced, "Khawaji, all my life have I been shikari, but
never before on shikar for the *namil* and the scarab."

To a newcomer Cairo had ceaseless interest, wandering about
during the day with Hassan, learning from him a few words in
Arabic, and at night, after dinner had been served in the hotel by
the silent, bare-footed waiters, sitting on the veranda, watching
the passing show, and saying "Mush ayiz" — "I do not want it" —
every other moment to a peddler. There were a snake charmer
with mongoose and cobra, a gullah-gullah man with his very
good magic, and a fortuneteller. I made friends with some of these
people, especially the gullah-gullah man and the seer. When a
troop of Australians invaded the hotel I drummed up considerable
business for my two friends. The fortuneteller expressed thanks
and in return offered to tell my fortune for nothing. He made a
horoscope with chalk on the pavement, and then looked at the
palm of my hand. Puzzled, he said, "Sair, I cannot tell your
profession. You are not a soldier, you are not a merchant." In
answer I pulled a vial full of pickled beetles out of my pocket
and showed it to him. Everything was clear then, and he said,
"Ah, sair, you are like me, a professor."

One morning the gullah-gullah man beckoned me to the pavement and showed me a lead half-crown piece that somebody had
passed him the previous evening. He had a sense of humor, for
he made a mark with it on the stone wall, tossed it over the fence
into an adjoining garden, and said, "And me a gullah-gullah
man!" Then he confided to me that his tricks were all really
sleight-of-hand, Allah did not help him; in fact, if Allah *would*
help him, he could charm money direct from the bank and would
not have to work at all.

The zoo at Gizeh could be reached by the tram that went on
to the pyramids. There was a small admission charge at the
gate. It was one of the most popular places in Cairo, not so much
for the tourists as for the residents. It was administered by an

English triumvirate, the Messrs. Flower, Bonhote, and Nichols. I called on them, explaining my interest in zoos, and was treated with great courtesy for a visit or two. Then, getting more garrulous, and talking about myself, which an Englishman seldom does, I mentioned that I was with Dr. John C. Phillips and was going on a cross-country trip with him. After that, the only courtesy shown me was so chilling I did not care to receive it. Something was wrong, but I did not know what it could be. However, I enjoyed the zoo itself. In an artificial but natural-looking lake was Sally the hippopotamus, and for a small gratuity the attendant would get a bunch of forage, call her, and she would take it out of his hand. A big cage contained dozens of hamadryas baboons. These are the large baboons with gray mantles, known to American circus goers who believe in side-show banners as "lion slayers." There were Addax antelope which live in the remote parts of the Sahara and are supposed never to drink water. Chameleons sometimes could be picked up on the shrubbery in the zoo.

Phillips had written ahead to me, suggesting that we get an Arab hunter who could also make bird skins, the idea being that he attend to the birds while I handled the mammals, reptiles, and insects. I told this to Hassan, he told it in the bazaars, and afterward throngs of would-be desert hunters and taxidermists hove in sight whenever I appeared outside the hotel. Hassan himself told me he did not think his health would permit him to make such a trip, but he would not recommend any one person. I got the idea of having a competitive examination, as in Civil Service, and announced that we would have a test on making bird skins at a near-by Egyptian locanda, or inn, at a certain time. Hassan and I kept the appointment, and there were a couple of dozen aspirants. The examination was easy to hold, because only two of them had brought their own specimens; one of them, a young Bedouin, had a pigeon which he had shot that morning, and the other, an elderly man, one that he had purchased in the market.

Ruling out all the others, I supplied these two with scalpel and scissors. Both of them had been on bird-collecting trips on one of the expeditions fathered by Baron Rothschild of England, and both of them did fairly good skins. The older man opened his bird at the side, but the youngster used the more conventional ab-dominal incision, and I chose him. His name was Abdul Simeon Aoubiad. He was tall, slender, wiry, and spoke reasonably good English mixed with French. He told me afterward that Hassan, an old friend of his, would have liked to come but was not feeling well "on account of a sickness he got from a lady," which rendered him unfit for travel and hard work. Abdul was about my age, a devout and philosophical Moslem, and quite an observant field naturalist.

Phillips eventually showed up. Mrs. Phillips had recovered and was on her way back to the United States. We made a trip to Munari's together, checked our equipment, and prepared to leave, but he wanted to visit the zoo and his friends there first. I told him how nice the zoo people had been to me till they learned I was with him, and how they had practically cut me dead ever since.

He said: "I can't understand it. Flower is a good friend of mine. Let's go out and see him."

There is an archway at the entrance to the zoo, and in it a mounted rhinoceros head and some other trophies. As we went in, Major Flower was coming out. Phillips said, "Oh, there he is now," and went over to speak to him. I stopped at a discreet dis-tance, but could see that Flower was glaring, and that Phillips's face reddened as they exchanged a few words. I retreated several feet, Flower walked off, and Phillips came back to me and said, "Did you hear how that so-and-so talked to me?"

Much later we found the reason. On Phillips's first trip to Egypt he had collected a small sparrow on the outskirts of the zoo. It seemed new to him, and he named it as a new species. It proved not to be, but Flower's acquaintances had twitted him so much about this American coming in and shooting a new bird from under his very nose that he lost his sense of humor about the affair and simply did not like Phillips.

Afterward, when we were in the desert together and it was necessary to pay a formal call on the local sheik, a thing Phillips did not like to do, he would send me. These affairs were a little difficult for one who had only a smattering of Arabic. One had to drink seven ceremonial cups of what would have been coffee had it not been made of parched corn, and engage in pleasantries through an interpreter. We would argue about which one of us should go, and I always lost. The only satisfaction I got out of these affairs was saying, "All right; I'll tell the sheik that I'm with you."

The three of us, Phillips, Abdul, and myself, left for Suez on the train one morning. Across the canal from Suez, our camp was ready, one large square-based tent, a tiny cook tent, and a toilet tent of canvas. In accordance with the arrangements we had made in Cairo, the tents had been pitched by the Bedouins, who were to take us across the desert. There was a sheik in charge of the Arabs, and a man for each camel.

It was after dark when we entered our tent, which was lighted by a kerosene lamp and contained a small table and two cots. Outside was a roaring as of a dozen lions. This came from our camels, seventeen of them, making more noise than seventeen animals ever made before.

We lunched the first day at Ain Musa, said to be where Moses once put some branches of a tree in brackish water and turned it sweet. It has since turned brackish again, but the camels enjoyed it. And we enjoyed our lunch of boiled pigeon, bread, and an orange. It was hot, so for a while we stayed in the shelter of our tent, but were driven out by pestiferous flies. These appeared every time we got in the shade, but they avoided the sun — as we should have liked to do. They were the flies that crawl about stickily over your face and try to get into your eyes. A wave of your hand is unnoticed, and a direct swat is usually a miss. This is the fly that carries so much of the trachoma of Egypt and Western Asia.

Many date palms edged the pool, and natives were carrying large bunches of blossoms from one tree to another. This was new to me, but Solomon explained it: "Sair, a date, to have baby dates, must be vaccinated — just like a lady and gentleman."

After lunch the ride continued until nearly sunset. Our main caravan had passed us, the Arabs eating only in the morning and at night, and our camp was set up and the tents ready to move into when we reached them. An American flag flew from the top of our tent, and a Turkish one from the cook tent, which was also sleeping quarters for Abdul, Solomon Demetrius — the drago-man — and Algeciras, our cook. Here I had my first experience of the sheer delight of a drink of water. During the day it was so hot that at noon, when we drank water with our lunch, I was as thirsty afterwards as before. During the entire journey, while we must have perspired profusely, our skins remained perfectly dry, but when the sun went down, the air chilled. This is true of the deserts of the world, and when you drink water then you can almost feel it soaking into individual corpuscles of your system.

The second evening the camp was again waiting for us, and before dining we put out about sixty traps for small mammals. Around the roots of each of the scrubby plants was a pile of earth blown there by the wind, and everywhere were holes in the ground, nests of jerboas and other desert inhabitants. Jerboas are the little jumping rats of the desert, with long hind legs and tails and the forelegs so reduced that sometimes, when they are in zoos, people ask if it is true that there are mammals with only two legs. We baited the traps carefully with oatmeal which we had brought from America for the purpose, that being a standard bait used by collectors of similar species in the United States. I wondered how we would get all the skins taken care of the following morning, but that proved simple because none of the traps had anything in it. The next evening, at Wadi Ghazel, we repeated the performance, but baited some of the traps with bits of dried dates and caught half a dozen jerboas. These specimens we skinned, stuffed, and dried, the drying process being unusually easy in that climate.

Camel caravanning is as much a contemplative man's recreation as Isaak Walton's fishing; one rides "joggedy-jog" two-and-a-half miles an hour, eight hours a day, as regular as clockwork. Moving slowly along there was time even to practice Arabic with Abdul. I would repeat a sentence after him, and Awad, my camel boy, would repeat the phrase to the camel man in front of him, who would repeat it to the one in front of him, till it had reached the whole length of the line; then it would be shouted back till it reached Abdul and me again. Sometimes it brought inquiries also; for instance, I learned to say "I am very angry." That went up the line, but as it came back, the question came, "But what is the Khawaji angry about? Allah grant it is not at us."

One evening when we had dismounted from the camels and were resting in front of our tent, Solomon Demetrius came to us. He had told us so many tales as we traveled through the desert that we had become suspicious of them. He was the son of a dragoman, and his father had been the son of a dragoman, so these legends had been repeated by word of mouth through generations. We would see a ruin, and Solomon would tell us: "That is a ruin of the ancient Egyptians. It was captured by the Crusaders and afterward taken away from them by the Saracens." To us, it was a pile of stones and we had no confidence in his statements. He always had a great interest in the entertainment of what he called "the passengers" — Phillips and me. This evening in the Wadi Mughara he said: "Sairs, down in this Wadi there are many mines, mined by the ancient Egyptians for turquoises. The Egyptians made some markings there. One of them is very famous. It shows an Egyptian with a whip in his hand and his foot on the neck of a slave."

Phillips said, "I've heard about that. Let's go and see it."

We went down the Wadi. On the side of the hill were many mine shafts, each with a pile of rubble below it. We climbed one after another. There were ancient markings and hieroglyphics there, but we did not find the one we were looking for. Quite disgusted, we came back to camp. We had with us three guidebooks: Exodus; Stanley Hall's *The Land and the Book* (such a tiresome book that Phillips said he did not blame Edward VII for some of his peccadillos, having had Stanley Hall for a tutor); and Baedeker. We opened Baedeker and found that the sculpture we had been looking for was noted, but unfortunately — completely unknown to Solomon — it had been cut out some years before and transferred to the Museum in Cairo. It shows a gigantic Pharaoh grasping the necks of a number of the vanquished with one hand, while he brandishes a weapon with the other.

We camped one night at the Wadi Gharandel, the Elim of Exodus. There was a well, the water six feet below the surface of the ground. In times past it must have been much higher, because there were records of ducks having lived there. Here for the first time we found birds — wheatears, martins, Bonnilli's warblers, and sand partridges. These sand partridges, known as "see-see birds," made an agreeable addition to our fare, which came mostly out of tin cans. Phillips said the partridges were the only fat things in Sinai except himself and me. We had an occasional chicken, for we carried live ones with us in crates on camel-back. When we made camp, the chickens were let out to forage, but before dark they would come back to their crates.

The vegetation here was very sparse, and mostly in the form of scrubby bushes a couple of feet high, which grew singly or in small clumps, at the base of which sand collected, forming little hummocks. Most of the insects were among these bushes, or were dug out of holes in the sand where they had retreated to avoid the heat of the day. While walking about looking for specimens, I often noticed that ticks came out from these hummocks and followed me. It was possible to attract them by stamping on the ground in the vicinity. If I changed my direction, they would do likewise — always at a frantically rapid pace for a tick, but one about equal to the slow walk of a man. It seemed ridiculous to be pursued in this manner, and I often walked slowly, watching them follow me. As long as I remained within a distance of ten or twelve feet, they would continue the pursuit. Those which I permitted to reach me crawled about for a little while and then dropped off without biting. Most ticks adopt a policy of watchful waiting, but this habit of running after their host adapts this special species to desert life, with its absence of trees and grass on which the tick can wait until the host passes by close enough for it to drop off and attach itself. The tick was later identified as *Hyalomma aegyptium*, and one of its hosts is the camel.

There was a day's march along the coast under high cliffs. Not a gull or a shore bird was in sight, nothing but dead shells on the beach. From time to time the camels had to walk through sea water, sometimes a foot deep. They didn't like it, and set up a bellowing.

On the afternoon of the eighth day our camels changed their gaits with a bang, and were off at a terrific trot, despite our efforts to slow them down. We had come to the Wadi Feran — the Vale of Rephidim of the Old Testament and sometimes called "The Pearl of Rimai." A beautiful stream of water flowed through a gully for about three miles and then disappeared. The camels had sensed it from afar and we had some bad jolting before they came to it, stopped and filled themselves up. While camels can go for considerable time without water, after three days of thirst they become meaner.

Our tents set up in the oasis, we settled down for a week of collecting. The stream itself was five or six feet wide and a foot or so deep, and flowed rapidly down the canyon, which was banked by high and rocky hills. A low hill, in the middle of the range El Meherrat, had on it the ruins of an ancient church, built to commemorate the spot where Moses stood with arms upraised in supplication while the Jews smote the Amalekites. The few Amalekites left lived in flat-topped stone houses, which we did not care to enter even for entomological collecting, as they were full of fleas. The windows of these houses open to the outside instead of to the inside as they do in most Moslem countries.

The cliffs near by are full of graves, and the cells of anchorites who lived there in the early Christian era. There was a tiny chapel presided over by a Greek monk, and above the gate were a cross and a crescent. Here and on Mount Sinai the cross and crescent could be displayed side by side, for both places are holy to Christian and Moslem.

The monk was a heavy-set man. He knew no English and I knew no Greek, but he welcomed me with an outstretched arm. I went in, and let him help himself from my tobacco pouch. He and I sat together in his room, smoking and beaming at each other, and saying nothing. He pointed to the pictures on the wall. Here were rows and rows of Greeks in orderly military formation, banners flying, attacking a disorganized army of Turkish soldiery who, with heads bowed in fear, were running away. Later on, in Turkish territory, I saw the same picture reversed, with the orderly Turks pursuing the disorganized Greeks.

Collecting perked up. We found spiny mice, that have some of the hair coarse and sharp, but the skin itself so delicate that it seems to have no more texture than wet tissue paper. They were the most difficult animals to prepare for a museum that I have ever handled. There were also a big gerbil, a silky gerbil, and a long-footed gerbil. These are small rodents, some of them with bushy, squirrel-like tails. Once when I had too many to prepare I handed one over to Abdul, who ordinarily did all the bird skinning. After he had worked with it a few minutes he turned to me and said, "Sir, his feathers are just like silk."

There were some rat snakes and some sand snakes, and Phillips shot a Butler's owl, the third specimen of its kind ever known.

The famous monastery of Saint Catherine, five thousand or so feet above sea level, although at the base of Mount Sinai, was built by Justinian in 530 A.D., in memory of Saint Catherine of Alexandria. He gave the monks one hundred Roman and one hundred Moslem slaves, with their wives and children, and their descendants still are the working people of the monastery. Curiously, they are for the most part Moslems, but not regarded as of the true faith by the neighboring Bedouins. The monastery is a huge fortresslike building, formerly tenanted by many monks, but when we visited it there were only about twenty-five, mostly from Crete and Cyprus. Cypress trees shade part of the garden, and there is an ancient well — undoubtedly the one where Moses helped Jethro's daughter water the sheep, as it is the only well in this part of the world, though there are a few small and irregular springs in the near-by mountains.

There are rooms in the monastery for pilgrims and other guests; we preferred to pitch our tents outside and, as it were, lead our own lives.

The father superior received us, and fed us great spoonfuls of currant jelly washed down with date brandy, for though the monks are under strict discipline and do not touch alcohol in general, they are allowed this *arak*. It burns one's throat even when diluted with jelly.

We hunted for ibex, still fairly plentiful in the higher mountains despite five thousand years of continual hunting and no game laws. Phillips saw a couple of small ones, but a newborn specimen was brought to us alive and we secured a number of fine horns from the natives.

There was plenty of shade and there were numbers of birds, but no species that we had not taken before. Near by were scattered tamarisk trees, the plants that produce the manna of the Old Testament. Scale insects attach themselves by their beaks, and suck the juice; this is then secreted, and solidifies into a round flat cake, sweet in taste. The monks try it out and sell little tins of manna for tourists to take home. Many scale insects have this habit; in some parts of the world they inhabit sugar cane and secrete the sap in such large quantities that bees use it for honey, so much so that some years ago one of our Pure Food and Drug laws insisted that confections made of this be labeled "Made from honeydew" instead of "honey."

There is a small burial area in the garden. This contains soil brought from the Holy Land, and when a monk or a pilgrim dies he is interred here. Eventually his skeleton is removed into the crypt. There was a huge pyramid of skulls at one end. The bishops rate little boxes set in niches in the wall, and the skeleton of one authentic holy man, Saint Stephanus, clad in a shirt and a skullcap, stands guard at one side.

We decided to go to Omm Shomar, a high mountain a day's camel ride south of Mount Sinai. About halfway between the two places we were astonished at seeing a solitary Arab coming on foot in our direction. He was dressed in a short skirt instead of the usual long robes, and Abdul recognized him in the distance as a fellow hunter. As he approached we saw that he carried under his arm a wire rat trap with a live jerboa in it. We had passed Arabs on their camels at different times; they had talked with our boys and the rumor had reached Tor in the southern end of the peninsula, some days' walk from us, that there were strange foreigners hunting for things like rats. This man had hurriedly captured his specimen and walked across the desert to ask for a job as guide. He had assumed that we would go to Omm Shomar to hunt ibex and had calculated the time so well that he met us just before we reached the mountain. We did not need a guide at the time, but Phillips was so impressed with the ingeniousness of the man that he hired him. He stayed with us for a couple of weeks.

The country was barren and we saw nothing but a few desert larks and crag martins. We camped at a high elevation and from the top of one of the peaks the view was unlike anything we had ever seen before. The south end of the Sinaiatic Peninsula lay below us like a relief map. To the west one could see about fifty miles of the Gulf of Suez and through field glasses make out steamships. To the east were the Gulf of Aqaba and the low mountains of Midian. The general aspect was terrible, desolate, and grand. We found little life in the hills but did see one eagle soaring overhead, possibly looking for ibex.

On our return to Saint Catherine's Monastery we heard exciting news; there had been a rain, the first one in three years. At the Wadi Gharandel we had had a light shower, and were told that it was the first time anything like that had happened in eleven years. Phillips laid the scarcity of animal life to an unusually great lack of water at this season.

We finally reached the shore of the Gulf of Aqaba, and camped opposite Pharaoh's Island, on which is a ruined castle of the Crusaders' time, said to be the farthest south that they ever reached. There were opportunities for a bath here in the Gulf. I went in neck-deep and suddenly becoming shark-conscious swam to shore. While I dried myself under a sayal tree, Phillips went in, but there was a fish swimming near the surface and in circles coming closer and closer to him, so he got out again. I twitted him:

"Why, you didn't even swim. *I* did."

He replied grimly, "I noticed you swam mostly in one direction."

Across the Gulf we could see the forbidden land, Arabia, and even make out one small village near the beach. When I jokingly suggested to Abdul that we swim over, he replied most seriously:

"That is holy land, and any Arab would consider it a great shame to himself if he did not kill you there."

We shot some sand grouse. Abdul made specimens of them and Algeciras roasted the flesh for us to eat. In this way nothing was wasted, and they were delicious.

Outside of an occasional bird, a sand viper that one of the Arabs picked up, and a few lizards, we collected little. The lizards I would often shoot from the top of the camel, with a .22-caliber pistol bored smooth for shot. Awad would toss them up to me to be placed in a bag until evening when they could be properly pickled. The Arabs, seeing me shoot so successfully with a little gun, and not knowing what shot was, said, "If the Khawaji can shoot like that with a little gun, what might he do with a big one?"

The Arab keeps his other robe under your saddle as padding, and the tenants of the robe migrate to you. These are known as body lice. I wanted some for the Museum, so preserved a small vial of them, mostly taken from Phillips's stomacher. They are in the Museum now and properly labeled: COLLECTED ON DR. JOHN C. PHILLIPS IN SINAI. He told me the reason I had less than he did was because I was too dirty. The collection was enriched once in a while by Solomon bringing me one between his finger and thumb, saying, "Sair, here is another flea for you."

His knowledge of English, while ample, had some curious twists to it. If he did not understand, he would put the palm of his hand to his forehead and murmur, *"Bgwan."*

Abdul noticed this, and remarked one evening: "Solomon does not speak the English too good. I hear him say *'Bgwan.'* "

"What does he mean, Abdul?"

" 'Beg me puggin,' sir."

The shore of the Gulf was strewn with dead shells, but there were no birds. Arabs came into our camp one evening bringing the saddle of a gazelle, and we had a sybaritic feast. Our water, carried in new casks, had become quite foul, so we decided to celebrate with a bottle of Evian, a case of which we had brought in the event of sickness or other emergency, and at our request Algeciras brought us a bottle. We wondered how our supply was holding out, as once or twice before we had celebrated in the same way. We asked Algeciras to investigate, and tell us how much there was left.

"There are two bottles, sairs, but one of them is broken and the water has run out."

Evidently other bottles had cracked and been thrown away, and we had to resign ourselves to drinking the water from the casks. We filled the casks at various springs, but it always became bad-tasting; Phillips thought it was due to having been put in new casks.

There was a good spring at Ain en-Nuheibeh, and here was a tiny fortress manned by three Egyptian soldiers. Though Sinai has an area of about ten thousand square miles and was inhabited by six or eight thousand nomadic Bedouins, it was a peaceful land. These three soldiers, living in a stone house, represented law and order to the entire peninsula, but back of them was the might of the British Empire, and Lord Kitchener. The latter was feared and respected by all who knew about him; moreover, they firmly believed that he knew all about each one of them, individually. In Syria, later, a missionary told me about sending a letter to a friend of hers in one of the bazaars in Cairo. Another man opened it, and when she went to Cairo, she called on him and reprimanded him. He was abject in his apologies and promised never to do such a thing again; when she left he pleaded with her, "Please do not mention this to Lord Kitchener."

The three soldiers greeted us as we passed their house, made some inquiries about us, and then to our great astonishment refused a few packs of cigarettes that we offered them. As we left their station I dropped some on the ground; looking back, after a hundred yards or so, I saw that they had strolled over and were picking them up, but they were avoiding any appearance of bribery.

At the extreme tip of the Gulf is the village of Aqaba, once a thriving and prosperous city on the main roads from north to south, one through Sinai to Egypt, and the other a pilgrimage route to Mecca. Little remains of the old grandeur except the Turkish fortress, a large, rectangular building with massive walls and each corner protected by a tower. The native houses are strictly Arab in style, a house alternating with a garden; both are protected from public view by high stone walls with an occasional Standard Oil tin built into the masonry.

The Kaimakan gave us official permission to set up camp on the beach at one side of the village, where he and his assistant, Feisal, a young Arab from Mecca, would visit us each evening and give us news from the outside world, received by telegraph. He told us of a war between the United States and Mexico, and asked us who we thought would win. He should have been war-conscious, for immediately in front of the village there stood out of the water a mast of what had been a Turkish boat, sunk by the Italians in their recent war.

We were in Turkish territory here, and the Towarah Arabs who had been accompanying us now departed with their camels and baksheesh.

The eight days we spent at Aqaba were the most profitable of our trip. They were made not only possible but necessary because our caravan, expected from the north, did not show up. There had been a robbery and some killings on another caravan ahead of ours, and hearing of it, our men took a divergent and much longer route.

We collected many birds: among others a crake, a specimen of the very rare Audoin's gull, as well as other gulls, and a couple of garganey teal. One extraordinary sight was a flock of Levant sparrow hawks coming north up the Gulf. We figured that there were between fifteen hundred and eighteen hundred birds in the flock, larger than any we had ever heard of. Among the palm trees were many smaller birds, including the beautiful European bee-eaters, who were engaged in overeating. A swarm of small sand beetles, emerging from the ground on their mating flight, filled the air with a buzz and furnished provender that must have seemed astonishing to the bee-eaters in this arid land. We found the awkward hopping thrush, a little bird that hops along and seldom takes to flight. There were many fan-tailed ravens, which have a curious flight and sometimes "tumble" like a roller pigeon. They have a rich and musical note. Migratory wagtails that ran about our camp showed us how they got their name.

The garganey teal were skinned by Abdul as usual, and we ate the meat. The following evening at dinner there appeared on the table two more birds, one large, one small, covered with a rich brown gravy. We assumed that Solomon had bought them in the little bazaar in the village. I cut a piece from the larger one; there was something wrong — it was as vile as anything I have ever tried to eat; but I wanted Phillips to have his share of any luxury. He liked his game much higher than I did. I hurriedly swallowed it and wished I hadn't. Phillips took a bite which he spat out on the ground, and asked:

"Do you know what the hell this is?"

I didn't, and we called in Solomon and inquired.

"Sairs, these is them two ducks you have shot today."

Phillips asked me, "Did you shoot a duck today?"

I had not, and neither had he, but he had shot an exceedingly fat gull and I, an exceedingly lean land rail.

To the Arab the dog is a foul creature and the greatest pests we endured were the local dogs. They are completely neglected and are the epitome of hunger. We set our traps, large and small, and every once in a while a dog would get into one. He would snarl as we approached, but grabbing him by the neck we would release him from the trap and set it again; often after being caught and hurt by the steel clamps, he would immediately return and get caught again.

Our caravan finally arrived with its tale of the robbery, so with an entirely new body of men, this time Palestinians and Syrians, accompanied by two Turkish Army soldiers assigned to us by the government, we loaded horses instead of camels and started north, climbing a long rise toward the Syrio-Arabian plateau. The weather became cooler and it was windy. At the end of one day we came to a camping place. There was an old Roman well from which the boys were already drawing water, but Phillips and I looked down into a deep canyon and saw what appeared to mark a stream: a long line of oleander bushes. We were camping on a wind-swept flat, and Phillips asked Solomon Demetrius, "Why do we not camp below in the canyon, where the bushes are?"

Solomon told him, "Sair, there are many bad roberts in the canyon."

Phillips said that we could take care of the "roberts" and Solomon replied, "But sair, there is no water."

That settled it, and we camped where we were, but the next morning as Phillips and I wandered down on foot, collecting as we went, and ahead of the caravan, we found a rushing stream of clear water. It would have been a lovely place to camp and collect, and we discounted the robbers as something that Solomon had imagined.

Climbing up, we came upon our first crude cultivation: little grain patches, the size of a spare room in a boardinghouse, with grain growing on what looked like a bed of rubble — no soil in sight. Our soldiers calmly drove their horses into these little patches and let them graze — which is one reason why the Turks were not liked by the Arabs.

Phillips, Abdul, one of the two Turkish soldiers and I stopped for lunch. Suddenly there was a sound of shooting up the trail and out of sight. Abdul broke our silence with, "Maybe the Arabs make war." There was nothing for us to do but go ahead and see what was happening, so mounting our horses we started in the direction of the noise. My horse was hard to control with the reins which I held in my left hand — my rifle was in the other — and my helmet slipped forward over my eyes, leaving me in the unenviable situation of galloping into what might be a battle, blindfolded. By shouting loudly at Phillips I got him to slow down his horse. My horse then slowed down and I got myself re-arranged. Soon we reached a group of excited people, men of our own caravan who had gone ahead.

The shooting we had heard had been done by them to attract our attention, but lying on the ground was our advance guard, an Arab soldier from Medina, who had gone forward with Demetrius. The camel belonging to the soldier was gone; Solomon and his horse had disappeared. Our soldier had been ambushed and left for dead by robbers of the Zaida tribe. They did not shoot Solomon but were going to cut his throat, when he fell on his knees and began praying aloud. Instead of killing him, they took from him what cash he had in his money belt, the money belt itself, and all his clothes, even his turban with the tassel on it, and gave him a kick in the direction of his horse. Like a he-Godiva, he left for Maan, the nearest settlement and one with a Turkish garrison. They had even taken from him a huge and obsolete revolver that he had been fond of brandishing, especially when native dogs came near our camp.

He made the trip to Maan in a little over four hours, not sparing his horse. It took us nearly two days because of our wounded guard. He had been shot through the abdominal muscles and the small of his back, which appeared to be a mass of shattered bone. He was paralyzed and in great pain. We gave him pill after pill of morphine, but each time we tried to get him into the litter hurriedly made from four tent poles and some canvas, he would shriek in agony. We kept giving him the narcotic until he was so thoroughly numb that we could wrap him up, swing him alongside one of the horses, and continue on our way. We camped in a gully. The remaining soldier climbed to a high place above us to keep watch, and we got a night's rest.

The wounded soldier seemed about the same the next day, and Phillips, who himself was a medical man, said that if we could only get him to Damascus where the French surgeons in the hospital could work on him, they might possibly save his life, though he would always be a cripple. Abdul explained that being a soldier he would much prefer to die. In the middle of the morning we were met by a troop of Turkish cavalry, who said that Solomon had arrived safely at Maan and told his story. We reached there early in the evening, and put the wounded soldier in the local barracks, on a stone bed. He was interrogated by the captain, and more so by an elderly, bearded Bedouin. Both of them showed more interest in the identity of the murderer than in the wounded boy, and Abdul told me that the soldiers would go out and burn many camel's-hair tents and seize camels and sheep in retaliation, but that the elderly Arab, the boy's uncle, would go out with the intention of getting the head of the murderer as a solace for the boy's mother.

The army took charge of the soldier and sent him on the Hejaz railway to the nearest military hospital, but we heard afterward that he had died en route.

Officials detailed another guard to go with us, this one a very black Nubian soldier of fortune. We climbed still higher and from then on were in the land of Moab, the natural history of which, according to Phillips, consisted of a pipit once in a while and a tree every other day. Moab has been the scene of so much history and fighting that ruins were commoner than vegetation. From time to time we jogged along what was left of a stone slab road that the Romans had built from Jerusalem to Aqaba, but most of this had been covered centuries ago by blown sand.

CHAPTER VIII

The Holy Man's

Donkey

We did no more collecting till we reached Petra, the city of the old Nabataeans, and one of the most interesting places in the world. To get there we rode down a steep canyon, with abrupt cliffs on each side from one to two hundred feet high. The path itself was sometimes only ten or twelve feet broad, really only a narrow slit in the sandstone rock that towered on either side. From time to time there were visible the remains of an aqueduct cut into the side of the rock, and we suddenly came to a ravine at right angles to the one we were descending, and were confronted with an enormous temple with huge pillars cut out of the cliff. This was called "Pharaoh's Treasure House"; then we passed an amphitheater cut into the side of another hill, with a seating capacity of about three thousand. We camped in the central valley beside what was left of a large temple of the Roman period.

From our camp we could see rosy red walls of sandstone in every direction, and cut into them were hundreds of tombs and temples, ranging from the simple excavations of the Edomites, and even of their predecessors, to the imposing carved edifices of the Nabataeans, Greeks and Romans — a tremendous amount of history in one place and only an archaeologist could tell who had built what.

The interiors of the temples were large, cavelike rooms dug out of the cliffs; the façades were carved into elaborate entrances, with pediments, porticos, and pillars of the various architectural periods. Some of the pillars — as much as two hundred feet high — were only partially cut out from the wall, others stood clear of the rock, and many of these were worn at the base by the eroding action of the blowing sand.

On top of a near-by mountain was a holy place of very oldest times, where a stone obelisk and the sacrificial altars for burned offerings stood as they did in the days of the ancient Jewish priests.

We were fortunate in not running afoul of the Arabs who lived above the entrance to the sikh, or ravine, and had been described by other travelers visiting Petra as the most rapacious of all people. Phillips and I, by the way, were the eleventh and twelfth Europeans who had come to Petra since its discovery by the German archaeologist Burckhardt in 1812.

The hunting call of a hyena is mournful in open country. When the animal is in a steep-sided canyon near you, and bursts into sound, it is like ten thousand insane laughs reverberating as one. The first evening we heard one I was alone in the tent, Phillips having gone out to speak to Solomon about his misbehaviors of the day, and the day before. This took some time. The hyena's call made me feel a little creepy back of the ears, and just then the front flap of the tent was pulled aside and a ragged native walked in. He was gurgling something, and did not reply to my "Good evening," but walked slowly toward me, so that I could see the whites of his eyes — of which there was a lot. I repeated my greeting, he repeated his gurgling, and when he was about five feet from me I put my hand on the handle of a revolver on the table, whereupon he fell on his knees, bowed his head in the dust, and kept on muttering. Solomon came in at this point, lifted him, dragged him to the tent's entrance, and pushed him out. His explanation was, "He is insane, sair. The heathen Mohammedans think that when a man is insane it is because Allah has taken his soul to Paradise. When he gets there it will be given back to him

Petra

all clean, you know, with no sin on it, because it has been in Paradise all the time."

No good Moslem would have molested such a person. The soldiers always on guard at the tent door would perhaps have opposed a dozen Bedouins who tried to come in, but would not touch this blessed person.

"But Solomon," I asked, "why did he come in my tent? What did he want?"

"Sair, I think he asked for a piece of bread." Probably that was it, because he left promptly after Solomon had given him a loaf of the camp-baked bread.

In the canyon there was plenty of water, some vegetation, and an abundance of bird and animal life, including many migratory birds — goldfinches, black-capped warblers, and blue rock pigeons, the latter wary and hard to collect. We saw our first Palestinian sun bird, a beautiful species, really African in origin, which comes up through the Dead Sea basin sometimes as far north as Beirut in Syria. In the cliffs were colonies of noisy rock sparrows, and some Tristram's grackles, with a beautiful melodious song. There were rosy finches, too; these had never been recorded outside of Sinai, and later when studied proved to be a new subspecies.

While Phillips and Abdul hunted birds, I turned over stones looking for insects and other creatures, and found a little burrowing snake new to science, afterwards named *Leptotyphlops phillipsi*. In the late afternoon I set out a line of small mammal traps, expecting a great catch. This I did for only two nights, because we found that the jackals would rob every trap and destroy whatever had been caught. These jackals, which abounded, apparently spent all their lives in a state of near starvation. It was disgusting to prepare the skin of one which we trapped, as it was full of vermin and skin sores. Once when I stuck my eye over the crest of a hill to see what was on the other side, I saw two jackals jumping around and apparently having a great time playing, but closer observation showed that they were frantically trying to make a meal off grasshoppers.

Out from Petra we journeyed for two days to reach Kerak, another of the numerous towns that the Moabites built on hill-tops, and the legendary home of Ruth and Naomi, and of David. This was the site of many ancient battles of the Moabites and their enemies, as well as of the Saracens and Crusaders.

The Turkish ruler, the Wali, invited us to dinner in his home, an old stone building. It was an experience new to us. The Wali sat at the head of a long table with Phillips and me on either side of him. His son, recently returned from college at Beirut and speaking good English, acted as interpreter for us. The meal was elaborate, sixteen courses, some of them unrecognizable by us, but all of them good. As a dish was placed in front of him, our host would dip in and take the first bite, smacking his lips to in-dicate that there was no poison in it. Then it was passed to us, and after we had dished out a portion, the plate was placed on the floor against the wall. After the meal we went into an adjoining room and, squatting cross-legged on stone benches, smoked our bubble pipes. A baggy-trousered guard ostentatiously pulled a curtain across the door leading to the dining-room, and drew a curved sword, which he held across his abdomen. While we smoked and talked, we could hear the chattering of the women of the harem who were enjoying "second table" at the dinner.

Among the local officials were a number of Syrians, aides to the Turkish governor. One of them sold me a couple of gold Byzantine coins which he had found in a box buried in one of the temples at Petra. He had, he said, thrown away the box — which, of course, would have been worth many times the value of the coins themselves. Some of these Syrians spoke reasonable English, and all of them wanted us to take them back with us to the United States.

North of Kerak was a beautiful spring on the upper edge of the Wadi that leads down to the Dead Sea. The spring was at an elevation of a thousand or more feet above sea level and directly above the Dead Sea which is 1300 feet below the level of the Mediterranean. Here we came upon history in the making. In the valley below us there were a few tents and some partly built houses of reeds, carried from the shore of the Dead Sea. The people were Berbers from Tripoli, who, refusing to live under the Italian flag, had obtained a grant from the Sultan of Turkey for an area of land to start life anew. Much of the region we had been passing through had been settled under similar circumstances. Some of the civilizations had disappeared and others grown great. We talked with some of the Berbers, one a blue-eyed, yellow-bearded veteran who had lost one arm in the war.

They had great reverence for their sheik.

We went down the Wadi and camped on the flat peninsula that projects into the Dead Sea in a northwesterly direction from the coast. Phillips was especially anxious to visit this spot because it is the only home of the Moabitic sparrow, a bird resembling the English sparrow but smaller and gaudier, with a yellow spot on either side of his throat. Few birds have such a limited range as this species.

This was May, and the Arabs were harvesting grain to take with them when they went for the summer to the better climate of the uplands. Birds abounded; we got turtle doves, blue rock pigeons, Hey's partridges, Egyptian quail, shrikes, larks, wheat-ears, goatsuckers, and three species of swallows, but above all a nice series of the sparrows we had come for especially.

We had taken only a small shelter tent for this side-trip, and during the heat of the day, when we were in for a rest out of the hot sun, we found a rich harvest of insects which had also come in from the sun. Among the lower vegetation were colonies of an ant (*Polyrhachis simplex*) that uses its young to spin silk to line the nest, and also to make little sheds on the branches to shelter the leaf hoppers (Membracidae) which are attended by the ants and evidently serve, like aphids, as milk cows. The only nest

I found was beneath a stone. It contained many larvae, some of which lay on the ground and some on a delicate sheet of silk. On nearly every tree near by were the little "cowsheds," and we saw the ant workers carrying the larvae up to spin the silk which would stick together the vegetable particles that makes the shelters.

When we returned to our camp on the plateau we went again to call on our Berber friends, and of course asked about the sheik. My informant told me, "He went to Mecca last night to pray." Now the caravan road went right by our tent, and our boys would have certainly noticed a caravan passing. I did not understand how the sheik could have gone without our hearing about it, but it was explained that he would retire into his tent, close the flap, and send his spirit to Mecca to pray. Sometimes he would go back to Tripoli in spirit and bring his people news of their friends and relatives there. When we went back to Kerak we asked our acquaintances about this and were told that the sheik, a holy man, could do such things. As the Wali explained it to me through his interpreter son — "Just like Jesus."

Phillips was not feeling well, so we started north, stopping briefly at Madeba, at an elevation of twenty-five hundred feet, to look at an ancient map, done in mosaic in the pavement of an old Greek temple. It is the oldest existing map of this part of the world. We camped one night at the foot of Mount Nebo, and climbed it in the morning to get our first view of the Holy Land, standing beside a pile of stones that marks the spot where Moses stood for the same purpose. We could see the valley of the Jordan, and, beyond it and past the northern end of the Dead Sea, the mountains of Judea.

The following morning we descended into the valley of the Jordan and had a gruesome farewell to the land of Moab. Some of our caravan were ahead of us, and as we approached them they stopped us, gesticulating for us to have a look at something by the roadside. It was the corpse of a recently murdered man. He had been the servant of a merchant who was also killed by bandits, but the merchant's body had been taken away. This one had been simply stuck into a crevice in the rock, where it was slowly drying. His *kaffiyah* hung at a rakish angle over his face, and beneath his body was a pile of empty pupae of carrion flies.

We crossed the Jordan and that night camped on the refuse heap of Jericho. I say "refuse heap" advisedly, because Solomon would always put our camp on the outskirts of a village so that "the passengers could enjoy the city and the ruins." This was our last night's camp together, for next morning we lunched on the Mount of Olives overlooking Gethsemane, and in the afternoon rode into Jerusalem.

At the hotel we bathed and changed, and were shaved. Phillips had grown a nice, straight-haired black beard; mine grew about an inch and then turned curly. Before dinner, as I stood at the doorway of the hotel looking out at the street, a fellow guest standing there told me that he had seen a caravan come in town a little while before. There were ibex horns, skulls, and guns fastened to the saddles. Two bearded Europeans led the caravan, and it must have been a hunting party; did I have any idea who it could have been?

Phillips was very weak and decided to go to bed for a few days. I first made the rounds of the city and the holy places with Abdul and a Moslem guide, and had everything explained to me from the Moslem point of view. Later, when Phillips was better, we made the tour again, this time with a Christian guide, who placed more stress on the Biblical stories and had less to say about Mohammed.

There was little natural history to observe in Jerusalem itself; but I did, as King Solomon recommended, consider the ways of the ant. Two species were abundant in the city, one of them a big-eyed red hunting ant (*Cataglyphis viatica*) running singly over the ground searching for other insects; the other a grain gatherer (*Messor barbarus*) plodding in columns to and from its crater-mound nests. Either or both of these species might have been referred to by the great king.

· Phillips was not well enough to do any more fieldwork, and decided to return to the States, leaving me to continue the work of the expedition in northern Syria. We packed our collections to ship to America, cut down our tentage and paraphernalia, paid off everybody except Abdul and Algeciras — the latter was to serve as both cook and manager of the new caravan — and left for Damascus by carriage.

We passed Jacob's well to the right of the road, and the parcel of ground, purchased by Jacob, where Joseph was afterward buried by the Israelites. His tomb is in the little valley, and small offerings are still burned by the Jews in hollows in two columns of the tomb. The well was still in use, and looked as it must have looked when Jesus talked to the woman of Samaria, but we were told that the Greek Church had bought this and would undoubtedly build a church over it, so that in the future visitors would have to go down into a crypt, after paying a fee, to see a landmark that had stood for centuries without benefit of clergy.

Mohammed thought it best to look at Damascus only from a distance lest a close view of its charms lessen his delights in the anticipation of Paradise. He could have avoided any such diminishment by staying at the hotel where Phillips and I stopped. Phillips was still weak and decided to spend a couple of days in bed before going down to Beirut to take his steamer. Abdul and I did the town together. There was a great deal to see in this, the oldest city in the world, still thriving and prosperous. Guidebooks tell all about that; but Abdul announced one evening that the most famous dancer in all Syria was going to dance that night at a certain theater, and could we go? "Hootchy-kootchy is what you call it, sir," he explained.

I had seen the hootchy-kootchy in circus side shows and dime museums, and it never came up to the description given by the man who sold the tickets. The idea of seeing such a dance in its very birthplace was exciting, so we went to the theater and had a little box to ourselves, where we sat smoking a rented bubble-pipe, chewing melon seeds and spitting the husks on the floor as the other Damascenes were doing, and waited for the show.

The curtain eventually parted. There was a semicircle of musicians who played the overture. I am not a musician, but I could swear that there were not more than four notes in the long, dragged-out piece they played. Then the star appeared. She was dressed from neck to ankles in a robe; the naughty thing was that she had her face exposed — and it wasn't such a pretty face at that. She advanced to the center of the stage, made a noise with some castanets, and then the orchestra performed. She waved one arm, snapping the castanets, and the orchestra played again. Abdul explained that she was acting a play, telling a story about an Arab and the girl who loved him. He sat entranced during the whole performance, but as it went on and on interminably, I grew tired and bored, and when we left I felt that the Orientals were a moral people but quite tiresome. The dancer had given only one short "wiggle" during the long evening.

The following day Phillips left for Beirut and his steamer, and at the railroad station I said good-by to a wonderful companion, and a great naturalist and sportsman. I was relieved to hear later that he had recovered his health on the way home.

With a smaller caravan, I started out on another collecting trip, this time with donkeys to carry the paraphernalia, but I had issued to me a horse, "a real Arab horse, sir." He may have been real, but he had a habit of falling down on every occasion, so I let Ali, the boss hostler, ride him while I rode a donkey — one that didn't like to be ridden.

We headed south, camped at a little village called El Katana, where we did some trapping and Abdul collected some birds. When we camped, as I have said before, on the refuse heap of a village, the inhabitants came out to look at us. They were not hostile; some of them were friendly and had relatives in the United States, and they inquired if we knew them, and how were they getting along? The second night's camp was at Rasheya, at the base of Jebel esh-Sheikh, the Mount Hermon of the Bible. We hoped to collect on its flanks. Tents were set up, and I was waiting for dinner, when a group of citizens approached. This had happened every time we had camped near a village since the start of our trip, and I was tired of it. I lost my temper. I shouted "Get out of the way" and threw my Baedeker into the tent. It grazed the nose of one of the bystanders. I stalked into the tent and pulled the flap shut, calling to Abdul, "Get rid of these natives."

At dinner Abdul came to me. He had been talking to some of the people, whom he had chased with a stick. He said:

"Sir, they are too sorry. They have come from the missionary living in this place with an invitation for you to be his guest in his home while you are here."

I was ashamed and the next morning called on the missionary, Reverend Najib David. He represented a small church congregation in Illinois. He had never seen them, nor they him, and yet through their Sunday-school mission society they were supporting this mission in Rasheya. I apologized to him for the way I had acted the evening before. He beamed and said: "I also have traveled. It was natural."

Ministers, like traveling naturalists, have their troubles. From the flat roof of his house he showed me four villages, each, he explained, with a different religion and all of them hating each other. There were Druses, Moslems, Baptists, and even Presbyterians. To the left of the desk in his study was a window, and to the right, in the wall, the mark of a bullet. Somebody had shot at him one evening. The bullet would have pierced his head if he had been there, but, as he explained, the Lord had been with him that evening; he had been sick at his stomach and was not at his desk at the usual time.

He invited me to visit the mission school; I told him I would come the following day, but he said, "No; the students are all waiting for you now."

The little girls were bunched on one side of the schoolroom, the boys on the other. He introduced me, speaking in the vernacular, and then a little boy came up and handed me a great bouquet of flowers — "This is from thee boys." Then a little girl handed me another bouquet — "This is from thee girls" — leaving me standing there with a large bouquet of flowers in each arm and very conscious of my mud-caked boots, disreputable costume, and three-days' beard.

We decided to climb Jebel esh-Sheikh, at least partway, to hunt the Syrian brown bear that is said to live there, as it did throughout Syria in Elisha's day. I asked the guide, "Are there bears here?" and he said yes. "And are there rabbits?" "Oh yes; they are just as common as the bears." Whether or not this was true, I do not know for we saw neither. But our camp was one I shall never forget. Our mule caravan wound up the narrow trail, crossing the snow that lay in heavy drifts across the road. In late afternoon we made camp at nine thousand feet altitude, alongside an eleven-foot snowdrift, a little below the ruins of Casa Antar. We were on a small flat, shielded on one side by a vertical patch of rock, exposed on the other to an intermittent wind, cold and heavy with humidity. Our animals, turned loose, foraged as best they could on the scanty vegetation of the slopes. Our Damascus boys dug roots for a fire, near which they huddled, and tried to warm legs innocent of socks and unaccustomed to the cold of the mountains. Abdul and I strolled upwards to a narrow ridge to get the lay of the land and plan the next day's operations. There was a dense fog, but from time to time the wind blew a clear spell and in the light of the late afternoon we had glimpses of Damascus to the east, with the Hauran plain beyond; of hog-backed, snow-ribbed Mount Sanin to the north; the valley of the Litany flanked by the Lebanon range to the west; and in the south Lake Huleh and an indistinct dark line that marked the vegetation on the banks of the Jordan. From where we stood, one can see Galilee, on clear days, and even make out the mountains of Judea.

It was natural, with the landmarks of religion's origins at our feet, that our conversation should wander from bears and the cold. Abdul told me of Mohammed and I told him of Saint Paul.

Abdul was a broad-minded Moslem, tolerant of everybody (except the natives of the district we happened to be in). He once gravely admitted to me: "Bibi Miriam (the Virgin Mary) that the Christians love, I think she a very good she." And our talks together are the only arguments on religion that I know of where anything ever resulted but bad feelings and sore throats.

Later, when dinner was over and I had crawled into the tent and lay on a straw mattress, putting all the clothing available on and over me in a futile attempt to keep warm, Abdul left the campfire for the canvas shelter, and wrapped in his robes came in beside me. Our talk drifted from the Christian school at Cairo which his two sons attended, to the Moslem priest who had guided us through the mosque at Jerusalem. We spoke of the hermit who had cursed me enthusiastically from his little cell in the side of a cliff when I, unaware of his existence, had shot a bird sitting on the cliff not too far from his venerable self. He had almost exploded when I replied sweetly in a pious Arab phrase that Abdul had taught me.

Then Abdul asked me a pointed question: Were some Christian stories, like some Moslem ones, perhaps a trifle stretched?

A dismal rain had set in outside, and a drop of water leaking through the tent top caught me in the eye at that moment. I wiped it out and found fault with the tent and the weather, which was less embarrassing than answering. Then Abdul told me, in dialect that I will not try to imitate, an old Arab story — the tale of the tomb at Wadi el Sah.

"On the outskirts of Damascus stands a tomb of remote antiquity and proven merits. Worship there, if accompanied by an offering, worked great benefits, especially to the aspirant of the green fez and the title Hadji. Each year when the pilgrim caravan started on the holy journey, the road to Mecca, many were the visitors and generous the gifts. The good hermit who presided grew prosperous, and his duties of providing blessings from the tomb and accepting donations multiplied until it was necessary to engage an assistant. The name of the latter was Mustapha, a bright lad and diligent, a constant help to his master. But he had one ambition: He must some day himself make the pilgrimage. At the starting of each caravan for the south he besought the monk, with tears in his eyes, and (unless he differed from all others of his race) with many gestures and many loud words, to be allowed to accompany it, 'Just this once, O master!' But the master, reluctant to lose him, postponed the departure season after season, year after year, with promises, promises being abundant in those olden times and not entirely unknown in the Orient even today.

"Time passed, Mustapha grew a beard, and became more importunate, until finally his venerable master saw that he could deny him no longer and gave him permission to go; also a donkey to carry him, and a bag of dates for food. Mustapha in ecstasies joined the caravan, and none talked more loudly and joyously than he when, after a kiss and with the blessings of the bearded sage at the tomb, the long line of camels, donkeys, and horses headed into the desert toward the Mohammedan holy city.

"The tribes of the desert are small, but great is their pride and mighty their ambition for glory. And what could be more glorious than an attack on *the* caravan, the big, the annual Damascus caravan. No harm is intended, for they are good Moslems in their light, and there is little chance of plunder, but what better sport than to hide in little groups among the rocky crests and fire with short-stocked, brass-studded rifles into the host below. Before the confusion subsides they are away, out of sight and danger, and then in the years to come they can boast, 'We, our small number, ourselves, did stop the caravan for the space of an hour and did cause great confusion among the pilgrims.'

"In a narrow sikh, unevenly bordered by vertical walls of stone, hid men of the Zaida tribe. When the caravan had all but passed they fired. For a moment there was wild confusion, then a return of shots, a scamper in the rocks above, and the caravan hurried on, helter-skelter. All but Mustapha. He lay on the ground in the shelter of a boulder, gazing fearfully about, while near by his mount with a heavy-bore bullet through its heart finished the sorrowful existence of an Arab's donkey. For a time our pilgrim was stunned by his loss. Then indignation towards an unjust Kismet surged over him and he fiercely shied a stone at the dead animal. Then another, and more, until finally, exhausted, he crawled back into the shade of the boulder, and sat. Night fell, and he gathered his robes about him to protect him from the cold night air of the desert, and slept. Next day, for other reasons, he put more and more stones over the dead, till finally it was covered, and Mustapha settled down complacently to await death himself.

"The tinkling of bells wakened him one dawn, and he saw approaching men and women mounted on camels in file, followed by a flock of goats driven by a boy — a family moving with its herd from one camp to another. Mustapha, doubtful of the best course to follow, raised his voice in grief mingled with fear of a cut throat. The mounted men saw, sitting by the road, a man in the garb of a disciple of a Holy Man, loudly wailing beside a pile of stone.

" 'His master, a Holy Man, has died, and he has made a tomb and weeps beside it,' said the leader. 'It is good to give to the holy. Peace to you,' and he spoke an order to his followers.

" 'God give you peace,' said the tearful proprietor of the late donkey, and the caravan moved away.

"A kid, hastily selected from the herd, bleated tethered near him; on the ground lay a bag of corn ready for parching, and a handful of tobacco tied in a dirty rag. He grasped the situation:

The passers-by thought the pile of stones covering the dead donkey to be the tomb of a Holy Man and had offered gifts. Mustapha was an opportunist. He took more stones and improved the tomb. Other parties passed; his loud wails brought more gifts, and tales of the new hermit in the Wadi el Sah spread from tribe to tribe, losing nothing in the telling. In that first caravan had been a man with an earache; after offering gifts at the new tomb, his earache disappeared. Mustapha prospered.

"Back in Damascus the guardian of the tomb at the edge of the city grew older. As the years went by he ceased expecting the return of Mustapha, and devoted all his thoughts to his own future. There is at Mecca one mosque, and all who worship there must afterwards forswear lying. Young pilgrims, who realize the difficulties this adds to a successful life, do not enter it. He had avoided it, too, on his first pilgrimage, but now, in the years of his decline, his earthly prosperity assured, he felt the call of a second and complete pilgrimage. The caravan road is long and arduous; he had journeyed on camel before, so this time it was excusable to take the train one way, as far as possible. From Damascus to Maan and then down, five days southward, to Medina, he went by train, over the formerly accursed railroad that had been built by Turkish engineers guarded by Turkish soldiers, under almost continual attack by the Bedouins. From Medina he walked to Mecca. There devotions and ceremonies mixed with the gossip so sweet to those of his blood and faith filled the days and nights. Theological arguments with priests from Afghanistan and the Sudan remained unsettled through tornados of oratory. The merits of various holy sites were compared and assailed and supported by whole-hearted demonstrations of arms and hands.

"With other gossip came tidings of a tomb, one in the Wadi el Sah on the caravan route, nine days to the north. Our holy man had not heard of it and asked for more news. It was known as the tomb of the beneficent Abu ben Idn, Father of Ears, and its fame had spread far and wide. He decided to visit it. After nine days his caravan reached the place, camp was made, and the old hermit strolled to the tomb. He asked to see him who was in charge, and was ushered into the presence of no less a person than Mustapha. As he recognized his former assistant, wonder gave way to admiration, and he took Mustapha in his arms. Prosperity was obvious, but beneath the old man's respect was an overpowering curiosity as to how all this had come about. Curtains were drawn, the attendant departed, and then the old man spoke to Mustapha.

" 'O son, I think thou shouldst tell me, thy father, something of this wonder. What Holy Man is enclosed in the tomb over which thou maintainest such well-paid care?'

"And then, seeing a look of hesitation in Mustapha's eye, he took the oath as priest to priest that the secret should still be a secret. Mustapha hesitated, and then said in a low voice:

" 'O father, he who is buried here is the jackass thou gavest me.'

"The old man started back, collapsed onto a rug from Teheran, gasped, choked, and then gave himself up to a fit of hysterical laughter. Mustapha waited abashed until the old man had recovered, and then asked reproachfully:

" 'But why didst thou ask me this? While thy disciple did I ever question who was buried in thy tomb at Damascus? It worked good things; surely that was sufficient.'

" 'Such a disciple,' said the old man. 'An honor to my teaching. So now unasked I tell thee the secret of the tomb where thou didst get thy training — my tomb. Give me the oath that I gave thee.'

"Inviolate names were uttered, beards mentioned as evidence of the seriousness and secrecy that must be maintained over the news that was now to be divulged. Then the old man dropped his voice, tried to restrain a sympathetic smile, and said:

" 'Son, my tomb, the tomb at Damascus, contains the father of thy jackass.' "

* * *

Coming down the mountain, we stopped in a small village, where I told the members of my caravan to buy a sheep for a feast. While they were negotiating the purchase, I sat in the shade of a small hostelry; then, as we were leaving the town, we were followed by everybody from near and far with but one thought in their minds: "Baksheesh." I had, naturally, given some to the proprietor of the hotel, and to the servant who had brought coffee, but didn't have enough for the multitude.

One boy was especially persistent, and disgustedly I asked Abdul, "Why, in the name of Allah, does this native, whom I have never seen before, think he is entitled to a gift?"

The two of them talked for a moment, and then Abdul explained, "He is a waiter at the hotel, and if you had stayed for dinner he would have served you."

We camped later at the Wadi ain Ata, directly at the base of Mount Hermon. Collecting and living conditions were good. One does not realize what "the land of milk and honey" means until he has traveled over the desert. Springs and little rivulets were everywhere, and occasional bits of woodland. Bird life was abundant, and we made a collection of small mammals, as well as numerous insects. Some of the latter, large ground beetles, were a nuisance because they would spring the small traps as they devoured the dates with which we had baited them. However, they were popped into bottles as specimens.

A number of my large traps disappeared. I did not know who was getting away with them until one morning I saw a gentleman in baggy trousers pick one up and start along the road. Abdul was hunting for birds in the woods ahead of him and I shrieked at him, for the benefit of the fellow who had my trap in his hand: *"Drub el harami wusikh!"* ("Kill the dirty thief!") Then I had to rescind promptly in English, because Abdul had come out of the wood and lifted his shotgun.

I yelled at him, "Don't kill him, Abdul. Just get our trap."

The man dropped the trap and started walking off hurriedly,

but exchanging remarks with Abdul. I asked Abdul what he had said to the man. "I said, 'Wait a minute. I will hit you on the head with the barrel of my gun.' "

"Then what did he say?"

"He said, 'No. Can't you see I am in a hurry to catch my donkey?' "

At Hasbeya there was a neat, well-kept mission station, cared for by English ladies. They were not quite as democratic as the Reverend Najib David had been, because they fed Abdul with the members of the mission household while I dined in state with them on mutton, eggs, and great bunches of mulberries.

Later on, back at Rasheya, I told the Reverend David about the mission at Hasbeya and he said that as soon as more funds were available he was going to start a mission there himself. It seemed odd, because in his vicinity there were half a dozen villages that had none at all. I mentioned this to him, but he replied:

"Jesus said, 'Go to all parts of the world to preach the Gospel.' He did not say, 'Don't go where the Presbyterians are.' "

At Hibbaryeh the basement of an ancient temple furnished bats and many gecko lizards. I spent some time in there with a flashlight and shot specimens off the wall; when I came out I was itching all over very badly. I was literally covered with fleas, thousands of them; there was a bracelet of them around each of my wrists, all engaged in the favorite pastime of their kind. My camp was near by, beside a little stream, so I made for the water, throwing my clothes on the bank and yelling for Algeciras to come and get them. I told him to boil them. I should have said "Now." He thought day after tomorrow would be good enough, so my straw mattress and various other camp paraphernalia were inhabited from then on.

We crossed the Valley of the Litany — a beautiful valley and a beautiful river, with great groves of poplar and oleander — to the east slope of the Lebanon, camping here and there till we arrived at Shtaura. The trip was coming to a close and it ended abruptly at Shtaura, partly on account of a little indiscretion on the part of Abdul, who intended to do me a favor. I was half asleep in the tent when I heard some conversation outside, and Abdul's voice raised. Then I heard Abdul shout to Algeciras, "He is gone." Algeciras asked, "Did he take his soldiers with him?" The word "soldiers" woke me up completely, and at the door of the tent I asked Abdul who our visitors had been.

"Sir, that was only the governor of this province. I asked him: If he were sleeping in his house, would he want me, or you, to walk in uninvited to wake him up?"

I thought it best to move camp. We moved to Zahle, and on the railroad platform I paid off the Damascus boys, said good-by to Algeciras, and Abdul and I left for Beirut.

During our entire journey the messages that had been sent to the various rulers from Constantinople had worked wonders. We had experienced no serious trouble of any kind. But on the very edge of Beirut, when we stopped at a station, some soldiers came into the train and asked to see permits for the shotgun and the rifle which we had in the compartment with us. Unfortunately, these permits, which had never been asked for up to this time, were in the baggage car. A missionary who was in the compartment with us tried to explain matters to the soldiers, but they had orders to seize any firearms. I hurriedly scrawled a note to the American Consul in Beirut, explaining what had happened; the missionary promised to deliver it, and Abdul and I got off the train to keep an eye on our guns. We did not want them played with. The combination rifle-and-shotgun, and the good English shotgun, were valuable and delicate mechanisms. One of the soldiers tried to break the shotgun, to see if there were any shells in it, but he didn't know how. The lieutenant in charge was not feeling very well that day. I answered his questions as best I could, until, becoming tired and having difficulty understanding him, I asked Abdul to talk to him. He evidently misunderstood, and thought I had asked him to give the man a talking to, which he did, so loudly and so sarcastically that the twenty or so troops, gathered in an admiring semicircle, listened beamingly while their commanding officer got a thorough verbal raking. Finally he shouted to the two of us, "Take your guns and go."

A carriage had approached, the driver attracted by the commotion. We got in and started in to town, Abdul taking a final verbal shot at the discomfited officer.

"In my country," he shouted, "when guests come, we offer them cushions, and *you*," pointing with his finger, "did not even offer us coffee!"

The *Armand Behic*, of the French Messageries Maritimes, arrived and Abdul and I took passage aboard her, he for Alexandria and I for Marseilles. At the ticket office I had asked for a ticket through to London, with a stopover at Yvorne, Switzerland, where I had been invited to visit the great Swiss psychiatrist and entomologist, the dean of all ant-students, Dr. Auguste Forel. At the office, they could not find Yvorne on the map, or in the railroad schedule, so I took passage merely to Marseilles.

Abdul had done considerable shopping for his family, Syrian boys' jackets and trousers, and a rug, but nothing at all for his "she" or for the little daughter whom he had mentioned incidentally when he was extolling the virtues of his sons. I insisted on his taking a cheap coral necklace to each of them.

During our time together, we had discussed talismans, omens and superstitions, and he explained to me very seriously one superstition that he had heard often in the bazaars of Cairo, chiefly from Arabs who had never been to sea.

"There is nothing to make you sick on a boat," said Abdul. "I hear that they are comfortable and the food is good, and why should a little movement make you sick? That, sir, I believe is imagination. If you think you are going to be sick, you will be sick. If you think you will not be sick, you will not be sick."

We boarded the ship in the evening, Abdul a deck passenger sleeping in a chair that I had rented for him. There was a bit of a swell. Next morning after breakfast, I went along the deck to find him.

There, collapsed in the steamer chair, was the mummy that was always Abdul when not well.

"Ya, Abdul!"

Slowly, and apparently with a great deal of effort, he unwound yards of his robe. He looked a trifle green, so I patted him on the shoulder and said:

"That's right, Abdul; don't think you are going to be sick, and you won't be."

He looked at me as though I had stabbed him, and said in a low voice: "Khawaji, I am too sick right now."

I parted with him at Alexandria. He took his purchases, wrapped in the Syrian rug he had bought, ashore. I gave him his money, and his baksheesh, he kissed me on both cheeks, and we parted, in sorrow on my part, but not so much on his, for he was back in his native land. He immediately picked up a couple of dragomen, friends of his, and disappeared after asking Allah to give me peace.

He reappeared shortly, with his friends, and asked, "Please, sir, will you come to the customhouse with us? They are making trouble."

I went, and found that Abdul had declared that all he had with him were things vital to his life in the desert with me. These included the Syrian rug, the gaudy apparel for his sons, the two necklaces, as well as some other things. I explained to the customs official that Abdul had never been away before, did not know the rules and regulations, was really an honest man though ignorant in such a case as this. The official gave him an Arabic tongue-lashing, but let him go. After another, but much more hurried farewell, Abdul vanished.

At Marseilles, the railroad ticket seller had never heard of Yvorne, either. I had a letter from Dr. Forel in my pocket inviting me to visit him at his home, "La Fourmilière," and the post-mark was clearly stamped "Yvorne," but I could not find how to get there. Expressing my heavy baggage to London in bond, I bought a ticket to Lausanne. There was an Academy of Science there and I was sure that somebody would tell me where Yvorne was.

In the station at Lausanne, I checked my bag. The porter asked me if I wanted a guide, and I told him not a regular guide, but suggested that he walk with me, when his work was done, to the Academy of Science. Immediately he changed his cap for a hat and we started out. I explained my reason for being in Lausanne — to find out at the Academy where Dr. Auguste Forel had his home. The porter said, "Why, he lives in Yvorne."

"And where is Yvorne?"

"*Auprès d'Aigle.*"

"And where is Aigle?"

"It is a village toward the other end of the lake."

This problem solved, we had lunch at a restaurant looking out over Lake Geneva, eating quantities of green salad, which had long been completely lacking in my diet.

It was evening when I got to Aigle, and not wanting to barge in on the eminent doctor and professor just before dinner, I put up at a little *pension;* as the only guest at the time I received all the attention of the proprietress and her daughter. During dinner the daughter asked how long I was to remain in Aigle.

I answered, "Only overnight. Tomorrow I am going to Yvorne."

"But there is no *pension* in Yvorne."

"But I am going to be the guest of Dr. Auguste Forel."

Her answer was a pair of elevated Swiss eyebrows. She whispered something to her mother at the other end of the room, who looked me over very carefully. A few minutes later a face appeared at the little square aperture in the door between the kitchen and the dining room — cook regarding me suspiciously.

While I knew that Forel was the dean of all the European ant students, a neurologist, and a psychologist, I did not know that he sometimes took patients into his home and treated them psychiatrically, often through hypnosis. He had had some famous cases, including a prominent princess, so the entourage at the hotel naturally thought that I was queer and had come to be doctored. The princess, after her cure, became interested in ants, and went on an expedition to South America. In the catalogue of the ants of that region, her name figures prominently.

Next morning, carrying my bag, I walked up the road to Yvorne, where Dr. Forel welcomed me, introduced me to his family, and showed me the guest room. It was a thrilling week for me, reveling in his study with his ant collection. He would leave me alone for hours, while with a hand lens and a notebook I went over one species after another. Toward the end of the week he brought out some empty insect boxes and turned me loose in his duplicate collection. The result was between five and six hundred different species of ant, all identified by the master and all for my own collection.

His younger daughter, Inez, was engaged to a Canadian, and Mama Forel was busy giving her a postgraduate course in cooking. The doctor himself was partially paralyzed, as was his Italian colleague, Carlo Emery. The two of them, by the way, living on different slopes of the mountains, had started collecting and studying ants in their teens, and became aware of each other's existence, when, at the age of twenty, Forel published his first paper, *The Ants of Switzerland*, and Emery a paper on the ants of Italy. Forel had another dear friend, a professor in some German university, who was also paralyzed, and the old gentleman would refer to the three of them as "Der apoplectic trio." Because of his health he lived on a careful diet; there were scales on the table, and for breakfast, lunch, and dinner he would weigh portions of meat, dabs of vegetables, cheese, and salad. He explained that his blood pressure demanded a rigorous way of life, but at teatime, when Inez would produce the results of her lessons in cooking cakes, buns, and other teatime delicacies, he ignored the scales, telling me, "This time I can be human."

We would stroll together in the evening, he walking very haltingly. His French was difficult for me to understand on account of his semiparalysis, and mine was difficult for him to understand, but with a few German words, some Spanish, and an occasional English phrase, we got along.

In addition to his scientific studies, he had been the founder of the Bon Templar Society of Switzerland, an organization devoted to the cause of temperance. Everyone knew him: the driver of a little streetcar once saw him when we were walking, stopped the car, got off, came over to the sidewalk, doffed his hat and shook hands with him. When we said good-by I apologized again for my French, and said that when I returned, as I hoped to do some day, I would be able to speak it much better. He smiled and pointed at a brick moratorium in the yard. Earlier, he had shown me the little urn that contained the ashes of one of his sons.

"Perhaps old man Forel will be there before you come back to *la Suisse*."

As a matter of fact, we corresponded afterward for a number of years. Once he sent me a copy of a paper with a description of a new ant from Madagascar, and some months later a new edition of his *Ants of Switzerland*, with the note, "Is it not curious that this, my first work, should also be my last?" Three years after that, when I had returned from Australia, he wrote and asked a question or so on the bulldog ants which occur there, for, as he said, he was writing "a little popular book." This eventually appeared in four volumes. He did not die until 1931.

I shall always remember him as a stooping, bearded, heavily eyebrowed, kindly man, one of the truly great scientists of his time and one who cared as much for the welfare of his fellow man as he did for his beloved ants.

CHAPTER IX

Bug Doctor

I⊤ wAs NICE to be back at the Bussey again, but a horrendous fact was disclosed to me by Dr. Wheeler — whom I had previously considered a broad-minded master teacher and an inspiration. He now decided that my travels must stop and that I must get down to work. Our Syrian collections were sorted; Phillips wrote a paper on the birds; there were a few new localities recorded, but only one new species. Glover Allen did the mammals, Tom Barbour the reptiles, and Wheeler and I together worked on the ants. There were several new species among them, but nothing very exciting: Forel had recently published a paper on the ants of Palestine. He was a little frivolous with the Scriptures, and had taken a number of liberties, using the names of various Biblical characters for his new species of ants. Classes and laboratory work were resumed and I eventually finished the paper on the ants collected on the Stanford Expedition to Brazil, which was to be part of my doctor's thesis. I continued to collect in the environs of Boston, and to correspond and exchange specimens with scientists scattered throughout the world. Some of my earlier schoolmates had left and gone to their duties in Canada, Ceylon, East Africa, and the Philippines, while I sat there day after day, doing research on ants and related insects.

Railroad roundhouses, ladies' sewing circles, circuses, armies and navies, clubs, and universities have one thing in common: gossip. One rumor reached me. Dr. Roland Thaxter, who studied the little fungi that grow out of the joints of insects, wanted to go to Borneo to collect various small fry on which his beloved fungi live. He wanted somebody to go with him, somebody more or less robust, and one who was interested in beetles. He had told Wheeler that he thought a Sheldon traveling fellowship might be arranged for me to accompany him. This fellowship had been established by the parents of a student who had died early in his Harvard career, and was for the purpose of giving a year or so abroad, in research work, "to round out" the student, but could be used for original scientific work in the field as well. News of this stepped up my heartbeats, but Wheeler said not a word to me. Then one day, as I was writing the description of a new species of ant in the laboratory, somebody called my professor to the telephone. This was within hearing distance, but I paid no attention until he said: "Yes, Thaxter, I have made up my mind. He has traveled enough for the time, and I think he should finish his work and get his degree before going on a long trip in the field again."

It was the most unpleasant eavesdropping I have ever done. The world seemed completely demolished, but I said nothing about it, and a few days later Wheeler mentioned it to me.

His idea was that his students should not stay at the Bussey forever but should go out from Harvard and improve the rest of the world. That was flattering, but hard to take. I had no desire to spread education or civilization anywhere. I wanted to collect and study bugs and beasts.

My doctorate examinations were finished that year, May 1915, and I was granted a Sheldon traveling fellowship. Dr. Wheeler and the geologist Professor William Morris Davis had decided that Fiji would be the logical place to send two students, a geologist and an entomologist. The European war had broken out, so Europe was a very poor place in which to "round out" an education. Scarcely anything was known of entomology in Fiji, and Davis was especially interested in coral reefs — did they grow up or down? Darwin had said one thing, and Agassiz the other —

and not enough was known of the island group to tell whether it was of ancient or comparatively modern origin, though Guppy, the celebrated English geologist, had made a careful study of some of the deposits there.

The ants of Fiji were almost unknown. Eight species had been described from there by Mayr of Vienna, many years before, and some of them were named *schultzi*, which implied that an early trader or settler by that name had collected them.

While the Sheldon funds were liberal for those days, they did not permit a great deal of extravagance, and I approached Samuel Henshaw on the question of vials for entomological and other specimens. He had supplied me before with an exceedingly fine type of broad-mouthed vial, of such material and workmanship that never once had I broken the top off one while pushing the cork out with my thumb. I wanted more of them, but his reply was, "Haven't you a fellowship? Why not buy your vials out of that? Or, if you like, you might wash out a few thousand dirty ones and I might find you some corks for them."

There wasn't time to wash out a few thousand anything, and I was rather irritated, because after all I was going to collect for the Museum, though not compelled by the fellowship to do anything except my own research work. I murmured something about being able to buy the containers necessary for ants. A couple of days later Mr. Henshaw asked me to drop into his office the next time I was at the Museum. I did, and he apparently was feeling better.

He said: "How many vials do you want, and what size?"

I told him.

"When are you sailing, and on what boat?"

"On the *Niagara*, Canadian Australasian Line, from Vancouver, August 4."

"The vials will be aboard."

And they were. Also a brass engine headlight, and a barrel of a special calcium carbide to make an acetylene light to attract nocturnal insects — this a present from B. Preston Clark, who intimated that there were few of his moth specialties known from that part of the world.

I spent a week in Helena, visiting my mother, and old friends. My mother was anxious about my living with those Fiji Island cannibals, but I assured her that according to the data I had gathered, cannibalism had not been practised for twenty-four years. There was a stable government, and besides, practically all of the natives were Christians. I promised her that if there were any danger, I would be careful, for while there might be some romance in being eaten by a cannibal, there was certainly none in being eaten by a Wesleyan Methodist.

At Vancouver, the boat was late in sailing — seven maddening minutes late. As the whistle blew, all the pretty girls who had come aboard to see their friends off kissed them good-by and went ashore, leaving the rest with us. We sailed. The other Americans aboard the *Niagara* went only as far as Honolulu, and after we had left that port, the passengers at once assembled and indulged in a favorite British practice — committee forming. There was a Red Cross committee, a concert committee, a sports committee, and some others. Whenever I became interested in a book, some personage with a pad would approach and state that I was due to play partners with a lady I did not know at a game I did not know. When the game was finished the lady would thank me, which was British propriety, but cruel, because none of my partners at these deck games had anything at all to thank me for. It is distressing to lose games continually for courteous players who take it seriously, so I was much relieved when a passenger discovered that I looked like "someone who wrote." I spent a great deal of time thereafter in the writing room working ostentatiously and diligently with a pen. Friends of mine who, after correspondence lapses of one to ten years, received letters from me mailed at Suva, may now know why I wrote. A literary man must not be disturbed in his work by being called away to play shuffleboard.

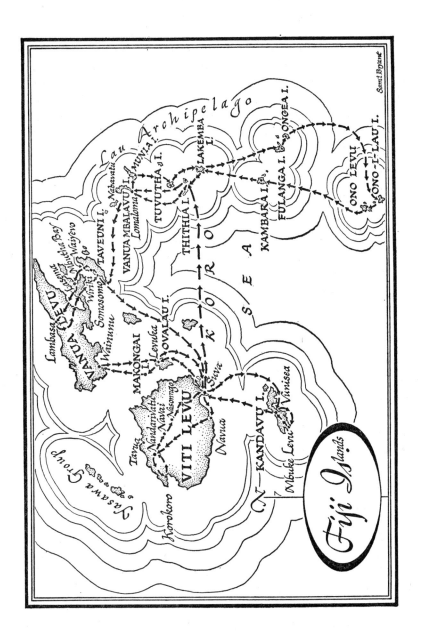

Fiji Islands

On the morning of the fourteenth day we saw the first of the Fiji group, and till late in the afternoon passed island after island, looming up gray and indistinct through a heavy fog that hung low over the water. Suva harbor is bordered by a reef, and we could see the long streak of white before the shore was sighted. We passed through the narrow opening with the surf booming against the reef on either side of the ship, and lay to, to wait for the port doctor. During momentary clear spells, the village could be made out, mostly small houses with oxide red roofs, a profusion of greenery everywhere, and in back, bordering part of the bay, rugged mountains. The shaky wooden dock was packed with natives, dressed in loincloths and cotton singlets. Each one was holding an umbrella, for it had commenced to rain, and they had their hair to protect. The Fijians' hair is worth protecting. It stands in a wonderful dense brush, sometimes as much as a foot in height, is beautifully cared for, and ornamental. It was the most conspicuous feature of the native at first sight, and I find, as I look back at those I knew, I remember each as much by his hair as by any other characteristic.

Porters came aboard, each with a government license number fastened to his belt. I motioned to two of them and they followed me to the stateroom to get my baggage. They said one word: "Mon'?"

In reply I opened the steamship company's folder and pointed to the government schedule of prices for handling trunks. They were perfectly satisfied. If it was in a book, it must be so. They carried everything to the customhouse, took the regular fee and a small tip, and departed smiling.

It was dark before we got ashore; the streets were poorly lighted and streaming with rain. In company with a doctor who was coming into the Fiji service I went to a hotel. The proprietor refused to accommodate the doctor's family because he had three small children. That took my breath away for a moment. On the voyage I had heard of the advancement of Suva, of its Carnegie

Library and of its automobiles, and I had expected to find it modern, but the "no dogs or children" idea was altogether too far advanced. It reminded me of home.

Further up the street the Club Hotel, run by the Cox family, took us in.

In the evening, dinner was served by barefooted, barelegged, bushy-haired natives, each clad in cotton undershirt and *sulu* — the waist-high piece of cloth that is characteristic of much of that part of the world. Dinner was brought; and at the end, for dessert, an English fruit tart. Aboard ship that noon I had taken an avocado from the dish and placed it on my plate, and then put it back, thinking that this avocado was from Honolulu and seven days old; that evening there would be plenty of fresh ones. On the menu was printed, "Fruit in season."

I asked the waiter, "What kind of fruit?"

He replied, "Fiji." I assumed he was defining the fruit, but he was telling me that that was all he spoke. When I pointed at the menu he disappeared and came back with a dish of canned cherries and apricots. The next avocado that I saw was a little less than two years later when we again docked in Honolulu.

Next day the acting governor, after an interview, gave me a letter to the acting Colonial Secretary, who introduced me to the native Commissioner, who arranged for letters to the native chiefs and European heads of districts. Then I called on the Government Entomologist, Jepson, who took me in hand and introduced me to Charles Henry Knowles, Director of Agriculture, an interesting man with a long background of West African experience. Knowles gave me a room in which to store my gear while I traveled, and the government sold me a license for my little .22-caliber collecting pistol, for ten shillings. I also met a Dr. Wright, originally of Trinidad, serving here in the Department of Agriculture, specializing in soil analysis but with general botany as a hobby. He immediately told me about "schools of salamanders" on the beach just out of town. There are few salamanders south of the equator, and none known from this part of the world; besides, salt water is deadly to these animals; so my first trip was with him to see these wonders. We walked up Victoria Parade, the main street of Suva, bordered on one side by stores and business houses, and on the other by large trees of a kind which folds up its leaves at night and hence is called by the natives *kau moce,* or "the tree that sleeps."

We reached the place where Wright had seen so many of the salamanders. They did remotely resemble the newts which he had known in his boyhood in England, but they were Periophthalmus, the little fish that lives equally well on land or in water, and does most of its hunting on the former. When frightened, it scurries into the water, usually making a quick circle and coming out again on a rock or on the beach.

However, Wright was a good botanist, and before my credentials and letters were delivered we took a number of short trips together. The seven species of ants that I found were those common to all tropics. The "crazy ant," common in houses where it can be seen rapidly running around the walls, was under almost every stone that I turned over. This ant is also found in timbered regions, and I have even seen it in some of Washington's hotels. The French call it *fourmi fou,* the Spanish *hormiga loca,* and it was interesting to find that one of the Fiji names for it was *nandi lea-lea* — all with the same meaning.

The telegraph wires in town were covered with spider webs of coarse silk, strong enough to hold sizable lizards. The spiders themselves were large, and brilliant yellow and black, quite formidable-looking.

A large wasp (*Polistes macaoensis*) was abundant. It had been introduced years before with hay from the island of Macao; in fact, almost everything seemed to have been introduced — mynah birds swarming everywhere, and the mongoose, both from India. The insect fauna appeared pretty tiresome, except for the introduced economic forms that created havoc with the sugar cane, bananas, and coconut palms. None of the coconuts was producing any nuts, because of a small moth named Levuana, a Fiji name, though the moth itself later proved to be not Fijian but Malayan in origin. Afterwards John Tothill, who had been at the Bussey with me, became government entomologist in Fiji. He secured parasites of the moth from Malaya and introduced them into Fiji. They controlled the pest so well that islands that had hitherto not been producing any coconuts commenced to do so — a nice example of biological control of one insect by another.

The human fauna of Suva was also largely introduced. There were English and Australians and New Zealanders and a few Chinese storekeepers. A large Samoan handed me his card: ALEX SAMOA; FINE AND FANCY WASHING DONE. These big, powerful-looking warriors were the chief washermen of the town. In front of the hotel passed Gilbert Islanders with short black hair and Mongolian features, and Solomon Islanders — small, dark, wooly-haired, generally wearing caps and trousers, which the Fijians themselves disdained. There were natives of Rotuma, with Semitic features — so much so that early explorers thought they had discovered one of the lost tribes of Israel; they are also said to be the best traders in the islands. And there were Indians, the gaudiness of their women's clothes and jewelry adding color to the cavalcade.

The local plants also had been imported, purposely or accidentally. Lantana, which in the north is a hothouse plant, grew there in dense thickets, and there was a vine called "mile-a-minute," and another plant with large green leaves growing so densely that one would walk half a mile around rather than through a patch of it. This was known as "Koster's curse." The story told me about it was that it had been introduced as an ornament by a man named Parr; but a journalist making notes had as guide and informant Mr. Koster's son; when asked who had introduced this plant, Koster replied "Parr," and the journalist named it "Koster's curse."

Young Koster, long since grown up, protested that he never referred to his father as "Pa," but always called him "dear old Dad."

Berthold Seemann, the botanist, who traveled in and described Fiji in 1862, stated that at that time there was scarcely any virgin forest on the islands, for the natives, in cultivating the land, had eliminated even such things as sandalwood, formerly an important article of trade. Wherever we went in the islands, there was little of interest to the naturalist in the cultivated areas.

Wilbur Garland Foye, also a Sheldon traveling fellow, was the graduate in geology whom Dr. Davis had chosen to study in Fiji. He had gone out on an earlier boat, and met me in Suva; from there on, we traveled together through the islands. Foye engaged a boy named Hosea, and the government assigned to me a native prince, or *ratu*, Joeli M. Kurnoodi. Both boys were excited at the prospect of the trip, because the Lau Archipelago, toward which we were headed, was strange to them and different from their part of Fiji.

The principal settlements of the out-islands were visited bi-monthly by a five-hundred-ton steamer, the *Amra*, an old boat that formerly had plied the Irrawaddy River in Burma. Because of the first officer's motherly attitude toward the boat and step-motherly attitude toward the crew, it was as clean and as well-conducted as a liner. We secured round-trip tickets, with stop-over privileges, and the four of us boarded her.

A regulation kept natives off the dock at night, but Joeli's friends, clerks in the various government departments and all high-caste boys, had secured permission to see him off. A dozen of them stayed on the dock till midnight, when we sailed, and all the time expressed their feelings in song. For the first time I heard the wonderful Fijian music which has no melody but depends upon harmony similar to a poetic chant. For Joeli and his friends, a voyage to Lau was a momentous occasion, with, perhaps, danger attached to it. A bottle was passed around at intervals as the eve-

ning progressed, and sorrow at the departure of a dear friend
grew and grew. Joeli himself was moved; he asked me for a
little money so he could give them another bottle. Just as the
boat was leaving most of them broke into tears as they sang —
in Fijian — "Shall We Gather at the River?" They shook hands
with us, over the ship's side, till we were out of reach. One big,
fine-appearing fellow, with tears streaming down his face, sobbed
"Good-by, Doketah" to me as though he were losing a lifetime
friend. We could hear them singing "It's a Long, Long Way to
Tipperary" in English until we were out of hearing.

The other passengers, knowing the ropes, had carried mats and
bedding from their staterooms to the deck and prepared to spend
the night in the open. Joeli and I went below to a small room with
two berths in it. It was hot, and I fell into an uneasy sleep — to
be awakened by a piercing shriek. I followed the example of my
hair, and rose, half thinking that something awful had happened,
but not sure that it was not a dream. Then it came again — a loud
"Y-ee-ah" from someone in mortal fear. I remembered Joeli and
called to him. An excited voice answered.

"Doketah, doketah, please to turn on the electric. I have seen
a ghost. My father — he come right to me." Then in a subdued
tone, "Please don't be sorry to me, Doketah. I think I have nightmare."

I went on deck and spent the rest of the night in a steamer
chair.

At Thithia * the steamer anchored and we went ashore in a
launch. Lying flat, with my head hanging over the bow, I got my

* When the alphabet was introduced into Fiji by the missionaries, certain
letters were given sounds different from those in English usage. C has the
sound of *th*; *b* is pronounced *mb*; *q* is *nng*. Thus the name of the famous
king, Cakabau, is pronounced Thakambau; and woqa (boat) is pronounced
wonnga. Fijian spelling was used by all the early travelers and I followed it
in my report on The Ants of Fiji. Recent maps, however, have substituted a
phonetic spelling; the island of Cicia, for instance, has become Thithia. On
the following pages I have used the modern phonetic spelling for geographic
names, but have kept the Fijian spelling for native names and expressions.

first close look at a coral reef, tier after tier of ledges, the top ones, in good light, colorful and tenanted by small, brilliant blue and yellow fish. Then came black depths. It was a fairyland panorama, though the great Charles Darwin thought coral reefs had been much overrated. Darwin was notoriously seasick; and of course the best way to see these reefs is by floating over them in a boat — which may have lessened his delight in them.

Vanua Mbalavu is the northernmost and largest of the islands which form the Lau Archipelago. It is about fourteen miles long and at its widest point nearly three miles broad. The central portion is composed of volcanic hills up to nine hundred feet in height, but a great deal of the coast is limestone, in the form of steep bluffs undercut and deeply indented by the action of the waves. Scrubby woods cover much of the island, but no real forest. Lomaloma, the chief and only important settlement, is composed of the residence and office buildings of the District Commissioner, a couple of European stores, a boardinghouse, and scattered native houses.

Mrs. Tripp, who took in paying guests, had rooms for us. She was part Samoan, and had been married to a European; her two daughters could have been a diagram for Mendel's theory. One of them was a pink-and-white English girl, rather quiet but passionately fond of tennis; the other was brown-skinned, smiling, and loved dancing, native or otherwise.

The Commissioner and medical man of the Lau Archipelago was Dr. St. Johnson, who had a little botanical garden near his official residence. He temporarily ruined his traveler's palms from Madagascar by trying to show me how, when you lopped off the broad leaves, water was available for the thirsty traveler. It must have been off season for traveler's palms, and after cutting half a dozen of them he gave up and I accepted his word for it. There was a hot spring near by, where Foye found the temperature to be 110° F.

Mr. H. H. Steinmetz, who had a Tongan wife, was the owner

of Munia, a near-by island, and he took us as week-end guests. There were about eleven hundred acres on the island, most of which were planted with coconuts, but he also raised all his own coffee, and kept a few cattle, chickens, and turkeys. His house was fastened down by two enormous iron cables placed over the roof and secured to stakes driven deep into the ground. Sometimes houses in this part of the world, if not secured, are lifted up by hurricanes and destroyed. His front lawn was full of little holes housing land crabs, some of which the servants caught with box traps and made into a delicious entrée.

Coffee was served at six in the morning; breakfast at eleven, a heavy meal with fish, turkey, suckling pig and yams. We had tea in the afternoon and at night a dinner even heavier than breakfast.

The overseer of the plantation showed me about the island. In one area were dozens of sea snakes, the flat-tailed, ocean-inhabiting relatives of the cobra. They had come ashore, probably to lay eggs. I tapped one of them with the handle of my insect net, whereupon he disgorged a long marine eel, evidently the chief food of these creatures. Despite the fact that they are equipped with poison fangs and a venom similar to that of the cobra, they never seem to bite anything except the eels on which they live.

Among little clusters of native trees that Steinmetz had left while clearing the land for coconuts, were black fruit pigeons. Later we shot some for food, and found that each had swallowed five or six large nutmegs. But there was little else characteristic of Fiji here — the usual ants, some geckos, and a tiny cricket living with one species of ant.

At the house we found that one of the children had caught a harmless snake, a boa, and had tied it in the leg of Mr. Steinmetz's pajamas. This was duly pickled and added to my collection. These boas are endemic to Fiji, as is also an iguana which looks for all the world like a small edition of our South and Central American iguanas, but is quite distinct from them and is found nowhere else. It is one of the curious cases of discontinuous distribution.

Large click-beetle fireflies, found in Fiji and related to those in tropical America, are the same type that the women in Mexico and Cuba put in little lace bags and wear in their hair at night. In my report to the museum I said that had they been found in the same locality they would have been considered the same genus, but the editor of the Harvard bulletin, a better beetle student than I, cut it out. There are also luminous centipedes in Fiji, and at night I would see them crawling on the outside of my mosquito net, two to four inches of moving flame.

Naturally I was trying to learn a little of the native language and the youngsters amused themselves by teaching me. There was one sentence supposed to mean, "Hello, my good friend, how are you?" They took so much pains teaching this to me that I became suspicious. It was *"Lea lea kaisi mbokola!"* Before using it, I tried it out on Joeli, who turned a Fijian green as he explained how awful the remark was. The Fijians had no real curse words; some were introduced with other European necessities long ago, but in the good old days the foulest thing one could say was the sentence I had just learned, which meant, "Crazy slave, cooked and ready to be eaten!" I never heard it used. One epithet also undesirable is *Kai cola,* or "Man of the mountain." This is derogatory because the Fijian bases his opinion of a person's culture on his ability to navigate a boat and the mountain people had none, so this became a word for stupidity. Different parts of the country have their own dialects, but someone in every village knows the dialect of Mbau, where lived King Cakabau when he and his cohorts ruled all the islands.

At Lomaloma Dr. St. Johnson let me fish in his fish trap. It was built of piles on the beach, funnel-shaped, so that when the fish came in with the tide over the reef they could not find their way out when the water went back, but stayed in an artificial pool about waist-deep. A number of fish were in it, two and a half to three feet long, and to secure one for dinner the fisherman waded into the pool and speared it. After numerous attempts, I got one, held it aloft on a spear, and climbed out of the pool. A look at it made me regret that I had gone in the water, for half a dozen like it had been swimming around, touching me. It, and I suppose the others, were armed with some of the worst, doglike teeth I had ever seen. Apparently they never hurt the cook when he went in, as I had done, to get a nice fresh fish for dinner.

Dr. St. Johnson took us in his boat to the north end of the island to visit Gus Hennings at Nabavatu, one of the show places of the islands. Anchoring in an exquisite little bay we zigzagged up the path to the house on top of the cliff overlooking the bay. It was a large cement structure, fronted by a long veranda, surrounded by coconut palms and small patches of bush, with pleasant paths, one leading to the cliff overlooking the bay and the clearest water in the world, spotted with little coral islands. While we were looking down and commenting on the beauty of the scene, a sizable shark swam slowly in, and as slowly swam out again.

Near the house was a vegetable garden, where grew cabbages, carrots and kohlrabi, in addition to the ubiquitous taro. Mrs. Hennings had preserved a supply of beef and pork, so life was luxurious at mealtimes.

Andi Mary, the mother of Gus Hennings, was a niece of King Cakabau. How many nieces he had I do not know, but from time to time we met one. The family of the great king is still revered by other Fijians, and while we were there a large group of natives from another village came to do homage to this niece. They brought gifts, a pile of mats and a whale's tooth; there was a feast where two pigs and a cow were consumed, and the old lady gave in return a bolt of calico. Fiji is a land of give and take. To refuse a request for supplies would be a shame that no Fijian would face, but also to ask for goods of which there is a shortage is in equally bad taste. To avoid this tabu, signs are hung out. When a piece of cloth is hanging conspicuously on a palm tree in a village, it means it is tabu for anyone to request cloth in that village. Sometimes there will be a mat, some tapa cloth, or an ax, to indicate a scarcity of those items.

The present Mrs. Hennings was a German woman, but Gus had formerly been married to a Fijian, and his daughter Seni Rewa (the Flower of the Rewa) was a most attractive girl. She had been educated abroad, and would dine with us in the house in European dress, then later, clad in a *sulu*, join her grandmother, who lived in a native thatched house.

Back at Lomaloma we ran into a bit of luck. The *Lotu Wesele* (*Wesleyan Mission*), a cutter of about five tons manned by Captain Tavita (David) Vui, was about to sail south to the very end of the archipelago, calling at one island after another to pick up the local missionaries and transport them to Viti Levu, where a big meeting was to be held.

We sailed out of the harbor in the morning, or rather during it, for the wind was against us so badly that towards late afternoon we put in at Susua, an island directly south of Lomaloma and near enough so that we might have crossed the narrow strip of water in a canoe and walked back to Lomaloma in an hour. If our crew had any sorrow at having to anchor for the night, it was solaced ashore, for a large shark had been caught, and, wrapped in leaves, was being baked whole in a big oven made of earth and stone. This long type of oven was formerly used by Fijians to cook their fellow citizens, but by this time it was used only for sharks.

Tuvutha was the first island that we visited where there were no Europeans, and our reception was typical of what we were to receive wherever we traveled in native Fiji. There were eighty-one inhabitants on the island, and all of them, except the women who were working in the gardens, stood on the beach to welcome us. The chief of the village handed my letter of introduction to his aide, a man who could read, called in Fijian the "eye of the village," and he was surrounded by all of the group, who listened as he read it aloud. The chief then led us into his house; he himself moved into another one, and we unpacked to stay until the wind shifted.

His house was the largest in the village, and stood on an elevated earth platform. It was about thirty feet long, twenty broad, and sixteen high, and was built on a framework of roughly hewn rafters tied together with native rope made of coconut fiber. The thatched roof was more than a foot in depth, as were the side walls, which were reinforced with reeds woven with fiber. These houses are as comfortable as any in the tropics, though there was no furniture except a trader's chest in one corner, and a built-in bed. The bed consisted of four uprights with crosspieces on which were placed a thick thatch of coconut leaves and a layer of half a dozen woven mats, so arranged that the edges, ornamented with fringe of blue, red, white, yellow, pink, and black string, were in rows to show off the coloring. Mats of pandanus leaves on the floor completed the house, which was typical of those in the archipelago. It was scrupulously clean, and this was also true of the twenty other houses and of the village itself. Later we learned that the former chief had been demoted by the District Commissioner for not keeping things in order.

At one side of our house stood a small, tent-shaped thatched shelter which served as kitchen. It was provided with cooking utensils — iron pots, a teakettle, several wooden bowls, and a pile of coconut shells for cups. Dinner was served shortly and, again, was typical of the fare we were to have for many months. A file of six women entered the house, and each set on the floor a large basket of boiled sweet potatoes. One of them carried a pot with a chicken in it cooked *à la Fiji*, that is, it was a mature fowl that had been killed, drawn, and boiled immediately afterward, served with the head and feet still on, the boiled eyes looking reproach-fully at one and the feet raised in a beseeching attitude.

The food offered us was really the food for the village for that day, but presented to us ceremoniously. After we had eaten, the rest was removed and served to the villagers. The chief explained to us that a recent hurricane had done a great deal of damage to the island; the gardens were in poor condition and the taro not ready to be gathered, so there was little to eat. The storm had destroyed a large part of the coconut crop, one of the mainstays of Fijian diet, and on some of the islands there was a real scarcity of food. The government had relieved conditions somewhat by the distribution of rice. Of course fish and other seafood were available, but during violent storms could not be obtained, and the natives required vegetables, and plenty of them. Taro, in Fiji, must be grown in well-watered areas, often in terraces on the hill-side; cooked, it resembles potatoes, and is perhaps as palatable as plain boiled potato without butter or gravy. The average native can consume quantities of it merely boiled and without seasoning of any sort.

A native police sergeant, whom I knew later, had been with the Fijian contingent to London in 1897 during Queen Victoria's Diamond Jubilee. I asked how London had appeared to him, and he answered:

"You like Fiji? When you come to our villages we give you all kinds of food we have, so you have plenty to eat, yes? But I think sometimes you would like something we cannot get here, yes? It was the same with me; I liked London, plenty to eat, plenty of beef, but I did want some taro."

Collecting was not good, though in a termite nest I found a little beetle that later proved to be a new genus of termite guest; I named it Lauella after the archipelago. There were five kinds of ants on the island, all of them the usual widely spread tropicopoli-tan forms. In fact, during my entire stay in Lau I found only two species of ants that might be considered typically Fijian. There was an occasional boa, and many lizards, one of them a large gecko, abundant everywhere. I would see it in rolls of native mats aboard boats, which explains how it has traveled from island to island.

The smallness of the number of both insects and other land inhabitants which I found was probably due to the dry season; but still, Lau is a poor field for the entomologist. Had I seen only this archipelago, and not visited the larger islands, my report on the fauna would have been as short as that of the Englishman of a fine family who, not being good at anything else, was ordered to write a report on the manners and customs of the Fijians. He spent some months among them and finally wrote, "Manners, none; customs, beastly."

In listing the contents of the chief's house I omitted its chief glory, a kerosene lamp suspended from the rafters. The letter of introduction which we had presented, and our deportment in the village, impressed the chief. On our first night he ordered the lamp to be lit, and he invited as many of the villagers as could get into the house to spend the evening. At first there was an air of formality, but this was broken by a young lady offering to Foye, most ostentatiously, a pillow on which to sit. Foye was suffering from two terrible boils, and he sat with difficulty. It was evident that the boils had been part of the village gossip that day, and everyone laughed heartily when the pillow was presented and the ice broken.

Long after proper bedtime, someone suggested music. There was no hesitation on the part of the three girls in the house. They left immediately and returned a few minutes later, having changed their *sulus* for more brilliant blue ones, smeared their torsos with coconut oil, and decked themselves with garlands and bracelets of banana leaves. They sat in a row. A boy, with a log in front of him and a stick in either hand, made up the orchestra. One stick was thick and one was thin, and as he drummed on the log the music went *chink* chink, chunk *chunk*. Then Wainisi,

the leader of the singers, commenced in a voice that seemed hor-
ribly coarse at first, but was subdued when she was joined by
Nani and Marana, the other two, in a song that was spirited,
although it had little latitude in tone. However, the three voices
blended in surprisingly good harmony. The end of each verse
was abrupt, and, until one became accustomed to it, jarring.
This is one of the characteristics of Fijian music, and has been
likened by a European to the sound of someone walking near by
singing loudly, and suddenly falling into a well.

The subject of the *meke* was King George's visit to India: his
departure from England, life on the steamer, a hurricane at sea,
and the reception in India took a great many verses, and we
were tired long before it was over. Finally the three girls stopped
singing and clapped their hands to signify that the *meke* was
over, and our visitors left the house, bidding us, as they went,
"*Samoce*" — literally, "There is sleep."

One of our fellow passengers on the *Lotu Wesele* was a native
missionary. He decided to stay over Sunday to conduct services
and to baptize a child. There was little for us to collect on the
island, and our store of food was gone. We had expected to reach
Lakemba in three days from Lomaloma; it actually took eight —
but we were content, partly because the captain was worried
about the weather, and partly because it took only a few weeks
in the South Seas to acquire "*Malua*" (by-and-by), sometimes
called "mat fever." (Latin Americans get by with "*Mañana*.")

At one side of the village was a miserable little hut, a store kept
by an elderly Hindu, a Madrasi, who had come out from India
years before as indentured labor, but was now a man of business,
and seemed to be living in unenviable circumstances. The Fijians
did not like him and he was ostracized completely except in
strictly business matters. We bought his stores — four cans of
Manchurian salmon, a package of matches, and some curry
powder, leaving him with nothing to do until he could get in a
new supply. Several times we saw him walking aimlessly about,

and during the church services on Sunday he came to the village and stood listening to the singing.

Sunday morning the entire aspect of the village was changed. Everyone was dressed for church, the women in pinafores, and the men in cotton singlets in addition to their *sulus*. The Fijian is rigid indeed in his observance of Sunday. In the morning, when we had finished breakfast, I asked the chief for a coconut; he looked about the house and found none. When I pointed to a near-by tree that was loaded with them, he looked at me in surprise and said, "*Siga tabu*" — "sacred day." That answered me. No native would climb a tree until Monday, but we did find some coconuts about the village that had already been picked. Thereafter on Saturday nights we always saw to it that there were plenty of nuts on hand for Sunday, because we were afraid of the drinking water and depended on coconuts to quench our thirst.

When Seemann, the botanist, had approached Lakemba years before it was Sunday. The boat could not land, and the ship had to sail back and forth the entire day. Seemann offered to go to church himself if landed, but the captain said no; it was as much as his position was worth to desecrate Sunday by landing a boat.

One admires this deep devotion, but sometimes it can cause complications. For instance, there is the *palolo*, a marine worm which exists in countless numbers deep among the coral reefs of the South Pacific. At the egg-laying season, for one day only, it comes to the surface in billions. Not all of the worm comes to the surface; it divides, and the egg-laying part comes up, the other end staying at home to develop new egg-laying apparatus for the following season. They appear at a certain phase of the moon that the natives know, and at that time all the people of the village go out to be ready. Several inches below the surface, these worms cover an area of many miles, and are scooped up, taken ashore, roasted, and provide a sumptuous banquet, with enough, and more than enough, for everybody.

I heard about this, and wondered what the Fijians would do on the very rare occasions when this plethora came in on Sunday. This has happened, and the Wesleyans steadfastly refuse to gather them. The Catholics are required to attend religious services on Sunday, and are not supposed to do unnecessary work, but scooping up *palolo* is not on the prohibited list. The same problem arises if the worms come up on Saturday, for the Seventh Day Adventists are as true to form as the Wesleyans. This could happen only once in many years, and I am almost sure that the Catholics would give some of the delicacy to the others, because food has always been a "give-away" among the natives.

Except Vanua Mbalavu, Lakemba is the largest island in the archipelago, about five and a half miles across at its broadest part, surrounded by a fringing reef on the east side, on which is the boat passage, a dangerous one where seven ships of various sizes had been wrecked during the previous eleven years. We made arrangements with the English trader to stay with him, so the chief sent us a present of half a dozen chickens and enormous quantities of vegetables. The trader was T. O. U. Stockwell, and his wife was a Tongan girl, most attractive and intelligent. She was an unusually good cook, too. One time, however, she put on the table for dinner a cake that had fallen, and muttered a Fijian expression, "As tough as Dr. Baker's boots."

Dr. Baker was the last missionary eaten by cannibals although a few others had been killed. In 1860, the doctor, who was most unpopular with the chief on the coast where he was staying, proposed to make an expedition into the interior. The chief immediately sent messengers carrying a whale's tooth to the chief of the village where Dr. Baker was going. It was presented and received with the usual ceremony, but when one accepts a whale's tooth, one cannot thereafter refuse any request that the donor makes. The request, in this case, was to kill the missionary. The chief did it, and not wanting to waste meat, had him roasted, divided and sent some to his various friends. To one headman in the village he sent a leg, encased in a Wellington boot which the missionary had worn, and he and his tribesmen, while enjoying the delicacy, complained afterward about the toughness of the "skin." The coast people thought this was a good joke on the stupid people of the bush, and it became a common Fijian expression.

With Hoodless, the English schoolteacher, and a group of boys, we visited a cave about which I had heard much talk. We walked to it through barren, low hills, and clusters of ironwood trees and pandanus palms. In the valleys were taro, tapioca, and coconuts. The cavern itself was a good size, almost a tenth as long and as high as had been described to us. There was a broad passage into a chamber about one hundred feet across and forty feet high; this led into a second one over two hundred feet long and fifty high, with large stalactites and stalagmites. The path into it was broad, evidently an old stream bed; chambers three and four were similar but smaller.

The roofs were studded with bats, and I collected a number of them by standing in the dark and swinging my butterfly net while the boys threw torches at the ceiling. With these torches of coconut leaves we were able to get a view of the cavern. The floor was soft and loamy, and sparkled with silver-colored objects. At first I thought they were bits of mica, but closer examination showed them to be millions of almost microscopic moths, living most probably on the guana of the bats. Specimens of the moths were duly collected, and are today reposing in the Museum. There are two more caves near Lakemba; one we did not visit, and the other consisted of a single grotto beautifully festooned with stalactites. It was about thirty feet across and as high as broad. There were bats here, too — the same species as in the other cave; but we saw none of the small moths.

Collecting was miserably poor. There were butterflies, a few bees and wasps, and the usual common ants. Even Foye got tired of whacking his hammer on coral rocks. We had already been named by the natives: Foye was *Tuki Vatu* (Hammers Rocks), and I was *Vuni Wai Ni Manu Manu Lai Lai* (Doctor of the Little Things That Fly, or the Bug Doctor).

We wanted to leave this part of the world, where we felt that we had almost exhausted the possibilities, especially at this season. But there was no way to get back, and Captain Tavita and his crew told so many exciting things about Ono-i-Lau, their home island, and the last one in the archipelago, where there would be "many little things for the doketah to put in bottles," that we went there.

It took a day and a night to reach Fulanga, because a gale blew again. The sails were half-reefed, and our crew sang hymns most of the night. In the morning we reached the bewitching harbor of Fulanga. A narrow entrance through the reef led into a protected harbor, dotted with tiny islets of coral. Geologically, the whole area of the bay was once covered by a bed of coral. The sea, cutting through, divided it into small islands and these have been worn down and rounded by the action of the waves, and the lower parts abraded, so that at low tide they stand out like so many gigantic mushrooms, the larger ones with wind-stunted palms on top.

A hurricane two years before had blown down the larger houses and destroyed the coconut crop. The people were desperately poor, and were eating a "bread" made of mangrove pods macerated with water, beaten between stones and then boiled into a barklike substance, which was as tasteless as some of our widely advertised breakfast foods. Here, instead of using money, I gave the boys who collected for me pieces of pilot bread, a sort of hardtack, smeared with jam. We tried some of the mangrove bread and also some *yavato*, the roasted larvae of a large wood-boring beetle. They were about the size of one's little finger and had a nutty flavor like other edible beetles. Insect larvae are eaten generally around the world by primitive peoples and *gusano de maguay* of Mexico is even tinned for export.

The chief gave us a fly swatter made of coconut fiber fastened to a stick, something like a feather duster. There were few mosquitoes on the island but swarms of flies. Other islands had so many mosquitoes that the flies must have had a hard time of it, for air can contain only so many winged creatures. Though I loved Fiji, I will say that it is the damnedest place for mosquitoes and flies anywhere in the world — except perhaps certain parts of Montana, which I also love. There are fleas, too, and sitting crosslegged in a native hut I often amused myself by picking them off my clothes one by one, or sometimes two by two. If the fleas, or the mosquitoes, or the flies, carried any fatal disease, there would be no Fijians and no European settlers. Yellow fever and malaria have never reached the islands, though the mosquitoes do carry the minute worm that causes the horrible malady elephantiasis.

There was such a paucity, however, of insects in which I was interested that, as we zigzagged from island to island, when going ashore to collect I would take just one vial with me.

At each island there were gifts of food, songs and dances in the evening, and then presents, usually beautiful mats. We gave what we could in return, from the stores we had brought along. Our boys joined in, and Joeli bashfully appeared one morning without his shirt; he had given it away the evening before to a new acquaintance, but he explained to me that to hold the respect of the natives for our party, he really must have another one.

Ongea is a group of islands, two large and many small ones, mushroom-shaped, conical or domelike, similar to those at Fulanga, all encircled by a broad coral reef. The village is on the main island. The chief was out in the woods when we arrived, but we took possession of his house, a small hut built of boards and elevated on stilts instead of on the usual earth mound. With a half-dozen boys I walked through the near-by forest and found a few small black and white butterflies and some leaf-cutting bees, but little else.

The woods contained large trees, some of them a hundred feet high. At one place we passed through a veritable forest of papaya trees. This is an introduced species, having been imported by early settlers. It grows like a weed wherever started and furnishes a melonlike fruit, luscious to the taste — if you like it, I don't — and of considerable merit as a digestive. Papain, derived from the seeds, is similar to pepsin in action, and the chief ingredient of some of our best digestive pills. Natives and Europeans wrap the leaves about meat before cooking it, and say they make it tender. Papain is known to be an effective meat tenderizer, but I am certain that none of the chickens served to us had been treated that way.

We passed several small parties of women returning from the gardens. As we approached, they stepped to one side of the path and flopped to the ground, where they sat with heads hung down and eyes averted, till we had gone by. This is a position of respect. A native will never stand in a house where a chief is present, but gets down as he enters and crawls to his sitting place.

When we returned to the chief's house, the entire population of the village (about eighty) passed us on their way to church, each carrying a hymnbook under his arm. The services in this case consisted mostly of singing.

There were a number of wild goats on the island, descendants of a pair liberated some ten years previously, and they were sometimes hunted with dogs. Naturally, the natives had no names for domestic animals when they were first introduced into the islands. So they imitated the names they thought were given them by their owners. Hence, the dog is known as *come-ere* — when not called *kali*, the scratcher — and the sheep is *sipi* and the horse *ossi*.

We had seen many chickens around the village. In the evening we asked if we could have some eggs. These are not generally eaten by the Fijians, and are reserved for invalids and sometimes children, but the town crier walked through the village shouting at the top of his voice: "Listen, all men and women, to the things I call. Collect some eggs and bring them to the *papalagi* (foreigners)." They brought in one or two at a time until we had quite a supply, but then a thought occurred to me. They might have taken them from setting hens, and I asked Joeli if he knew how to tell a bad egg from a good one. He did, and with the aid of a lamp he found baby chickens in all but one or two of them. It had to be carefully explained to the chief that what we wanted were untenanted eggs, for eating purposes. Whereupon the town crier paraded through the village again and each native who had brought us eggs came to get them back, offering to return the trifle we had paid for them. I hoped the eggs got back under the brooding hens in time.

We slept on the boat that night, and got under way in the morning, but were overtaken by a native in a canoe, who brought a big pair of entomological forceps that I had carelessly left behind. Later we heard that after our departure the natives held a long prayer meeting, beseeching the Almighty that no harm should come to them on account of our visit. There are always rumors in war time, and Foye and I, by our actions, had aroused suspicions. We were foreigners, and one of us was spending much time in the study of coral reefs — perhaps finding a way for submarines to come into the harbor? And the other, with a powerful light at which he pretended to pick up little insects attracted to the glare, might he not be signaling to the enemy?

Another day and a half of steady sailing brought us to Doi, one of the three islands that make up Ono-i-Lau. The natives were practicing for a big *meke-meke* to be given when our ship left for the north a week later, a farewell ceremony for the missionaries who were to sail with us. The wife and daughter of the chief were preparing for the dance; blue *sulus* were put on, then their hair was combed and oiled, and a liberal lot of oil rubbed on their torsos. Garlands of leaves were hung around their necks and more oil added. Out of a small leather purse, the girl took some brilliant red powder and arranged it in large blotches on her hair, and a dab on each cheek. As it was a practice affair, and quite informal, the tiny tots in the village stood about and imitated the movements of their elders' arms and hands. When the party was assembled, the dancers stood solemnly in a row. After waiting for some time for things to begin, the chief told me that they wanted to have their pictures taken. Nobody likes having his picture taken as much as a Fijian. When I got out the camera, everybody in sight would stand still, like so many grenadiers, so much so that sometimes it was difficult to photograph a bit of landscape without too many natives in the foreground. Often I merely pretended to snap pictures until my self-appointed models had dispersed.

Captain Tavita, a couple of the boys, and I crossed to the big island Ono Levu in an outrigger canoe equipped with a sail made of matting, and sped through the surf to the beach. Tavita had told us an American lived here, and sure enough, there he was on the beach, dressed in trousers and shirt and hailing us in good English as we approached. Alf Williams was his name, and he was the village storekeeper. A Negro cook from an American whaler had, in times past, remained behind in Fiji when the ship left, married, and settled down to grow up with the country. Alf was his grandson. There was considerable Fijian blood mixed with the African, but the blood of the latter race is dominant when mixed with Fijian, and both the storekeeper and the children might have come from Africa. He received us in the hospitable manner of both races, and took us at once to his house, where tea was served by Mrs. Williams — the small Williamses, typical little pickaninnies all, gazing shyly at us as we ate. We had hot biscuits for tea, baked according to a recipe that had been handed down through three generations.

At the store, we hoped to lay in a stock of food, but Williams was anxiously waiting for one of Stockwell's boats, the *Dorine*, with supplies, because his stores were sold out except for a little rice, some curry powder, and perfume. Our boat had brought a case of kerosene for him, and his store was soon crowded with natives, each with a quart bottle.

As was customary, the chief gave us his house; this one had three rooms, and a broad veranda three fourths of the way around. Inside were several fighting clubs of the olden days, some of them beautifully carved. He served a supper of fish-head soup, boiled fish, sweet potatoes and breadfruit, and afterward we sat around talking and smoking, each member of the party provided with an empty meat tin for a cuspidor.

The natives of Ono-i-Lau treated us graciously, and sometimes informally, as when the youngsters invited us to the beach on a squid-spearing expedition. These squid, a foot or so long and swimming forward or backward with equal facility, were seen by the light of torches, which some of the party were carrying. I had to wear shoes, not having the reinforced soles that Fijians have on their feet, and I wore a bath towel instead of a *sulu*. The children taught me how to twist it to keep it from falling down, but when it did, exposing my BVD's, there were shrieks of laughter, and one of them would pick it up and help me put it on again. Spearing squid is a lot of fun, though I did not get any myself, not being able to judge the refraction in the water, but every once in a while one of the boys or girls would take my spear and impale one.

On Sunday we went to church, and to our surprise were taken to chairs on the pulpit platform, and informed by Joeli that we were to make nice speeches, which he would translate as we went along. Foye, being quite a churchman, gave a good account of himself, at least his talk was splendid in English, but both of us had some trepidation as to how Joeli had translated it. Mine was short, and consisted of a brief comparison of Lau, the land of abundance, and the Holy Land itself with its scarcity of food and water. In the question period at the end of the service, one of the natives asked, "Why don't all the people from the Holy Land come here where there is plenty?"

The *Buli* (chief) and the local missionary were going to leave when we did, and the farewell celebration, the first formal *meke* we had seen, filled the last day and night. There was subdued excitement in town in the morning, and everybody wore an extra lot of wreaths. Under a mango tree in front of the *Buli's* house long mats were arranged in a square, with a table and a bench at one side. The more important men of the village sat in a row at another side, and on a third side was a man with a flat stone about a yard square and a small rounded stone to serve as a hammer. At the far end was a huge wooden bowl and handfuls of coconut fiber to act as mixer and strainer for the drink we were about to have — *yanggona* in Fiji, *cava* in the rest of the Pacific. A sack containing dried roots was brought out, and a speech made over it by the *Buli's* right-hand man. The roots were tossed on the big stone and crushed with the smaller one; the resulting mass was dumped into the big bowl, mixed with water and kneaded. When properly mixed, it was strained through the coconut fiber. A coconut shell, half filled with the liquid, was held up, and the man who had poured it shouted "*Ka ko heg?*" ("Whose is this?") and the town crier called the name of the man to whom it was to go. The recipient drank the cupful at one gulp, slapped his thigh, and yelled, "*Moci, moci, moci!*" ("Empty, empty, empty!") Whereupon everybody else slapped their thighs and yelled, "*Vinaka, vinaka, vinaka!*" ("It is good!")

The cup was filled again, and the same performance repeated. The first cupful from each bowl went to the *Buli*, and as the party went on, he got rather more than his share. At first the drink tasted to me like mild soapsuds, but it became more pleasant and refreshing as time wore on. Too much of it causes a sort of nerve paralysis, so that the drinker lacks co-ordination. It was said to be the custom to invite newcomers to Fiji to partake of it

Macromischa Fiber Nest from Haiti

A Yanggona Party in Fiji

copiously just before a tennis game, which contributes to the amusement of the bystanders, and the chagrin of the man trying to hit a ball. The mind stays clear and there is no thickness of speech.

After the *yanggona* party had started, a *meke* troupe arrived and commenced to dance, the men in one group doing the dancing, the women singing. The missionary took his place at the table, and the town crier made an appeal for funds. There were dancers from four villages, and while their costumes varied, the girls all wore heavy skirts of leaves, one of them ornamented with some spoiled rolls of camera film that I had thrown away. From time to time the *yanggona* server called "*Ka ko heg?*" and amid the dancing and singing, and the town crier's speech about money, the people came to the table and made their offerings.

Then the missionary read a list of their contributions to the expense of his journey to the conference, such and such a town — or such and such a man — so many pounds, so many shillings. There were no sixpences or pennies, and yet this was in a group of islands where often an entire village was unable to change a pound note for me. The entire collection came to sixteen pounds, ten shillings.

When the *meke* was finished, the dancers squatted on the ground and clapped their hands as a sign that it was all over. One of the girls dashed out of line and threw a *salu-salu* (wreath of flowers) around my neck. I did not know what this meant, but Foye blushed.

In the evening, the young people gave another *meke*, putting much energy into it, the boys singing war songs accompanied by shrugging of the shoulders and grimacing, and the girls singing songs of Samoa and Tonga with abandon, tossing their garlands into the air and onto their heads. Some made and lit for us *salukas* — strips of tobacco rolled in dried banana leaves; we made and gave some of our cigarettes in return, and I saw one girl light hers and then put it between her toes till the song was finished. More *yanggona* was served, and we had a glorious evening, finishing with a hulalike dance, the first we had seen in this part of the world. When the dancers gave their performance directly in front of the *Buli*, he hung his head and murmured, "*Sadruka*," which means literally "I am beaten," or, "This is too much." It finished with a dance of hands and waving leaves, without music or words.

When we left in the morning, all the villagers were down to see us off. There was some show of emotion between the captain and his wife and daughter, and between the *Buli* and his sister. At Kambara the next day, we landed in the rain. Here an Englishman, Willy Baker, lived with his wife and father; they gave us a little house of our own, and after we had changed into dry clothes invited us to tea.

Baker had taught some of the children to speak a bit of English, and one of them, extending his hand to me, said, "Sixpence, sir, please?"

Fijians are not beggars, even when children, and, surprised at this, I asked what he had done to deserve sixpence. "Nothing, sir. I was just cadging."

Kambara is essentially an island of forest, save for a narrow strip along part of the coast which is sandy and flat and covered with coconuts, backed by precipitous cliffs of coral. In the interior the natives have cleared enough land for their gardens. We took a walk inland with Mr. Baker. From the highest hill (about four hundred and thirty feet) we had a fine view of a valley with an even covering of big forest. Fruit pigeons were everywhere and their guttural hoots always to be heard.

Here, I found two black carpenter ants that proved to be new and the first uniquely Fijian species I had come upon in almost three months of collecting.

We went on to other islands, but each one was much like the last. When we sailed parallel to reefs and close to them we would troll, the lure being a beef tin, flattened inside out, and occasionally we would draw in, hand over hand, a *walu* or a *sanka*, averaging about three feet long and making delicious steaks roasted in the little oven on deck.

Before I started for Fiji, Outram Bangs had given me some money to hire an assistant who was to make a collection of bird skins. Bangs had explained to me that the Chinese are all good bird-skinners and I could hire one for practically nothing. But unfortunately for the bird collection, all the Chinese in Fiji were merchants, and better able, financially, to hire a Harvard traveling fellow than he was to hire them. The idea of making a bird collection had to be abandoned. We saw many, for we were constantly passing islands uninhabited except for birds. An occasional heron would be standing on a reef. There were smaller herons among the mangroves; flocks of gulls were usually in sight, as were terns, noddys, and man-of-war birds, with their long tails, high in the air. Near the beach would be whimbrels, a kind of curlew, sojourning in Fiji to avoid the winter of Siberia. There were other migrants, among them the American wandering tattler, far from its breeding grounds in Alaska. On the wooded hills large Pacific pigeons, black above, with glossy green wings and a large knob on the bill, were heard continuously. Some we got for eating purposes were filled with nutmegs, probably so that they could digest the surrounding mace and then disgorge the nut itself.

Porpoises would follow us for hours, and once a Mola with its head and part of its body out of the water circled the boat several times, as though it were looking us over, with its eyes as big as saucers. These fish are sometimes eight feet or more in length, and nearly as deep as long, with compressed bodies and very short tails. Sluggish and apparently stupid, they spend much time basking on the surface but descend to great depths in search of food; their stomach contents are often fishes that never come near the ocean surface.

The crew and our passengers would sing night and day, often

hymns, but also the abrupt Fiji harmony and Tongan melodies. One song appealed to us especially — it was a sailor's song to his sweetheart on departure:

> Blow, wind, blow;
> But dry that tear from your eye;
> Because the same wind that blows me away from you
> Will blow me back.

We requested this so many times that Captain Tavita demanded that we also sing, to them; and furthermore he stated that they would not do the sailor's song again until we had. Foye and I canvassed our musical memories and found that we knew only one American song in common — George M. Cohan's "It's a grand old rag . . ." Foye could sing, I couldn't, but I added noise and we went through one verse and two choruses with energy. There was deep silence for a moment after, and then Captain Tavita explained to his crew, "Now that is the way the *kai tovati* (United People) sing."

As we sailed into the harbor of Lakemba, there was a welcoming committee (not so intended, of course) composed of ten little girls. They were far below the bobby-socks age; they had no bobby socks or anything else on. They sat on the side of a schooner that had been submerged to rid it of cockroaches — a common practice in Fiji, but not common enough — and they were singing in English and with childhood lustiness "God Sav the Kink."

Back at Lakemba, we heard about the *Winifred*, a cutter that was to come in, load copra, and return to Lomaloma. We engaged passage on her, and gave a farewell party to the crew and our fellow passengers of the *Lotu Wesele*, availing ourselves of the abundance now to be found on the shelves of Stockwell's store. In addition to some canned gristle (labeled beef), and "genuine" pink salmon — common trade goods and known and liked by all the natives — we had tomato soup, pork and beans, and gooseberry tart. The beef and salmon met with favor; the beans were eaten one at a time and not more than a half-dozen by any one guest; the tomato soup and gooseberry tart were avoided politely. But our dessert of tea (a bitter syrup of boiled tea leaves poured over half a cup of sugar), pilot bread, and an abundance of jam was greedily and appreciatively eaten.

We took our baggage out to the *Winifred* in a punt, glanced into the hold full of copra and cockroaches, and decided to stay on deck. Captain Willie headed for a point, and got there regardless of waves, so we were wet most of the time. Dr. St. Johnson and the Tripps greeted us at Lomaloma and gave us tea and mouth-watery cake, which we ate until we were ashamed of ourselves — and then ate three pieces more.

CHAPTER X   Human Meat Is Sweeter

THREE MONTHS in Lau had been a delightful experience. We had developed sincere affection for the people, who had taken us wholeheartedly into their homes and lives. We had learned enough of the language to stumble through it. But zoological collecting had been miserably poor, and when the *Amra* came, we boarded her for Taveuni.

The *Amra* seemed a much better ship than it had on the outward passage. It was clean and the food was good, and the first officer a splendid fellow to argue with, as neither of us agreed about anything. Taveuni is one of Fiji's largest islands and one where I hoped to find some land fauna. There were many European planters here, each plantation fronting the sea and backed by high hills, and the steamer stopped at each one, a sort of rural delivery system. The shores were covered with coconut palms, but the densely forested mountains beyond gave promise of some real collecting.

Disembarking at Somosomo at noon, we were taken into the *Buli*'s house, but without the enthusiasm to which we had been accustomed. Rumors that we were German spies had reached Taveuni and the *Buli* was worried about us. But there was a Swede in the village who served us tea, tinned fish, and a lot of gratuitous information. He took us to a bathing place in a little stream that flowed by the town; while we soaked in a pool of cool, clear water, he informed us that he was the greatest authority on the South Seas, on ants and plants, that he loved the moon and the stars and every blade of grass — "even if you gentle-

226

men should be doctors of science, I know more about it than you do." Then he told us that he had been a strong man among men, a tiger trainer in India, and had sailed with Bully Hayes, the noted blackbirder and pirate of former days. He had lived among the Eskimos, had fought cannibals; and he hated the English, who charged him eight shillings for a two-shilling bottle of gin. Later, at the house, when he had had a little more eight-shilling gin, he explained:

"When young, such a strong man I was. Like lightning, I would kill a man and think nothing of it. Strong like a bull, and brave like a lion, I would take two young men like you, bang their heads together, and throw them over the roof of the house."

We were glad we had delayed coming for so many years.

With more gin, he grew more vindictive about England and made a number of statements that an alien, living in a country at war, should not make. In the morning, somewhat subdued, he said to us rather plaintively, "Didn't I give you food? I would not refuse food to a dog that was hungry. And you will not say what I said about the English? You see, if you do, they will kick me, and then I must kill them, and then see what you've done!"

We found later that most of his adventure stories were true.

Dr. R. S. Trotter, the government medical man of the district, had invited us to stay with him at his house near by at Waiyevo. The Somosomo people, possibly afraid of carrying the baggage of such desperate spies as Foye and I were supposed to be, showed no inclination to help us move. Through an interpreter I asked, "Are there any men in this village or only Fijians?" This prompted Tolu, the chief's right-hand man, and another native to come with us, and the two of them poled a little boat with our gear and ourselves to the landing. Foye went up the hill to the government house, and returned shortly followed by an assorted crowd of prisoners from the local jail released temporarily for the purpose, and the not very lame, halt, and blind from the hospital — all of whom helped carry our baggage. The doctor was out but his Hindu servant made us tea, and we settled down in the luxury of a well-screened house, with a large veranda, situated in a clearing with other government buildings — the magistrate's house, the hospital, and a wireless station.

It was here that I had my first really good collecting day. The cleared areas were covered with a tangle of weeds almost impossible to walk through, but a little stream made an excellent roadway, up which I walked for a couple of miles and reached some real forest, the trees covering the narrow ravine of the stream. Spiders were everywhere and as one walked in a foot or so of water one was continually in their webs, which were close to the surface of the stream and practically invisible in the shade; the spiders themselves seemed to be floating through the air. On stones along the edge were other spiders, one a large flat one that when startled would jump on the water and zip across to safety.

The coast of Taveuni is a succession of native villages and European plantations, each with a stream of mountain water near by. The houses were on elevated areas and the coolie settlements and copra-drying frames were near the beach. Mackenzie, a planter, invited us to visit his place, and the first day he came in bringing a phasmid, a "walking stick," ten inches long. The largest I had ever seen before was in Texas, and only half as long, though in the East Indies they grow even larger than in Fiji. They are foliage feeders and stand on a plant in a way that makes them look like part of the bush itself. They eject, sometimes for several inches, a milky fluid which the Fijians believe will blind one but which is actually no more than a strong irritant.

Insect and other life was plentiful. We would go with Mr. Mackenzie inland where his Indian laborers were clearing; the vines were so dense that they had to be cut and removed before the trees on which they tangled could be felled with axes. There are several species of snakes in Fiji, one of which is mildly poisonous, and the Indians brought some tree snakes, a boa, and another walking stick, and I commenced finding more ants that I believed could be there.

On the fallen trees were hosts of beetles, mating, laying eggs, or just sitting there. Mackenzie pointed out a Myrmecodia, the first I had ever seen, which he had cut down six weeks before, thinking it some kind of orchid, but he had been driven away from it by the ants which occupied it. These ant plants occur in many parts of the South Seas and the East Indies. Of parasitic habit, they are usually large, green, irregular, bulbous objects, full of chambers which are always full of ants. The ants have made their colony there since the queen moved into the tiny bulblet, and the colony grows with the plant. It was easy collecting, because one could slice them open with a whack of a machete and expose the chambers. Most of them were inhabited by a very small ant (*Iridomyrmex myrmecodiae*) that gets its name from the plant. While it did not sting, it was annoying by its very numbers, hundreds of them running over me.

There was evidently an epidemic of a relative of our own seventeen-year locust, because the shed skins of their nymphs were everywhere.

When we left Mackenzie, we went part way by launch and the rest of the way on foot, arriving at Waiyevo about eleven at night. Dr. Trotter told us that he had arranged for us to go to a lake on top of the almost unexplored mountain range, and we were to leave at three-thirty the next morning. We started at four, while it was still dark — the doctor, the District Commissioner, a planter named Drury, Foye, and six natives — and walked along a trail toward the big bush. After two and a half hours of climbing, Foye's barometer showed we were at twenty-three hundred feet. We could see below us the forest spreading down to the clearings near the shore, and beyond the settlement was the bay of Vanua Levu, with the reef showing very distinctly from our altitude. The bush about us was thick and dripping wet, every stem and branch covered with moss and lichens.

A little higher up we could overlook the crater lake, which was in a valley about five miles long. We walked, or rather waded, sometimes up to our shoetops and sometimes up to our waist, in a mixture of water and mucilaginous algae which gave our path the consistency of thick tapioca pudding.

Large ground orchids, four feet high with a spike of white and purplish blossoms, were common along the edge of the bog. One plant was especially conspicuous, a vine which completely covered trees and shrubs. It had glossy leaves, bright red bracts and peduncles, and masses of delicate white flowers. The natives called it *tagimocia*. It was such an interesting plant that I made a sketch of it, from which it was afterward identified as *Medinilla waterhousei*.

The lake itself had abrupt banks. There were said to be eels in the lake — quite probable, because eels occur everywhere. A drizzle had set in, but some of our party decided to have a swim and dove in. They pronounced the water cool. The rest of us climbed onto a pile of fallen reeds and ate bread smeared with jam and rain.

In the bush were many more Myrmecodias, mostly high up in the trees. Our natives would climb, drop them down, and they were all tenanted by the same kind of ant. Under stones in very wet earth, however, I found two specimens of a primitive ant which later proved to be a new genus and was named after my professor, Wheeleripone.

The moment of greatest excitement came when Dr. Trotter saw a frog sitting on a branch of a tree directly overhead on the trail. This was one of the specimens that Tom Barbour at the Museum had especially wanted. The native Fijian frogs belong to the genus Cornufer, differing from most frogs in their method of developing young. The eggs are placed on the undersides of leaves. They are large, and within them the little tadpoles develop, eventually emerging as fully formed, though minute, frogs. Formerly abundant throughout the large islands, they have been almost exterminated by the mongoose. This had been explained to me in the same way a dozen times when I asked natives about them. In fact, I talked so much about frogs that they supplemented my name of Bug Doctor with *Ka Savia Na Botu* (Who Wants Frogs), *botu* being the common name of the frog, though I found three other names in different parts of the country.

Having at last found a frog, we took elaborate precautions in catching it. I deployed the rest of the party in a circle in case it jumped to the ground. The branch was carefully pulled down. The frog sat quietly, I picked him up, wrapped him in Dr. Trotter's handkerchief, and took him home to pickle him in some of the small supply of grain alcohol that I had brought for such a purpose.

In the trees above us were flocks of a little lorikeet, green in color except for some red markings on the cheek, throat, and thighs, and yellow at the tip of the long tail feathers. We also saw a pair of red-breasted musk parrots. These, including the tail, are about a foot and a half long, bright green on the back and wings, and bright red on the head and breast, one of the most colorful of the parrot family. Besides these two species there were flocks of collared lories, crimson-red below and green and black above. These were in the clearing and clustered in the tops of the coconut trees.

Before leaving for Fiji, I had copied the descriptions of the endemic ants that had been described from there, all ten of them, and after a few days in the bush — reached always by following one little stream or another — I found that I had collected nine of the ten known ones, and a number of others which were probably new to science. I presumed this was the case with other groups of insects, with which I was less familiar; and later on this proved to be true.

Each day I would stroll along the beach to a new stream and follow it to a new part of the forest, in a continual state of exultation over the abundant and interesting specimens. Beneath one stone that I had just turned over were dozens of little wormlike objects, that darted forward half an inch and then lay quiet. A touch of the forceps showed that these were not worms at all but little threads of a viscid matter. They were moving and seemed to be alive, but I could not make even a remote guess what they were till, looking more closely, I saw dozens of small black ants lying perfectly quiet, and from each of these was exuding a "worm." The ants at first were indistinguishable from the black earth on which they were lying, and it was a gland secretion that I had first noted. Many ants do secrete from their anal glands, but none in a manner like this, and the result must be quite a disappointment to small ant-eating creatures who come into such a colony, for they would soon get tangled in these sticky threads.

Except for too much rain and far too many mosquitoes, Taveuni was a dream island. Each day many new things turned up.

At Wiriki, a small, well-laid-out village, there was a large two-story cement house where lived the priests of the local Catholic church. The church itself was an imposing structure, fronting a clearing that extended to the sea; there was a statue of the Virgin, and in front of this an active fountain. Inside were good pictures of the Stations of the Cross, each nicely framed and fastened to the wall. The holy water basins, made of the largest of all known clamshells, Tridacna (which grow up to three feet in length), were cemented to the wall, and above each of them was a small, oval piece of china with a painting of one of the Stations. Some lively mosquito larvae disported in the holy water. The floor was covered with large native mats, on which had been left the prayer- and hymnbooks waiting for the next service.

The natives, I think, had dismissed the idea that we were spies, because they showed us every courtesy, even to carrying us across the little streams to avoid getting our shoes wet. While standing on the edge of one of these streams, a native saw me, and as usual came over, bent down, and indicated I could ride "piggy-back" across. I did, but I was nervous about it because he kept stumbling and whistling through his teeth, indicating he was in some sort of trouble. When he dumped me on the other side he looked all right, and I burlesqued his limping and whistling. He looked at me reproachfully, then waded back into the stream and from the bottom brought up a double handful of snails, each with its shell covered with long sharp spines, enough to annoy even the sole of a Fijian foot. Then, of course, I was sorry for having made fun of him, but glad to have the shells as specimens. They were Neretina, and afterwards we found them to be common in the fresh-water streams where we collected. We parted friends, and when I left him he was drinking from the creek in Fijian style — not putting his mouth into the stream but throwing the water by quick scoops into his mouth. This custom has persisted from the old fighting days, when it would not have been safe to lie down beside a stream to drink.

On this same walk I found a coconut palm so bent that I could reach one of the nuts, which I twisted off. I was awkwardly trying to clear one end of it so I could get at the milk when three young Fijian women appeared. I heard one of them say "the Bug Doctor," so they knew who I was, but I did not know that I was violating one of the laws in Fiji by stealing coconuts. I had actually purloined a nut belonging to one of the girls. I found this out later; they did not tell me, but one of the girls took my knife and skillfully opened the nut, and the four of us used it as a loving cup.

An interesting story was told me later about this girl, illustrating the pride of the Fijian. On one of the streams was a long deep slide in a trough hollowed out by the water, and one could sit in this and "shoot the shoots" for about twenty feet, tumbling into a pool at the end. When the girls were playing in this manner, it was considered proper for the men to remain out of sight, because there is no nakedness in Fiji except among the smaller children. But one day a *ratu* of considerable social importance, but a playboy, thought that he would surprise the girls. With a friend, he hid in some bushes in which they had left their *sulus*. This was to be a huge joke on my friend of the coconuts, a princess in her own right. When she came to get her *sulu*, she saw the two young men sitting there. Instead of getting flustered and hurriedly putting it on, she merely threw it over her shoulder and walked away in her nakedness, the implication being that she considered the observers as of no more importance than so many dogs. The *ratu*, shamed before his people, actually left and made his home on another island. This inherent dignity and pride is evident throughout Fiji. Sometimes as a joke I would ask, "Are you Solomoni?" Or, "Are you Rotuma, or New Zealander?" Always I would get the reply, *"Kai viti"* ("I am a Fijian") — delivered as proudly as Saint Paul in court saying, "I am a Roman citizen."

Sometimes the rain was so heavy that we could not go out, but stayed in the doctor's house, and I found that a lot of my big specimens, such as walking sticks and large grasshoppers that I was attempting to dry, had molded completely. This mold is the curse of the collector in the wet tropics, and a far worse one to the curator of a collection. Jepson, the entomologist in Suva, had done a great deal of work in getting together the different species of mosquitoes of the islands; some had gone to London, where they had been described, but he had kept a duplicate set for reference. He had not looked at it for some time when he showed it to me, and remaining in the box were rows of pins, each holding a little square of cardboard, in the center of which was a fungus garden with here and there a mosquito's leg or wing protruding. I had with me a few metal insect boxes with a hollow around the rim so that the edge of the cover would be firmly inserted. This was lined with cotton on which one could pour creosote, which is a good preventive of mold after the specimen has been dried. I had pinned some of the walking sticks in these boxes and left the top a little ajar, and whenever there was any sun I put them out in the sun, but even then, what the mold didn't get, the ants did, despite powdered naphthalene in the boxes.

One rainy day I turned to the doctor's medical library and found a report on the disease filariasis, based on the work of two young British doctors who had studied it in Lau. Of course we had seen much of it, especially among some of the elders, where one or both legs were swollen till they resembled the lower part of an elephant's leg. Pretty girls sitting cross-legged and doing the *meke-meke*, with their inimitable gesturing of the arms and hands, often displayed swollen, unsightly ankles. Little attention was paid to it because there was nothing one could do except leave for the north as soon as there was the first sign of this disease. But in this report I was astonished to find that everyone we had known personally in Lau was afflicted. This included the whites, the half castes, the chiefs, and the missionaries; I could recognize our friends by the initials placed before the statement of each case. One lady who had complained to us of a weak ankle had filariasis of the ankle, and there were other cases that I could recognize from the description as well as from the initials.

The disease is caused by a worm that gets into the lymphatic system and prevents the ordinary stoppage of undue growth, so that any part of the body may become infected. The worm itself is carried by mosquitoes, and I think in mosquito egg cases, which are often found in water in cement tanks in Lau and in Kandavu in Fiji, as well as in the New World in Barbadoes, the Guianas, and eastern Brazil.

Except for filariasis, dysentery, and yaws, there were few diseases at all common. But in Lau, a child who did not have yaws was not considered normal; little attention was paid to those who did have it, though one would see tots covered with eruptions and sores.

We got the news once a day by means of the Colonial Secretary's report, sent by wireless to the government office and then read over party telephone lines that extended from one end of Taveuni to the other with a receiver at each plantation. At a given hour everyone would unhook his telephone and hear as much about the war and other things as the government wanted him to know. For local interest, the broadcaster put in notes for my benefit, such as "Frogs with hairy legs discovered at Mackenzie's place," "Montgomery reports strange creature day after day wading in middle of his stream and turning over stones on the bank," and even, once, "United States declares war on Britain."

One evening after a day in the bush I found my whole torso an unwholesome-looking pink. The doctor didn't know what it was but assumed that I had bumped into one of the poisonous plants, of which a half-dozen are known in the islands. The sap or the fine spines are most irritating, and sometimes cause severe illness. One of these trees, called by the Fijians *kau karo* (itchwood), can produce serious effects. One of the early settlers made a flagpole of one of these trees, about forty feet long and twenty inches in diameter. He pulled off the green bark, found considerable sap beneath it, and it was two months before he recovered from the irritation that it caused.

It was not easy to leave Taveuni, but we felt that we had done all we could at the time. We had a farewell party at the hospital, drank quantities of *yanggona*, and visited with the patients. One of these, an elderly woman, was dismayed when she heard that we had neither taro nor *yanggona* in America; she thought something should be done about it.

In the morning the patients again carried our baggage to the beach, from which a cutter took us, through a continual shower but with a direct wind, to Mbutha Bay on Vanua Levu, in about two hours. An English trader there took us into a hut, where we were able to change and get fairly well dried out. He then produced a feast of fresh wild pig, and currant pie out of a tin. The mosquitoes were terrific, but we did very well under our nets until a dog, also being tortured by the bites and apparently realizing what the net was, crawled in with me, followed by all the mosquitoes.

A mile and a quarter up a little river, an Australian named Solwey had a sawmill at a place called Lasema. To warn him of our coming, we sent Hosea with a load of supplies up the river in a punt, and we walked to his house. He was cutting *vesi*, one of the finest woods in Fiji, the trees growing to immense size. His men had cut an enormous one, nearly five feet in diameter, and were hauling parts of it out with a team of fourteen oxen, driven by a Hindu. He had an English vocabulary almost adequate for driving oxen (which do not compare favorably with mules), and when he reached the end of his knowledge of profanity he would shriek at them, "You bloody liar!"

As in Brazil, I had the opportunity of collecting in the tops of newly felled trees, and reaped a harvest of many insects I had not seen before, including colonies of twig-inhabiting ants.

In addition to his Indian labor, Solwey had a number of indentured Fijians working for him, engaged through a complicated process of getting a permit from the native Commissioner, and also from the chief. The boys received some coins, called *yanggona* or earnest money, at a farewell party in their native village; then they had to appear before the local magistrate while the papers were signed. They worked for twelve months at a salary of fourteen to twenty pounds a year, plus food as scheduled by the government, and tobacco and soap.

Leaving Solwey, we boarded the *Amra* again, and went by the ship's launch eight miles up a little river to a sugar plantation at Lambasa. Our engine stopped so frequently that the engineer anchored in midstream for an hour and took it to pieces and put it together again, after which it did not stop quite so often. It would get going merrily, then give an odd gurgle and break down. We had some English women aboard, and the engineer, fixing his eyes on the motor, uttered the most blasphemous and plaintive "Oh dears" that have ever been spoken.

At Lambasa the District Commissioner introduced us to Mr. Berry, of the sugar company; he introduced us to the head of the officers' mess; we moved into a room in the barracks, one of eighteen rooms placed end to end, and flanked on both sides by a ten-foot veranda, well-screened and comfortable. The men, young Australians for the most part, were a friendly crew. The mess, presided over by a matron, was reached from the barracks by a covered passageway locally called the "Tube," and furnished unusually good food, served by Hindu waiters. One of them tried to teach me the name of everything in the room in his own Tamil, but I was having enough difficulty learning Fijian.

Six miles up the valley were some hot springs, coming from an opening half as large as a barrel, freely flowing, and so hot that the hand could not bear the water. One spring was covered with coconut leaves, and a lot of coconut leaves were soaking in the water, softening to be made into native mats.

There are great extremes of climate in Fiji, and after the steady rains of Taveuni, we found Lambasa hot and arid. The mountains above, heavily forested, invited us, and we made a four-day walking trip, at first over red clay territory, similar to that at Lakemba, with thin growths of ironwood and pandanus palms. Beyond were Indian plantations, with rice fields, and with vegetables to sell to the mills. We were given wild pineapples, planted by settlers in the past and now abundant over many parts of Fiji, but, like other fruits, it is difficult to find one that has not been partly eaten by fruit bats. The juice was warmer than I thought a living plant could stand, but quenched our thirst very well. Some *yanggona* plants were pointed out to us by our guide who with his limited knowledge of English referred to them as "whisky trees."

A teen-age native boy came with me as guide and with him

I walked some distance from the stream. When I looked up from a log that I had been tearing to pieces in search of specimens, he had disappeared. The forest was dense and it was difficult to find the way back to the stream. That night in the village I asked him what had happened to him, and he replied, as though it explained all, "I found a *kavika* tree." This is the Malay apple, and produces a delicious fruit. There had evidently been some good ones on this tree, and the idea of a white man stranded in the jungle meant nothing at all in competition with a bellyful of the fruit.

The trail up the canyon was one of surprising beauty; the stream flowed over a rocky bed, and every now and then broke into a cascade down the precipitous mountainside. There were clusters of tree ferns and at the end of our climb to the top of the mountain, we could see the stream a thousand feet below us. Under rocks and logs there were short-tailed scorpions, and numbers of diplopods, the thousand-leggers. One of the diplopods, six inches long, was arboreal in habit, and I saw many of them twined around the stems of plants like so many snakes. These secrete a poisonous fluid, and I heard about their causing death to pigs that ate them.

There were some enormous trees on the summit and my guide, evidently having heard about tourists, handed me his knife and indicated that I should carve my name on the tree.

The house in the village was not clean, even though the women swept the floor with straight-edged fans — with which they afterward fanned me and the food I was eating. With bread, tinned food and pineapples, I drank a native tea made of lemon grass (*wai cabona*) while the small boys sat about eying the jam tin. When it was passed to them, they emptied it with their fingers, and spread the jam on slices of taro.

Two youngsters, my guides the following day, worked enthusiastically rolling over big stones to see them bounce down the mountain. However, toward evening, when I was in a gloomy spot in the woods gathering shells from a tiny stream, there was a loud whirring sound above us, evidently caused by birds. We could not see them, and the boys were frightened. One of them, with wild eyes, his hands clenched and his heartbeat showing plainly, kept saying in a whisper, *"Salako, salako!"* ("Let's go!") They were very quiet and subdued all the way down the mountain.

Peta, our guide of the following day, got us both lost, and he had to cut a trail, his idea of cutting a trail being delicately to trim a twig now and then. The forest was not bad as far as thorns were concerned, but in places vines were very dense and difficult. Once we passed a bees' nest, built apparently of wax, some fifty feet up on the face of a cliff. Eventually we got out of the bush to a camp where a couple of Fijian pig hunters were eating. They had with them eight nondescript dogs who were eating anything available, even coconuts, bananas and pieces of pineapple. Pork was not offered them.

On the way from Lambasa, down the stream, we had the usual trouble with the *Amra* launch, the engine stopped from time to time, but not the rain, which had us thoroughly soaked before we reached the steamer. At Taveuni we loaded forty head of cattle for the market in Suva. Waking from a doze in a steamer chair, I found my lap full of green, leaflike things which a planter had sent to me from shore as a joke. They were the famous leaf insects, or Phyllium, of the East Indies. Related to the walking stick group, they are broad, flat, bright green, and look more like a leaf than anything could without being one. Even the veins in their wings look like the veins of leaves. In Fiji, they live on guava plants.

In Suva, we stored our collections at the Department of Agriculture, and went by launch to Navua, a two-hour ride inside the reef all the way. A friend gave us a letter to Mr. and Mrs. Travis Rimmer, who had a plantation up the river and near a native village. Hosea, becoming more and more important, hired an assistant, and the two of them left in the morning for the village, carrying our gear. Foye and I walked along slowly, as usual, collecting. The Rimmers' house had evidently looked good to Hosea, and he had calmly deposited our baggage there. I don't know yet what the Rimmers thought of this, but they took us in and for a week showed us a hospitality rare even in the South Seas.

Wai natu (Water of Spirits), the home of the Rimmers, was on top of a hill, with a view south over the canefields to the ocean. On the east was a little valley in which a river made a bend, enclosing a field of bananas, and opposite were green-clad hills, with a mountain range in the distance, and one blue peak known as Vakorogasia. In the hills was a village of Solomon Islanders, relics from the old "blackbirding" slave ship days, who had settled there instead of returning to their native land. We later visited this village, and found it made up of houses smaller than those of the Fijians — each protected by a door and a lock, something unusual in Fiji and unknown in the Solomons. Rimmer told us that these people had acquired some bad habits and could not be trusted.

At the back of the house, where my screened room was situated, was a cluster of tree ferns, and beyond lay the forest, so that it was no long walk to reach good collecting grounds, nor did I have to fight through Koster's Curse and Lantana to get there. I could hear the soothing sound of tumbling water day and night. Below the lower of the two falls was a clear pool some twenty feet deep where I could plunge after a day's work in the bush.

There was a great deal of life in the forest, and some felled timber produced quantities of wood-boring beetles of various families. Under stones and in rotten logs were ants, different from those I had found on the other islands, one of these a primitive genus (Leptogenys), the female of which lacks wings; how it got to Fiji originally we do not know, but the individual ants do not travel far now. It was interesting, and exciting, too, to find a different species of this genus on each island, and several species on the larger islands.

At night we tacked up a piece of white calico on the back of my veranda, placed an acetylene lamp in front of it, and until the moon came up, the cloth was an animated scene, covered with moths, large black-and-white spotted caddis flies, beetles, and half a dozen ants for each of the other insects, all busy, as I was, in collecting. The caddis flies seemed quite helpless when seized by ants, and would give up without a struggle. Some of the moths would permit themselves to be dragged along by their antennae without even flapping their wings. The same moths, when placed in a killing bottle, would often flutter around enough to knock off their scales and destroy their value as specimens.

Boxing Day was observed in Fiji, as well as in London, New Zealand, and other parts of the Empire. About a thousand people congregated on the beach at Navua, mostly Fijians and Indian plantation workers, but with a scattering of Europeans, some of whom had come from as far as Suva for the races. There were five pony races. I bet on a horse called Buddha, and came home poorer by one sovereign. Hosea caught the fever and spent the evening gambling among the Indians, losing not only the proverbial shirt, but his money and everything else, even the coat for which he had recently paid a guinea. I advanced another shirt to him and some cash, and he returned much later with his coat and two pounds ten.

Near by the Hindu festival of Tajia was going on, in which the gaily bedecked little temple, or Taj, was carried by hand, preceded by a band composed of drums and cymbals, and a couple of men pretending to have a sword fight as they walked along. Some booths had been erected in the square in which the Taj was placed; and a merry-go-round and three Ferris wheels, all handmade of wood and all propelled by man power, were popular with the children and women who brightened up the landscape with the brilliant pinks, greens, and yellows of their dresses. We were warned not to go too close to the temple because some areas in the vicinity were temporarily sacred, and white intruders had been known to get hurt for going into the wrong places.

Travis Rimmer had been a surveyor before settling down on his plantation and had told us many tales of the interior, especially about Nandarivatu, which means "Bowl in the Rocks." This is the highest part of Viti Levu, and hence of Fiji, and it could be expected that the flora and fauna would be different. Foye decided to go to a group of islands, the Yasawas, while I went to these mountains. There was a railroad train from the coast to near the base of the hills — as far as I know, the only free railroad in the world. When the franchise was granted by the government it was with the understanding that passengers would be carried free, and they are, one day a week. A grocery box on a little flat car was comfortable enough as we went across the broad level plain through the cane fields. A missionary with his own grocery box shared my car and immediately hoisted a large black umbrella. My contempt for such a sissy — though he seemed a large and powerful man — gave way later to admiration and envy, because it most certainly was a hot ride. At the end of the road was Tavua, a cluster of government houses and a couple of stores near a mangrove swamp. The government bullock cart met the train, to take supplies and mail to the District Commissioner at Nandarivatu, so I put my heavy baggage on it, and then started on foot up the eleven-mile trail.

The government rest house at Nandarivatu looked good and I went to the front door planning to screw up my courage and get double portions of everything for dinner; everything, I knew, would be canned lamb's tongue and sardines. But nobody came to the door. There was a Fijian in back of the house cutting grass with a sickle, and he informed me, more cheerfully than I thought necessary, that the *Marama* had gone away. Did he expect her back that evening? "No. Perhaps Thursday."

But this was Monday. That meant a three-day wait, so I went to the house of the District Commissioner, Mr. Spence, who received me very kindly for a man who had been wakened from his afternoon nap. It was embarrassing to me because my letter of introduction to him was in my baggage, which was on his bullock cart without any official permission. He took me to the home of a trader, Rudy Vollmer, the son of an old German resident of Levuka, who had married a niece of King Cakabau. Rudy was married to a Tongan girl and there were two children: Hans, who looked as though he might have arrived recently from Hamburg, and Letila, a beautiful little girl completely Polynesian in appearance and mannerisms.

Rudy Vollmer had a prodigious appetite for *yanggona*, and would drink so much of it that he would lose his powers of coordination completely. I remember once when it took a dozen attempts for him to get a piece of bread from a plate onto his own; the children and his wife laughed heartily as he reached for the bread in the wrong direction and finally Mrs. Vollmer put it in his hand.

A combination house and store was built on the edge of a cliff and was very comfortable, until there came a day of rain, followed by a strong wind which actually made the house rock. My room in the back part rattled more than a room should when it is hanging over a cliff, so I spent most of the night in a chair by the front door of the store, looking apprehensively at lamps, spades, and buckets that were hanging on the wall and swinging chiefly in my direction. The next day it was worse, and the District Commissioner sent word that we were to expect a "blow," as his barometer was falling rapidly. Inmates of the local jail, escorted by the police, hurried over and boarded up the windows. We packed up our things and put them beneath the store counter and hurried — or tried to hurry — to a native house where all the local people had assembled for protection. The house was propped up by strong posts inclining in the direction from which the hurricane was supposed to come. The mats had been removed and the floor covered with straw.

There was a heavy fog, sometimes cleared by rain which hit the roof like machine-gun bullets. The air inside the house was full of mosquitoes, we had no nets along, the place was crowded and a little girl covered with boils cried all night long from the pain, while the wind and the rain kept up.

Besides the Vollmers, the only one in the hut who spoke English was a Hindu *babu*. He sidled alongside me and conversed in English. His first question was, "Who do you think will win the war?"

"The Allies, of course."

"No," he said. "I have heard that the Nizim of Hyderabad has had secret correspondence with the Sultan of Turkey." This was handed to me as of equal importance to the sinking of the entire British fleet.

"What will you do after the Allies are defeated?" I asked.

"We will drive the English out of India."

"I have been told by an old Anglo-Indian that if the English would leave India, there would be a Moslem king in Delhi, and that the Moslems would come down from the north and eat up the Bengalis. What about that?"

"Oh, no, sir. England would never let them do it."

The morning was clear, dry and beautiful; no great damage had been done to the village; a number of trees had been blown over, but not so many as I had expected. Delicate palms were standing up in the sunshine as though nothing had happened. The tops of the fallen trees yielded a dozen or more species of ants I had not seen before; one large black carpenter ant with a broad and flat node, different from anything I had ever seen, was to be found — but only one by one. It was exasperating not to be able to find the nest of what was undoubtedly a new and strange species, evidently a twig-dwelling one. There were several in the top of one tree lying on the ground. I put the larva of a beetle near one in the hope he would take it to his nest and thus show me where it was. He did take it, and laboriously climbed off the twig onto the ground, and over to another tree, which he climbed up till out of sight.

Myrmecodias were abundant and all contained ants — not the usual Iridomyrmex, but half a dozen other kinds; and in one nest were a number of interesting beetle guests, with rounded bodies, and slender heads carrying clublike antennae. One beautiful slender red-and-black ant proved to be a new genus. I afterward named the species *senirewae* after the "Flower of the Rewa," the daughter of Gus Hennings of Lomaloma. There were nests of these in the Myrmecodias, but one short, stubby, glistening ant standing on a tree trunk was the only one of its kind taken. It proved to be not only a new genus and species but a new tribe: Archeomyrmex. Heavily sculptured, and with spines on it, it reminded me of some of the extinct species of three million years ago found in the Baltic amber.

The forest about Nandarivatu is large and beautiful and one of the few places where the *dakua* or kauri tree is found. The natives sometimes tap it for the gum, which is used in varnish.

There were good roads and trails about, and something new for the collection every few feet.

A few miles away, a Mr. Friend had an estate with a herd of seventy-five cattle. He knew the dialect of the mountaineers, and his translating for me helped out a lot. He liked to ramble in the woods, also; we spent days together, and climbed Mount Victoria, the highest peak in the islands. There was fine forest at the base, which as one ascended turned into low canopied woods thickly covered with moss and giving the area an archaic look similar to that on the hills of Taveuni. It seemed as though we were traveling in a region that dated from before the appearance of insects on earth. I finally found a few elongate, bluish rove beetles in the moss, but nothing else.

The village of Navai lay below, near the base of the mountain, and we stayed there overnight and the next day. It was cool, and there was an open fire in the hut, but no chimney and no place for the smoke to escape — except some of it in my eyes. The girls of the village that night insisted on a *meke* despite the fact that two of their guests were completely asleep and the third one (myself) half so. Their only ornaments were leaves and oil, and it was so chilly that the latter had to be warmed before it could be applied.

Isikeli, my local guide, was a good woodsman and apparently loved to climb trees to bring down Myrmecodias which I duly slashed open, bottling the contents. Once, as we stood at the base of a giant kauri pine, with gum oozing from its side, he asked for a match. He thought it would amuse me, as well as himself, if he set fire to the gum and burned up the tree. He did not get the match.

The road back to Nandarivatu was a broad one, made three years before by the government and freed from stones which were placed along its edge. I turned most of them over and reaped a harvest of small fry, including land snails, ants and other burrowing insects quite new to my collection.

The last big thrill in ant-collecting came at Nandarivatu. To the north there were cane-covered hills cut by canyons with streams in them, and some forest on the sides, and it was below a waterfall that I spotted a long-sought ant, the only one of the ten recorded from Fiji that I had not found before. A large ant, nearly an inch long, was running over a damp spot and disappeared into a hole beneath a stone. Turning this, I exposed a populous colony of Odontomachus. I had begun to think that the original describer had made a mistake in its land of origin, but after this I found numerous other colonies, always in the canyons and always in the vicinity of waterfalls.

On our first stay at Navai, my attention was drawn to an old man who was different from all other Fijians, because when I pointed my camera at him he turned away. I asked Friend what the matter was, and the old man replied that he thought he was too old for the childish frivolity of having a photograph taken. He did not know his age; he was thin with deepset eyes and a meager gray beard. His ears were pierced to hold bits of coral, and he was dressed in an old artillery coat and a cloth *sulu*. Friend had evidently given him a good impression of me, because when we returned to the village he greeted us in a shrill, squeaky voice and we sat together late into the night, talking, with Friend interpreting.

His old name, that of the devil-devil days, had been Vuniacawa, but twenty years before, when he had joined the mission, it had been changed to Anitavasa. He was the only one of the old people who would talk about the man-eating period of the earlier days. There had been a fight here less than twenty years before, and Spence had told me some of the details. The village of Natikula had been on a hill near by and the old man had lived there with thirty-four others. He told them off by name to me, and described the fight with the inhabitants of a near-by village (now also vanished); the last attack resulted in the death of four men, two of whom were eaten. My friend had been the right-hand man of Tui Nadraw, who himself had stopped the custom of eating victims. I asked about the *tavoras*, or devils in the forest. He told me that there had been many of them, but with the coming of the missionaries most had disappeared; one important one still maintained residence on Mount Victoria, though he was rarely seen. Anyway, the devils had stopped kidnaping young girls from the villages. Isikeli had seen this devil, and the expression on his face and the way he pointed with his fingers showed that he believed in it firmly.

Vuniacawa said it was the missionaries, and not the government, that had stopped cannibalism. He also told me that I would taste good. But when I asked him which was better, a *kai lotu* (missionary) or a *kai viti* (Fijian), he answered without hesitation, "*Kai viti*," and then added, "*Bully-macow* (canned beef) is no good. Human meat is sweeter." He talked as one who had had plenty of experience and a good memory.

There have been many explanations as to the cause of cannibalism: revenge, religion, superstition, the idea of absorbing the strength of the eaten victim. Expecting to get a long and interesting explanation I asked frankly:

"Why did you eat men?"

And I got the laconic reply, "To have some meat with our vegetables."

Friend came with me on the fifty-five-mile walk to Korokoro, which we made in five easy days. Mr. Spence inspected the prisoners in jail — most of them there for having dirty huts — and selected a dozen of the huskiest ones, half to act as porters for the entire land journey and the others to return from Navai with a supply of yams for the prison kitchen. My luggage, in grass baskets and an ancient cloth "telescope," was carried on poles and covered by a thatch of banana leaves that kept the contents dry. We came down from the high forested mountains, through rolling hills, and then into flat, banana-growing country.

The mornings were clear, and we collected as we walked along; then we lunched at the side of the road, and started again. Rain came each afternoon, sometimes heavy, sometimes merely a drizzle, but always enough to get us thoroughly soaked by the time we reached the village where we were to spend the night. A rubdown and a change into dry clothes preceded dinner and a night's sleep. In the morning our dry clothes were carefully put in the baskets covered with leaves, and we put on the damp ones of the previous afternoon, which soon dried in the heat of the sun.

Nasonngo, reached in the evening of the first day, was one of the most beautiful villages we had come upon: entirely native in structure with forty-five houses scattered among enormous boulders quite as large as the houses themselves. As we entered the village we noticed a piece of rag flying from a high pole — it would be tabu to ask for any cloth there.

Friend knew the natives, and must again have given them a complimentary account of me, because that evening there was a new kind of *meke*, known as a *grog* or "devil" *meke*, one from the old days, which theoretically was prohibited. A young boy chewed up the *yanggona* root and spat it into a bowl; water was added and the drink was ready. I swore off *yanggona* that evening, but was interested to see it made as in old Fijian days. Friend asked me not to mention this, as they were doing it to show me the old customs, and there was a fine of ten pounds sterling for the practice.

While the drink was being mixed a low dirge was sung by the men. This was followed by a merry song, and the toast to me was "Many little animals tomorrow."

After the *meke* was over and some leaves of smoking tobacco distributed, I tried — and successfully — to bring the conversation around to my favorite subject at that time, frogs. The chief said that in the old days there were many, and they used to take them to meetings with them, as well as other food, "But now we can't. There are none." Just then a man who was sitting in a corner electrified me by saying that he had some, four of them, with their eggs. Through the interpreter I asked where they were. They were in a *bully-macow* tin at his house. While knowing the Fijians usually did not lie even to make a visitor feel good, all the doubting Thomas in me came out, and I asked if I could see them. In reply, he left the house and returned a few minutes later with four live Cornufer frogs with twenty-two eggs in the same tin. My benefactor had found them on the underside of a leaf, and several of the men told me that they had sometimes seen them in hollow twigs. With the extinction of this species very probable because of the mongoose, it was a great thrill to obtain the specimens. I killed them carefully and then, before dropping them into alcohol, opened up their abdomens so that they could cure uniformly. There was deep silence while the operation was on, and then the chief asked why I had done that. Friend explained it, and the chief made the flattering remark to the people grouped in the house: "That is what doctors are for: to know everything."

Besides the frogs, I collected one of the most striking insects of the South Pacific (*Macrotoma heros*), one of the giants of the beetle world, a wood-boring species, the adult flattened, over three inches long, and with very long antennae. It was in a piece of rotten log that we pulled apart.

We stayed over another day to enjoy the excellent collecting in the vicinity, and four more frogs were brought in. Before I left, the chief expressed a desire to give me a *loloma*, or gift of friendship. Malaki, an ex-*buli* who had been sacked by the government for having two wives, brought me a lizard in a bottle; and the chief gave me a long two-handed fighting club, without the usual carving on it but with a human molar tooth imbedded in the head. It was heavy and I did not care much about it, but took it so as not to hurt his feelings. Later, in Suva, a resident there with a large collection of old-time relics called on me to see it. He glanced at it without much interest and tossed it carelessly on the bed, but the following day he commenced to worry about the fact that I did not have a pineapple club — that is, one of the fighting clubs with the head carved somewhat like a pineapple; in fact, he offered to give me one, which filled me with deep suspicion, because he was not known for giving away such specimens. I later found that my club was a rare type; it is now in the Peabody Museum at Harvard.

Walking in the mornings and slipping in the afternoons, when the rains had started, wading frequent streams (often preferring to wade because of the precarious look of the makeshift bridges), sometimes through forest, again through open country, and passing one village after another, we came down from the mountain country into the banana flats along the Rewa River. In addition to the wild pineapples along the roadsides, there was a profusion of passion fruit vines, laden with delicious and thirst quenching fruit. The seeds of these plants had been scattered "Johnny Appleseed" style, by an old settler, Joske.

In one of the villages there had been a measles epidemic and a child had died. His little brother, just recovering, played till long past midnight with a tin box tied on a string which I gave him, while the father lay on the floor being massaged by his wife. Some of the Fijians are excellent masseurs. Eleven men slept on the floor, while I was given a real canvas cot, a rarity here, and served with *lebo-lebo*, a bread made by grating green banana and boiling it in a banana leaf, not unpalatable though rather on the elastic side. Another bread is made by burying assorted vegetables in the ground and leaving them there till thoroughly fermented. I found tinned biscuits easier to eat.

On the outskirts of Koro Vatu my boys dressed up for our triumphal entry — Avelosi with a fluted-front dress shirt and his *sulu*, while Hosea removed the rag which had protected his fine head of hair. A little launch, the *Tui Kola*, left the following afternoon for down-river. We passed many banana barges and stopped at various plantations, each with a large pile of bananas, covered with leaves, waiting for lighters to carry them down to Suva. They were fumigated for insect pests on the way, and loaded aboard ships for the Auckland and Sydney trade. At one stop we took aboard an Indian prisoner, tied with ropes. He had torn a necklace off a little girl's neck and then thrown her into a fire. Lower down the river, bananas were replaced largely by sugar cane for the mill at Rewa, and we saw many fine horses and mules, quite different from the rugged mountain ponies which originally came from the island of Timor. There were also quantities of Brahma bulls.

CHAPTER XI

Whales' Teeth

Suva and the Cox Hotel seemed luxurious indeed, but Foye joined me there and we left almost immediately for the south island of Kandavu on the *Ului Lakemba*, a cutter fifty feet in length, provided with a cabin containing lockers, mats, a hurricane lamp, and a whisky advertisement for decoration. The captain and the mate (who had elephantiasis and a funguslike growth from his toes) were on salaries; the crew, all Kandavu men, were not paid, but had made the trip just to get to Suva. A mile out the wind stopped, and though we could see a heavy storm coming down the Navua valley and out to sea, none of it came near us. The mail steamer came in, unloaded, and passed us on its way out to sea again. Three times on the way to Kandavu, we were becalmed; each time the captain would speak entreatingly to *Ratu Cagi:*

"O good Prince Wind, can you not see we have foreigners here who, like us, want to get to Kandavu?"

Personally, I lost patience with the wind, or lack of it; the third time, on the third day, when we were tantalizingly close to our destination, I spoke up myself, shaking a fist in the direction I wanted the wind to come from, and harshly demanded: "Devil Wind, come here." The officers and crew were shocked but the wind did come — even though in the wrong direction; by a lot of tacking, we made shore at the town of Vunisea, where we were welcomed by W. D. E. Alcock, a young cadet in government service, and taken to his house. It was a frame structure on a hill, at an altitude of about three hundred feet, and from the front veranda there was a beautiful view of the Bay of Namalatta. From the height we could see that the middle of the bay was depressed, and surrounded by a ring of coral, really a submerged atoll. After-wards we spent many nights down there fishing.

Alcock's office was a large native house, screened and floored and furnished with tables, chairs, maps, a safe set in cement, and quantities of lockers to hold quantities of government papers. He alone represented the might of the British Empire on the island, acting as District Commissioner, judge, chief of police, and doctor for such cases as could be helped by pills. People seriously ill were sent to Suva.

Our first walk into the hills showed that we were practically back in Lau as far as people or other fauna were concerned. There were the same butterflies that we had seen there, similar ants and tiger beetles, and blue and scarlet parrots — always a flock of these in an ironwood tree just in front of the house.

We had heard in Suva that there was a government house be-longing to the Medical Department, and thought that it might be a good idea to "batch" there for a change, instead of going native. We purchased a case of provisions and put in a request to occupy the house. No answer came to this request, and weeks later, when we had been living in Alcock's house for some time, he showed us the official correspondence on the subject, all tied to-gether with a piece of genuine British red tape.

First came our letter: "We respectfully request permission to occupy the now vacant government house at Kandavu belonging to the Medical Department. (Signed) Foye and Mann."

The Governor asked: "Has the Commissioner of Works any ob-jection?"

The Commissioner of Works replied: "Provided Chief Medical Officer does not require building, and has no objection, I can see no reason why Doctors Foye and Mann should not occupy house. I suggest a deposit of ten or twenty pounds be left with District Commissioner who should deduct for repairs."

The Colonial Secretary added his word: "I suggest that sum be deducted for fumigation."

The Chief Medical Officer's contribution was: "I know nothing whatever of these gentlemen or their intentions in occupying the building. Until I know, am not prepared to let them have the use of it."

The whole correspondence went again to the Colonial Secretary, who sent it on to Alcock at Kandavu, with the following note, marked *Urgent:* "I understand the Doctors have left for Kandavu. Have they arrived? Have they asked you for quarters? Are they occupying same? How long are they going to stay? Have you any objection to their occupying quarters?"

Alcock had the last word: "Doctors Foye and Mann staying with me. (Signed) District Commissioner."

Alcock had come out as a cadet, second class, and been made assistant to the District Commissioner. As was the procedure at that time, he was given a year to acquire a reading and conversational knowledge of Mbau, the official language of Fiji, and also a passable conversational acquaintance with the dialect of the place he happened to be in. After an examination, he was made a First Class Cadet. As a Second Class Cadet, his social obligations had consisted of calling on the governor once a year in a carriage drawn by one horse. After promotion, the social call was doubled to twice a year, and there were two horses to the carriage. From then on, after other examinations, including British common law, the cadet was promoted grade by grade — an efficient system that produced a governing group in all of the colonies, which held together the British Empire for so long. This competitive system went on and on; the incumbent could be promoted eventually to the governorship, or he could reach a certain position and then stay there. For instance our friend Spence of Nandarivatu had been in the islands for years, but was apparently pegged at the rank of District Commissioner.

ANT HILL ODYSSEY

Alcock was not allowed to hold real estate in Fiji, or stock in any of the local enterprises. He could have got into serious trouble for showing me the correspondence relating to the vacant house, as it was "strictly confidential," but I did not betray him. Later, in Suva, I acted as go-between for him and a girl he loved, whose parents did not like him. Her name was Iris, and I carried letters from one to the other. Eventually they were married, and Alcock was transferred to Tanganyika, East Africa, where I met him again years later when he was a full-fledged commissioner of a large district.

He was an English public school boy, but this public school education did not include cooking, and he had been unable to teach the Fijian who catered to his wants. After I had been there for seven days, eating canned sardines on toast for breakfast every morning, I asked if I could invade his kitchen and make some cocoa. The Fijian's idea was to dump some chocolate in a pot, add water and sugar, and let it boil; the result was not good. I had brought with me from the States some powdered malted milk, and when I prepared the chocolate added a portion of this. Alcock couldn't understand why it tasted so different. The few Europeans who tasted the drink declared it was different from anything they had ever had, and half-believed my explanation that I stirred it six times to the right and six times to the left while cooking.

We attended court, with Alcock presiding. The police sergeant gave the oath. The witnesses sniffed at the Bible and looked uncomfortable, shifting their weight from one foot to another. A parrot flew into the courtroom, watched the proceedings for a while, and then flew out again. A couple of rats ran across the floor while the cases were being tried, cases mostly concerning sailing a cutter without a license, or keeping a dog without a license. Small fines were levied. Alcock told me of a curious case of mixed English and Fijian in court language: *ataka* is the Fijian

256

verb "to do," but there is no word for "bail," so the procedure was referred to in court as "*Vaka* bail-im-out *ataka*."

Near by, at Vanua Ava ("The Land Which"), lived E. T. Wilson, a settler who two years before had landed with his native wife, two children, and no money. He cleared space in the bush, put up a canvas shelter and planted his first crops, quick ones, of sweet potatoes, tapioca, and tobacco, financing the place with money paid him by natives for putting cement water tanks in their villages. He traded tobacco for some small yams to plant, and when I stayed with him he was the most independent man I have ever known. There were papayas in abundance, some cocoa, coffee from old plants in the bush, mangoes, soursops, and cherry guavas; *yanggona* for trade and for drinking; and in his vegetable garden maize, radishes, celery, lettuce, cabbage, tomatoes, several kinds of beans, carrots, beets, parsnips, eggplants, chili peppers, parsley and onions. These, with a few banana trees, a small crop of coconuts, and some of the wild edible plants near by enabled him to set a magnificent table. He even had pigs, which ran half-wild in the mangrove swamps and devoured crabs but were also fed on tapioca, sweet potatoes and sweet-potato greens. With wild pigeons and an occasional wild hog, with chickens, ducks, and plenty of fish, he lived exceedingly well.

The Wilsons had their homemade starch, coconut oil for cooking, vinegar made from bananas. They bought only sugar, salt, sauce (Worcestershire, of course), tinned milk, kerosene, and cloth which his wife made into clothes for them both. The furniture was comfortable, but homemade. The tea was *matadra*, made from a native wild bush, gathered in the field, fermented and then dried, and pleasant to drink. In the two years he had cleared about ten acres, brought running water in bamboo pipes from a spring to his house to provide a shower bath, kitchen supply, pig run, and some irrigation. He had built a comfortable sleeping house, a cookhouse, a workshop, and labor quarters to house the two Hindu employees. He had salvaged a cutter from the reef and from its wood had made himself a serviceable rowboat.

Besides his family there was living with him at the time an elderly Englishman whose cacao plantation in Samoa had been ruined by a hurricane; he had come to Fiji low in spirits and lower in cash, but with the idea of planting rare and high-priced medicinal plants for sale to the local Chinese. He was a great reader and a philosopher; for instance, his spectacles contained only one glass but he explained to me: "No matter; I can't see out of the other eye anyway." He had a small library; one evening, after I had been telling him about collecting in Haiti, he mentioned that he had a book on Haiti which he had had for some time and was through with. He gave it to me. It happened to be St. John's *Hayti or the Black Republic*, then and now a rare item.

I joked Wilson about being like Robinson Crusoe, but it was I who acquired Man Friday. One afternoon while I was collecting on a hillside my Fijian guide, carrying my knapsack, got into conversation with another native. After a short time he disappeared, and a new boy showed up with a large walking stick in his hand, gave it to me and inquired in *bêche-la-mer*, instead of Fijian, "This one he good fellow?" I told him it was, not understanding what it was all about; put the walking stick in a container, and started collecting very brilliant metallic wood-boring beetles from near-by leaves. He went after them, and soon had a handful, which he gave me. When I thanked him he told me, "Me boy belong you now. Every month he come, you pay me two pounds."

He was a Solomon Islander, perhaps a relic of the black-birding days, when many of his fellow islanders had been brought as labor. More probably, because he was young, he had left his own island for some good reason; he was from Malaita, where the really tough boys live. His name, Suniduni, was tattooed across his chest, but I called him Sol. He was five feet, two inches tall, thickset, powerfully built, with dark skin, short red hair (dyed with coral lime), bright eyes and a short lower lip that gave him a comical expression. In each of his perforated and stretched ear lobes were half a dozen bone rings. He was tattooed across the chest, nose, and arms, and had a knife scar on his right cheek and another on his right forearm. He told me with a great deal of glee how he got the scars. He and one of his compatriots were annoying a sleeping Solomon Islander by tickling him inside his nose with a stick. The sleeper awoke suddenly, jumped up and knifed Sol.

From then on he was with me almost constantly, and was an indefatigable collecting companion. He had one defect: A native guide always carries you across streams when you come to them, to keep your boots dry. On account of his short stature he was a complete failure at this.

Instead of being clothed in the conventional *sulu* of Fiji he wore a pair of brown shorts. These were replaced on his first payday by a more formal set of white ones with red stripes. These he wore when we were around villages, but changed into the old ones when we were in the bush. His most important possession was an umbrella that he carried with him wherever he went, offering it to me when it was raining, despite the fact that I had a raincoat. He would walk along behind me holding the umbrella carefully over his dyed hair and naked torso.

Alcock invited Foye and me to join him in accompanying the *Tui Roko* of Kandavu on an official trip of inspection of some of his villages. His name was Kingi Williami Nanovo, and he was a finely built Fijian and a high hereditary chief. His whaleboat was twenty feet long, with two sails and a jib, and was manned by a crew of five, all with ocher hair and each wearing a fluted *sulu*. We visited a dozen villages in the course of a week.

At one we breakfasted on prawns that had been cooked in coconut oil — delicious but exceedingly rich. At Joma I stayed on the beach collecting, and afterwards rested on the front steps of a store kept by an affable Chinese trader who served me a glass of *samshu*. While I was waiting for the boat, a group of tiny girls entertained me with a *meke*, sung softly and seriously. When I gave them a bottle of soda water they drank it with bliss written on their faces. One of the girls was tattooed on the arm with a row of dots and her initials, but I saw little good tattooing in the islands, except on one Fijian who had evidently been a sailor and had the picture of a snake on his forearm. When questioned he explained: "Sydney. Three shillings and sixpence."

In general, the people were courteous and often obsequious to the chief, but at Langu Levu we were taken in hand by a couple of comely girls who presented us with bowls of tapioca and papaya pudding, and then while we were eating it smeared our faces with talcum powder and ran away laughing. They later appeared during a meeting; one of them suddenly got up, walked to the chief, squatted in front of him and presented him with a turtle, the body made of a flat nut, the legs of four bits of matches, the head of a smaller nut attached to a matchstick neck. Some of the people laughed, but others looked horrified. I could not get the significance of the affair, but the presentation of a turtle was evidently something that should not be burlesqued. After the meeting was over, the two girls caressed our cheeks with a light cloth. I didn't know what that was all about, either, until I noticed the king with two smears of lampblack on his face. There were a few expressions of surprise, but mostly poorly suppressed giggles, and as we waded out to our boat the same girls followed us throwing water at us from coconut shells. The chief tried to look as dignified as a man can who is holding his *sulu* up to keep it out of the water and is getting splashed from behind. When the smaller of the girls ran after me the older one shouted, "No, he has a camera!"

As we got in the boat, Williami wrung out his *sulu* and muttered to me, "*Kai ca*" — bad people. I asked their name and to my astonishment was told "O'Connor." There had been an Irishman on Kandavu long ago!

One rain gust after another struck us on the way to Lomati. We would sail in a heavy rainstorm but could look ahead at a clear sunny spot and see, on the other side of it, another rain cloud ready to catch us as we came through. It was monotonous travel except for the sight of an occasional sea turtle. Once we sailed for miles through a mass of pumice stone which covered the water as far as we could see. We were told that this had resulted from a volcanic eruption in the New Hebrides two years before and the stone, lighter than water, had floated to the southern part of the Kandavu coast.

Landing, we climbed uphill through a grove of magnificent flamboyant trees to Lomati. There was a stone fence around the village, and near the church a table had been set up and five chairs were placed in a row in the shade of a big mango tree. The object of our visit was to settle a dispute over land between two villages, and the party was attended by all the villagers as well as the chiefs. The three of us, with the head chief, and a Chinese trader, evidently one of the important men of the village, sat on the chairs. *Yanggona* was served, and then a whale's tooth ceremoniously presented to each of us. These were on ropes of coconut fiber to go around our necks. A feast had been prepared; there was a large pig roasting on an open fireplace, but we were given a can of corned beef, the last word in luxury. This was followed by another presentation of food by the people of the rival village, Mbuke Levu; and then came speeches and arguments. While the speeches were under way I strolled with Sol along the edge of a forest, walking through tall grass mingled with the finest *yanggona* plants that I had seen in Fiji, and Sol pointed out a patch of *yanggona* which he said belonged to him and another Solomon Islander: "By-'n-by Chinaman him see, him buy."

Sol also showed me a fence that he had put up for some planter, with the remark: "No pay for it. Me see him, me kill him." "Kill," by the way, used by the Solomon Islanders, means to hit, and not to kill.

The argument over the land was settled, but I don't see how it could have been, because each faction had presented us with a whale's tooth with much ceremony. Because of the scarcity of them in the islands, they were usually returned the following morning. This time, however, the local chief, with a delegation, made a speech to me, saying that I had come from a far, far land, where we probably didn't have whales' teeth, so I was to keep mine as a gift, to remember the people of Lomati. It hangs today on the corner of a book shelf.

It was drizzling in the morning, but we started to climb up Mount Washington, the large mountain of Mbuke Levu, along a slippery trail and one with few trees to hang on to, so part of the climb was really a scramble. In order to make this trip *de luxe* we had sent some natives ahead of us with food and bamboo tubes filled with water.

The rain increased but we kept on, reaching the forest where it was easier going, walking on the soft moss that covered the path. Just before we reached the summit we met our boys coming back. They had decided that on account of the rain, we would postpone our climb, and they had either drunk or poured out our water. The others were irritated, but not I; here was a chance to show off by giving an imitation of Seemann, the botanist, who had climbed this mountain in the '60's and had had a similar experience. I told my companions that I knew how to secure water in the high mountains. They looked around for the water-bearing vine that we had used in other places and found none, but I found, as Seemann had, very large pitcher plants, each containing about a cupful of water. This, when strained through handkerchiefs to remove most of the insects that had drowned in it, made very acceptable tea. Our boys had made a small shelter and a fire, and we dried and warmed ourselves, and had lunch. There was a bottle tied to a tree, and a note in it stating that a party of natives from Nandronga had planted coconuts there twelve years before, but there was no sign of the trees. There was little collecting on the summit of the mountain; among insects, I found chiefly the blue rove beetle which always occurs in mossy places, but coming down the hill there were pigeons, parrots, and quantities of beautiful large landsnails (*Bulimus seemanni*), which had been discovered in that locality and named for the finder.

Back at headquarters at Vunisea, Charlie Caldwell showed up. He had come on the official government boat, the *Ranadi*, because a native had seen a German *sitima* (steamer), and the *Ranadi* had been sent out to investigate, armed chiefly with Caldwell and a rifle. I had heard of him and he of me, and at that time I had a suspicion he had been sent to cover my activities and to see if there was anything subversive about them. My large acetylene lamp, used to attract insects at night, threw a tremendous beam. Naturally, in collecting I would walk back and forth in front of it, and a schooner at sea, with German submarines in the sailors' minds, had reported the "signals."

A Fijian-born Englishman, Caldwell was the prizewinner of all athletic events, and at the annual tennis tournament all of Fiji would turn out to see who would play the finals with him. It was the same with swimming, boxing, and target shooting. The usual prize was a pair of pipes, one with a curved stem and one straight. He had dozens of these about his home, and as he smoked only curved ones and I the straight stems, I acquired a fine collection of British pipes. He enjoyed all physical exertion, except for the time when he was showing me how far he could jump backward in his stocking feet, and landed among some spiny starfish that I had placed on the veranda to dry.

It was getting time to leave Fiji. My letter of credit had so many of my autographs on the back of it that there was little space for more, so when the Kandavu mail cutter came in, Charlie, Sol, and I boarded it for Suva. The local people gave us a fare-well standing-up *meke*, and Saini, Alcock's laundress, dashed from her place in the line, threw a *salu-salu* around my neck, and gave me a hearty Fijian sniff, not the formal one on the back of the hand but a regular buster of a sniff — if a sniff can be a buster — just below my right ear, while the onlookers shouted *"Vinaka, vinaka, vinaka!"* although some were embarrassed by such wantonness on the girl's part.

In Suva, exciting news reached me. Months before, after the hurricane at Nandarivatu, when it was so rainy and disagreeable that nothing seemed to matter or could be worse, I had written to Mr. Henshaw at the Museum that it was larceny, murder, and numerous other crimes to be so near the British Solomon Islands — that poorly known and so inviting a land — and not visit there. The round-trip steamer ticket from Vancouver to Suva had cost three hundred dollars, but it was only $37.50 additional to Sydney and the steamship agent had told me that by paying the difference my ticket could be extended there and back. Then from Sydney to Tulagi there was a round trip fare of $110. This information had been given me before, and I retailed it to Mr. Henshaw, showing how economically one could get to new worlds. Suddenly came a cable: AM SENDING CHECK. USE THIS IN FIJI, THE SOLOMONS, OR ANY PLACE YOU SEE FIT.

That cable changed all plans. The check would undoubtedly come on the next southbound steamer, nearly a month away.

It was in festive spirits, therefore, that I joined in the big welcome the residents of Suva were giving to the *ratu* Sekuna, who had just come back from the European war. Sekuna, one of the top-ranking chiefs, had been at Oxford when the war broke out, and had spent his vacations in France. At first when he tried to enlist, the British were not taking "natives" into the Army, so Sekuna joined the French Foreign Legion, was wounded in action, hospitalized in England, and later attached to the British Army on the Continent, where there was then the spectacle of a descendant of King Cakabau, the most famous cannibal chief in history, translating French for British officers.

The whole town was a hubbub of dances and *mekes* and brass bands in his honor. Sekuna removed his uniform, resumed his *sulu*, and today is the ranking chief in Fiji.

A passenger on the same steamer with Sekuna, returning to her native Australia, was Madame Melba. She gave a benefit concert at night. Things were not going so well with the war in Europe, and we were all deeply moved when she sang the British anthem, especially by the verse that ended "God save us all!"

Captain Robbie, who was Madame Melba's uncle, had come to town to see her and to join in the celebration for Sekuna. I had met him first in Levuka, on my first trip to Lau; he was an old Scotch sea captain, long a resident of Fiji, Captain of the Port in Levuka, with a lifetime of ocean adventure behind him. It was a saying in Levuka that you could set your watch at eight o'clock in the morning when he and the schoolteacher came to the Polynesian Hotel for their eye-openers.

He was returning to Levuka the day after the celebration, and then going to visit his plantation at Wainunu, on the west end of Vanua Levu, opposite the region where I had previously collected on the same island. He invited me along on his cutter, the *Annie*, named after his wife. We sailed late in the morning, and had to lay-to at the mouth of the river nearly all night waiting for the tide. Mosquitoes came in clouds, hitting us in the face like rain, and we had no sleep at all. The captain optimistically kept wrapping himself up, his head enclosed in a shirt, but after two snores, never more, he would wake again and start scratching and slapping. From six at night until five-thirty in the morning we counted the hours — the captain by looking at the Southern Cross, and never more than a few minutes away from the time on my dollar watch. He sang an occasional chantey, and slapped mosquitoes, telling me in a mild Scotch accent what he thought about them, which was not mild. We told each other stories. His reply to my question, "Captain, have you ever heard the story of . . . ?" was always, "No gentleman has ever heard a story."

Friends had warned me not to bring up the subject of *daku woqa,* the fish god. The giant basking shark is still worshiped by some of the Fijians, who make offerings of *yanggona* which are sometimes retrieved by nonbelieving natives for their own use. But Robbie brought the subject up himself, and told me of his experience, which, he said, had given him a bad reputation. His boat, the *Annie,* was thirty-three feet long, and one day, as she was sailing slowly along, he felt a sudden bump and saw two large fins, one on each side, which had seized the boat. He went forward and saw about five feet of shark, upside down: and on going aft he noted the tail. This giant shark, which sometimes attains a length of more than forty feet, had turned on its back and seized the boat, possibly a mating gesture. It loosened itself in a few minutes and swam away. His friends, hearing the tale, looked at each other slyly, and the Captain was so embarrassed that the mention of *daku woqa* in his presence was strictly tabu.

A little before daylight we took off, tried to make a short passage inside the reef, but after getting stuck for a while came outside and reached Levuka in the rain at ten o'clock.

Ovalau is one of the gems of Fiji, mountainous and beautiful. Levuka, its town, is built on a hillside and some of the streets are rows of steps, always winding and with great masses of vegetation all through the village. Sol and I crossed the hills and reached a very narrow valley, where we followed a small stream that tumbled down in many cascades, with little tributary streams on either side and a couple of waterfalls. The high cliffs and jagged peaks, covered with bush and tree ferns, afforded good collecting, and we found frogs in and near the streams.

Ovalau was the island from which the collector Schultz had

sent his ants and other insects to Mayr in Vienna in the 1860's, so it is the type locality of the earlier known Fijian ants. It was exciting to find these species one by one, but I failed to find the large tick ant (*Odontomachus angulatus*), called by the natives the "*buli* ant," which was first taken here and which I had taken only at Nandarivatu. The mongoose had not yet been introduced here, nor had the coconut moth, so lizards were abundant and there were plenty of coconuts.

Levuka is really the Plymouth of Fiji; retired sailors have houses on the beach, always with a boat in the yard. The streets are thronged with all manner of South Sea folk, natives of the Solomon Islands, New Hebrides, Rotuma, Samoa, and Tonga, and quite a number of half-castes, so that the sophisticated residents of Suva refer to it as the "black-and-tan" city.

The Ovalau Club and the Polynesian Hotel are the rendezvous of sailors and traders throughout the islands; there is one story told of a woman writer who asked the manager of the hotel to let her hide behind a screen in the bar so that she could listen to the conversation and hear what sailors really talked about when they relaxed after a voyage. Someone tipped off the sailors and the conversation must have been good, but none of it ever appeared in print.

On one trail Sol secured some oranges and while we ate them he told me of a white man for whom he had once worked. Every day at five o'clock, he said, this man would give him "much whisky," and Sol, in return, would give him onions, so that the man's wife could not smell whisky on his breath. As he handed me another orange I fancied a hint was intended but I ignored it. He evidently took matters in his own hands that evening, and was not to be found the following morning when Robbie and I boarded the *Annie* and sailed with a light breeze toward Robbie's plantation.

The wind died down in midafternoon, and even the crew working hard with the long oars, which the Captain called "the ashen breeze," got us nowhere. We anchored, to await the wind, off the island of Makongai, on which is situated the government leper hospital. About three hundred patients, Indians, Fijians, and Rotumans, lived there in separate villages. We could see some of them, and the doctor's quarters. I fished over the side with a handline for red snappers and caught a few, while Robbie told stories of the old blackbirding days — the recruiting of native labor by one means or another from out-islands and bringing them in to the plantations of Fiji and northern Australia.

We got under way in the morning, passing a little island to the left where a famous priest of the old devil-devil days is buried, and offerings are still made to him, and reached Davuti Creek, navigable for cutters and launches as far as the landing of the plantation at Wainunu. Here Captain Robbie and Mr. Barratt, an old Darjeeling tea planter, owned jointly one thousand four hundred acres of land, hills and plateaus, six hundred acres of it under cultivation.

About two hundred acres of tea, the only tea plantation in the South Pacific, were here producing about sixty thousand pounds each year — none of it for export but all consumed in Fiji.

There were ninety Indian laborers on the place, and the plantation, according to local law, supplied a school and a teacher for the children. One saw these Indians in the early afternoon sitting around in the shade talking, apparently leading the easy, carefree life that people think tropical natives lead, but each of these laborers had done his "task" — that is, a fixed amount of work to earn his salary. Each was required to pick thirty-six pounds of green tea leaf a day. This, after being wilted, rolled, fermented, and dried, made about nine pounds of commercial tea.

The task system was applied to other duties around the plantation. A laborer had to hoe so many rows, or pick so many coconuts, for a fixed daily salary. More was paid for more work, and there was one woman on the plantation who picked as much as eighty-seven pounds of tea leaves a day. The boy employed to pick walking sticks from the coconut palms, and cut them in two with a pair of scissors, delivered for each day's work seven pounds of insects.

There were fifty thousand cocoa trees, producing only fairly well because the climate was not quite tropical enough and hurricanes are especially hard on these plants. In Fiji there are several indigenous trees that bear rubber, and Mr. Barratt had sent some of this to the market, where it brought the same price as Pará rubber, the finest of all. It was, however, more expensive to collect, as the latex came only from the tips of the branches, so he had planted sixty acres of Pará rubber. This was the first rubber plantation outside of Malaya and the Dutch East Indies. The latex was gathered in the early morning and set in pans of acetic acid (made from lemon and coconut juice) to coagulate; then rolled and smoked — the first rubber in flat sheets that I had ever seen. But Barratt complained: "You can't make any money out of rubber at three shillings a pound." When the war was over, rubber sank as low as four cents a pound, and yet plantations in the East Indies continued to survive.

From the river and numerous creeks, water was piped into the laborers' villages and used also to supply power for various types of machinery. There were some hot springs and one of them flowed into a large cement bathtub, enabling me for once to keep free from mosquito bites — not the spring itself, but the fact that I could grease all exposed parts of my anatomy with heavy coconut oil and roam the woods in comfort, though smelly, and then take it all off before entering the house by a thorough soaking and soaping in the hot water which ran continually through the tub.

Sol showed up one evening. How he got there I don't know, probably in a native sailing boat. He carried his knapsack and umbrella, wore a sad smile, and told me an incoherent tale about a policeman in Levuka. Glad to get him back, I believed him and forgave. He suddenly yelled at me, "*Mbu!*" He wasn't trying to scare me, but he had seen the betel nut trees that Barratt had planted beside a path. Barratt gave him permission to pick some, and he went after them as eagerly as a terrier after a rat, chewing them without the lime customarily used with this nut. He bit into one and commenced sucking it explosively. I asked him why, and he said it made him strong.

When it was time to leave Wainunu, we poled down the river in the late morning, and at night anchored off Whippy's Place.

Fishing was good off the cutter, and I got eight red snappers that averaged a little less than a pound each. Sol extracted the hooks, growling at those fish which had "swallowed him inside." Captain Robbie read by the light of a hurricane lamp, and it was a pleasant evening till we went to sleep. In the morning I found that cockroaches had eaten patches of skin from places on my hands, on my ankle and toes. A light wind in the morning pushed us along over a smooth sea, through a school of bonita jumping from the water: we passed many giant Medusae, some of them a beautiful purple and brownish cream in color, and sometimes more than a foot across. Beneath each, among the tentacles, was a school of little fish two or three inches long, or sometimes as much as six inches long. Frightened by our boat, they would dart out, but always hurried back again into the shadow of the velum and the tentacles.

The *Amra* was at Levuka and took us on to Suva. The *Makura*, bound for Sydney, was due in two days' time, in which period the collection was packed. The large specimens — lizards, bats, snakes, and larger snails — so as to preserve the bodies for anatomical studies, were wrapped in cheesecloth by groups, with their locality labels, and then packed in alcohol in five-gallon kerosene tins. The tops of the tins were soldered and the outsides painted with red oxide to prevent rust. The shipping agent took everything and sent it on to Boston, all except the hundreds of vials of ants, which were packed in a big cloth telescope to be taken by hand — and my hand at that. I paid Sol his accrued wages with a little extra so that he would clean up the rubbish I had left in the Agriculture Building, and the last I saw of him was that evening when he, and most of the Solomon boys in Suva, were marching up Victoria Parade carrying, trussed on a pole, a large pig which had probably cost his accrued three months' salary. Sol waved good-by at me as he went by, as did his companions, and I could imagine that that night and the next day were spent in roasting and consuming vast quantities of "piggy-pig."

A flurry of consternation came over me: Ordinarily the steamers were required to spend at least five hours of daylight in Suva, but this practice had been discontinued on account of the war, and I heard that the boat was due in at ten o'clock at night and would sail at two in the morning. The check on which depended the Solomon Islands trip was theoretically on the boat; so in desperation I appealed to the Postmaster General to get my mail as soon as the boat came in, and then to the head of the bank to leave the doors of his bank ajar so that I could cash the check. They co-operated, the check was delivered to me in the middle of the night, and cashed; the steamship agent modified my ticket, and I got aboard in time to sail.

CHAPTER XII

Bêche-la-mer

Iɴ Sydney there were three weeks before the Burns Philp boat would leave for Tulagi, chief port of "the islands." The first day, after depositing my hand baggage and the ants in the Hotel Metropole, I strolled down to the quai to the Mining Museum, where were the headquarters of Froggatt, the Dominion entomologist. He was not in, but his assistant, Bill Gurney, was there, and took charge of me for the rest of the day. That evening when I unpacked my suitcase and looked at the sheaf of letters of introduction that Jepson had given me, I found that I had already met everyone to whom they had been addressed, and a number of others.

The zoo was at La Perouse, and here were many species of living creatures that I had never seen alive before; also, outside the enclosure, were a couple of aborigines who, for a sixpence, would throw a boomerang.

To me everything was intensely interesting. Under rocks were ants that really should have been dead a million years before but that were very much alive, many of them with hot stings. Bulldog ants were an inch long, with large and sharp mandibles with which they grabbed their victim to gain a purchase for stinging. One of these bulldog ants, true to its continent, leaps like a kangaroo.

No matter how long people collect, something new is always turning up, and even in the outskirts of Sydney I found a new and striking species of a very primitive ant in which the sections of the abdomen, instead of being welded together in one large segment, as in the higher forms, are each distinct, a feature common to many primitive insects.

The *ti* trees were swarming with buprestid beetles and other insects. I could gather them literally by the handful, and in one of the ant nests were exquisite little beetle guests. One of these had golden trichomes on its thorax so brilliant that when the beetle was lying partly embedded in the earth I was attracted to it by the sun shining on these little bunches of hairs.

Froggatt gave me room in his laboratory, and offered to store the ant collection while I was away. Besides Froggatt and Gurney there was a small galaxy of entomologists about Sydney, in the museum and in the Department of Agriculture, and amateurs — one of these, R. J. Tillyard, lucky enough to hold a £400 Mac-Cleay fellowship. He lived at Hornsby and was especially interested in aquatic insects. He had built himself an octagonal greenhouse with pools, deep and shallow, with streams and waterfalls, in which he could keep his pets alive while he studied them. Wheeler had told me that Tillyard was the most brilliant of the younger entomologists of that time.

He was not very well; in fact, he was something of a hypochondriac. While collecting, he carried a huge knapsack full of bottles and cans, and once, when we were climbing a hill toward a railroad station, he stopped and very sadly told me, "I don't think I can make it." That was too bad, but I walked slowly ahead, picking up things here and there, when suddenly the engine at the station whistled. I hurried toward it, but was completely outdistanced by Tillyard, who spurted past me and up the hill, his gear clanking like all the pots and pans in the kitchen.

When he collapsed into a seat in the car he said, "I shall probably be ill for a week on account of this," but that evening in Sydney he was well enough to sit with me and talk insects till midnight.

Most of the time was spent in eucalyptus forest. It was cicada season and the sound of what seemed like millions of them made such a roar in the air that we actually had to raise our voices to be heard.

One evening while I was in my hotel room, there were some sharp raps on the door, and two young Australian officers entered with stern looks on their faces. They asked if it was I; when I admitted it, one of them ordered — and he didn't mean maybe — "You tell us what *Polyrhachisarten* means in English."

During the whole trip I had corresponded infrequently with Dr. Forel, who usually wrote me in French on postcards. But I had told him that I had been under suspicion as a German spy while in Fiji. That appeared humorous to him, so in a waggish way he wrote to me afterwards in German. Polyrhachis, from the Greek words "many spines," is a genus of extraordinary ant found throughout the tropics and noted for the silk-spinning habits of the larvae. There were none in Fiji, but he wrote now hoping that I would find many kinds in the Solomons, and had used a mixture of the scientific name and a German word. It was a little funny to me, but not to the two censors. I asked them if they had looked at a German dictionary and was informed, "Every bleeding one in Sydney." My explanation was satisfactory, and they sat down and had a drink with me.

I had picked up a little folder on the Solomon Islands in which visitors were described as most unwelcome. There were no hotels in the islands, and the traders and planters were said to be too busy to answer tourists' silly questions. One of the managers of the Burns Philp Plantation Company had also thrown cold water on my trip with "There are no hotels there, and you can't stay at our plantations." He explained about a couple of anthropologists who had stayed with natives studying them and had to be disinfected before his manager would even allow them near the plantation.

Despite this discouragement, when the *Mindini* sailed, four days late in the middle of May, I was aboard for the twelve-day voyage, headed for what was to me really the unknown, although

I had read that romance of early geography, the discovery and subsequent loss of the Solomon Islands.

In 1566 Mendaña, the Spanish navigator, sailed from Peru westward on a voyage of discovery and in 1567 came upon this group of islands. The largest he named Guadalcanal after his home town. The fascinating journal of his pilot, Gallego, describes a number of the islands and the "Indians" who inhabited them. The Spaniards dealt with the natives in the manner of the day: when they were presented with a pig in one village they took all the canoes away because they were not given two pigs. At some places they were received in a friendly manner, and at others greeted with showers of arrows.

In fact, the exploration consisted largely of a series of fights, though at places they were welcomed, and once even were presented with the roasted arm of a boy, sent to Mendaña. At other times they might have been presented with roast Spaniard also, because a number of Mendaña's men were captured, killed, and eaten.

After cruising about and endearing themselves to the natives by burning down canoe houses, which they considered heathen temples, they returned to Peru and Mendaña announced his discovery. He named the group the Islands of Solomon, because he had recognized their possibility as an agricultural colony, which he knew would not interest his people — but he hoped that by so naming them the Spaniards would think that this was where Solomon had got his gold.

It was twenty years before he was able to sail again for the islands, which he did with a fleet of four ships and four hundred colonists. They headed for San Cristoval, but instead came upon the Santa Cruz Archipelago, which they thought was part of the Solomons — a modern anthropologist would have known at once that this was not so. They founded a colony, and there Mendaña sickened and died.

There was constant fighting with the natives, and much loss of life by disease, so eventually the colony was abandoned and what was left of the group sailed away and arrived at the Philippines — one fourth of the number that had started.

At this time Drake and other English navigators were making an honest penny by seizing Spanish galleons and raiding Spanish territory, so the governments of Peru and of Spain hid all records of the Solomons, and they remained a lost archipelago for two hundred years.

Then news of it leaked out and other navigators — Dutch, English, and French — started looking for this land of promise, eventually refinding it, and incidentally discovering other Pacific areas.

For years the group was visited only by a few explorers; later traders came, bartering for pearls and some of the native produce, but chiefly for the purpose of blackbirding — that is, getting natives aboard ship and taking them as forced labor to northern Australia. In 1893 some of the islands were taken over by Great Britain; others were later assigned to Germany. Blackbirding stopped, head-hunting and cannibalism were frowned upon, and planters and traders moved in, among them the two large firms of Burns Philp and Lever Brothers, who secured thousands of acres of land to be turned into coconut plantations.

My fellow passengers on the *Mindini* were an interesting assortment: my roommate, a Pitcairn Islander, swarthy and taciturn, but reputedly a good artisan, as many of his people are; missionaries, old-time South Sea sailors and traders returning to their work, a Nova Scotia seaman on his first trip out, and government officials. Many of them had lived years in the islands; some of them had good imaginations, and they plied me with the usual misinformation given to "new chums" in the Australian region — delightful tales, of cannibals and head-hunters, green hard-shelled ants an inch long always walking singly on the branches of bushes, frogs with eyes as big as saucers, and an assortment of incurable and highly painful tropical diseases.

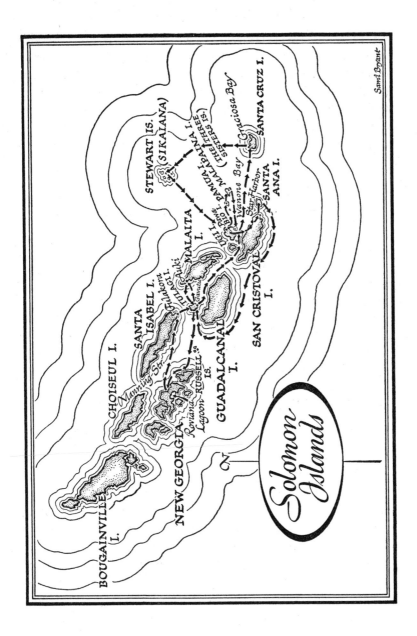

Solomon Islands

BOUGAINVILLE I.

CHOISEUL I.

SANTA ISABEL I.

Manning Str.

NEW GEORGIA I.

Roviana Lagoon

RUSSELL IS.

Tulagi I.
Talakona
Gavutu

GUADALCANAL I.

MALAITA I.

Ugi I.

Ulawa
Bio I.
Ivanore Bay
Star Harbor
SANTA ANA I.

SAN CRISTOVAL I.

PAMUA I. PAINA I.
(THE THREE SISTERS IS.)

STEWART IS.
(SIKAIANA)

Graciosa Bay

SANTA CRUZ I.

N

Sam¹ Bryant

One of the passengers was W. R. Bell, resident commissioner on the island of Malaita, the wildest of the islands. He had lived there some years, and the two fingers of his left hand had been lost before in the Boer War. In fact, he was quite healthy-looking for one who had been through his experiences, described by the others. He confirmed some of their stories — with reservations — and greatly reduced the size of the frogs' eyes. Furthermore, he invited me to stay with him.

At midday we anchored in the harbor at Tulagi, and were met by the doctor, who came out in a whaleboat with a crew of natives wearing red caps and *sulus*, one with a necklace of cuscus teeth, and others with armbands of plaited grass very tight around the biceps. There were native constabulary with them, distinguished by red belts. When the doctor had cleared the vessel a crowd from shore came aboard.

There were no ice machines in the Solomons and it was only once a month that a cold drink was available. Now, available it was, until long past midnight. An affable, friendly group they made, real pioneers in a new country, and before the very late party broke up I had received invitations to stay at more plantations and trading posts than there would ever be time for.

Governor Barnett invited me for lunch the first day. The government house in Tulagi had been built by a former governor, Mr. Woodford, who was interested in natural history, and had planted numerous flowering hedges. These were covered with wasps, and sipping nectar from the blossoms were two giant bird-winged butterflies (*Ornithoptera victoriae*), velvety green and yellow, and among the most magnificent of all insects. I had seen them listed at one hundred and ten dollars a pair, but had never owned one or seen one alive. At catalogue value, the two I picked off the bush amounted to as much as my round-trip ticket from Sydney to Tulagi. A number of species had been named *woodfordi*, but I did not realize that they had been named for this first governor of the Solomon Islands until Pugh, the government treasurer (as well as postmaster general) seeing my insect net, asked how soon was I going to "tike over."

After lunch Barnett's son took me for a walk in some near-by woods. The first catch was a little boa about eight inches long, coiled in a bush. There were fruit pigeons and white cockatoos, while each coconut palm housed some of the brilliant red coconut lories, and in the cleared spaces were little flocks of mynah birds on the ground.

Then the inch-long, green, solitary ant showed up. It was not an ant at all but an elongate tiger beetle with its elytra coalesced so that it could not fly, but walked slowly along on tree trunks or bushes.

Spiders, metallic blue and red and bearing spines, were everywhere. Froggatt had been to the islands some time before, studying a species of Hispid beetle that had been doing considerable damage to coconuts. It had proved to be a new species, was named after him, and was generally known in the Solomons as "the bloody Froggatt beetle." He had collected a few ants, one of them a large, slow-moving, heavily chitined, stinging one, also named for him (*Ectatomma froggatti*). This was in evidence everywhere, and there was a nest of the silk-spinning ant (Polyrhachis), in a long, flat web under an agave leaf, the first of this type of nest that I had seen since those in Palestine in the valley of the Dead Sea.

Around the settlement were quantities of the great flame-trees, which served as natural bait for the giant rhinoceros beetles whose larvae do so much damage to the coconut palms. The adult beetles congregated on these trees, where they could be picked off like so many plums, dumped into a receptacle, and destroyed with oil.

My reserve collecting gear was placed in a government bonded warehouse and the next day Bell, Captain Campbell (chief of native constabulary), and I boarded the police launch for Malaita.

We passed Gavutu, the headquarters of Lever Brothers — small islands off shore, most desirable real estate on account of the protection given against attacks of natives from the bush. A narrow passage, sometimes less than two hundred yards across, took us — past a group of naked natives fishing with spears — to the open sea, where thirty miles of sailing and steaming brought us to Auki, Bell's residence and government headquarters for the island.

After tea, Bell and Campbell had some shoptalk to do, so I took my knapsack and insect net and started toward the edge of the clearing. When I had gone no more than a hundred feet, both the men started shouting at me, "Come back!" I went back, and Campbell spoke quite sternly.

"I don't know the dialects of these people," he said. "Neither does Bell. If someone swings on you with a tomahawk, who the hell could write notes to them?" If I wanted to go to the edge of the forest I must take two guards with me. If I went in out of sight it must be four; and if I went more than a hundred feet I must have a dozen soldiers. Otherwise I could not stay on the island.

There was an average of a murder a day among the natives, and a white man was killed every once in a while. Campbell was quite serious about it. He told me that the salt-water people were all right, for a distance of about two miles to the east and five miles to the west; but the danger was in meeting passing natives from the bush. There was little open fighting, mostly attacks from ambush. At first I thought Campbell was trying to impress me, but after seeing some of the bush people I was very content to have constabulary along. Besides, the guards made excellent collectors.

After Campbell had left, Bell, with some of his soldiers, took me to a village, Bushrata, first passing the grave of a German who was murdered there four and a half years before while recruiting native labor. The grave was planted with crotons, and well tended by the government people. Then we marched inland following a small river, the Kwaibala, over a muggy trail, which got dryer and better as we climbed the hill.

The constabulary had been selected from different islands; in our group of twenty were represented various tribes from east and west, including black ones from Bougainville — so black that tattoo marks did not show, and they ornamented themselves with cicatrices, made by making incisions in the body and then rubbing the juice of poisonous plants in to make them swell into large and permanent bumps. To have too many boys from the same tribe was to invite them to gang up on the others and on the white chief.

The natives were much interested in watching me pick up specimens here and there — ants, beetles, spiders, tree snails (some of the snails were large and pearly white), gigantic grasshoppers, and the praying mantis. Polyrhachis nests were on nearly every tree. This area being fairly safe, and the police boys so interested, Bell let them do a bit of collecting for me, and I heard my first *bêche-la-mer* spoken in earnest.

"This small fellow good fellow?" referred to a beetle, and when I unknowingly grasped a nettle tree, I was told, "Him fellow tree him savvy bite'm man."

Loboy, the chief of the village, stood in a native taro patch — not glad to see us. He wore a trade hat, and a belt around his waist, the latter interesting because a trader had brought condemned German Army material to sell to the natives, and it was odd to see Loboy standing there clothed in nothing but a belt fastened by a large brass buckle inscribed *Gott mit uns*. He also had a woven armband with a clay pipe in it. The pipe was empty, as he demonstrated to me by putting it in his mouth and blowing loudly through it. A stick of trade tobacco was accepted with no expression. He had a quid of betel nut, with leaves and lime, in his mouth, tucked up on the inside of his right cheek. He spat from time to time and then chewed a bit more until the saliva

was the proper vermilion color. Then he turned, still expression-
less, and led us, limping on one bad leg, to his village. This consisted of a half-dozen huts, the largest belonging to the chief, and
built on an elevated platform with a roofed-in area in front. A
bow and sheaf of arrows, three spears and a woven basket were
all the furniture in sight.

Farther on was a cluster of three more huts. We saw some
people in front and shouted at them, but when we got there, no
one was in sight. An old woman informed us that everyone was
away working in the gardens, but Bell insisted that they were in
the house and ordered them to come out. They did, a squalid lot
of diseased people. Through an interpreter Bell talked with them
a few minutes; then they turned their backs and unceremoniously
entered the house again, apparently frightened at our visit.

This village was typical of hundreds on Malaita. Placed usually
on elevated areas for strategic reasons and separated one from
another by deep valleys, they associated little with each other
except in the matter of feuds, which occurred continually. Each
little district had its own dialect and could not understand that
of even its nearest neighbor. This resulted years ago in their
adopting the lingua franca, *bêche-la-mer*, when they spoke to
each other.

The chief of our constabulary was Alec, a Choiseul Islander
and a "brass hat" if there ever was one. A patrol sleeping on duty
might be let off with a reprimand, but Bell told me Alec recommended death for anybody caught laughing in ranks. It was he
who through a knowledge of several dialects and *bêche-la-mer*
was our official interpreter. He developed a line about me, informing the natives that I was a different sort of person — not a
trader, not a missionary, not a government official, but I would
pay good tobacco for worthless creatures of the woods. He invariably introduced me as follows:

"Him big fellow master, he 'nother kind; he no catch'm coconut, he no belong sekool, he no belong gov'ment. Suppose you

find some small fellow along bush he no good belong kai-kai [eat] you bring'm he come, him pay you along tambac."

Alec's explanation and my curious habit of picking up things resulted in action, for next day there appeared at Auki practically the entire population of the village, seemingly much more at home than when we had called on them in their bailiwick. They carried bamboo tubes and poured out from them small lizards, spiders by the cupful, insects, and land shells, taking their payment in pressed sticks of tobacco that were the chief medium of exchange at the time, and showing no emotion either of thanks or dissatisfaction. Then I took the group and played for them some Billy Williams songs, his laughing ones, on Bell's phonograph. When Williams laughed they understood it and some of them almost smiled, themselves. Later, when I got to know them better they would come down and one of them would speak for the party: "We want to hear him fellow sing-sing."

Bell and I visited little villages one by one, till eventually there was scarcely a day when natives did not come in with specimens. When I collected, with my army, military discipline was relaxed. The boys would decorate themselves with forbidden ornaments, flowers and sticks in their hair, sticks through their noses and anything that attracted their attention shoved through the already prepared ear punctures. There never were more enthusiastic collectors. Not knowing what it was all about, they got a thrill out of it, and tried to make fun of my ignorance. Whenever big monitor lizards would hurtle through the bush (and hurtle they did, knocking down small bushes and rattling through the leaves) the boys would sink to one knee, rifles ready for action, and then look over their shoulders at me to see if I was properly impressed at their readiness in face of danger. It was not so impressive as if I had not already known that things that hurt you in the jungle are little apt to make a preliminary noise.

After I got to know him, Bell was a pleasant host, but he had lived long in the tropics and through frequent attacks of malaria had acquired what is generally known in these countries as "a liver."

In the morning he was grumpy. His remarks were "Yes" and "No," till I learned not to give him any excuse for making such answers. After lunch he would mellow a bit, and with afternoon tea he became pleasantly human, laughed at my jokes (they were old American ones but new to this part of the world) and told me about his experiences both in the Solomons and before that in the South African war, where he had once been tried for cowardice, and later on given a medal for valor. In the first episode, he said he had retreated with a small group of soldiers after trying with one pompom gun to take a hill which had been secretly occupied by two companies of Boers.

After dinner he would reminisce even further. Once he told me the story of the stomachers in South Africa. Trying to reduce the amount of enteric troubles the soldiers were having, the Army issued woolen abdominal bands with instructions for everyone to wear them. This was lived up to so loosely that the colonel made an inspection one morning, asking each soldier if he had his stomacher on. The invariable answer was "No, sir," and the invariable reason given was a far-fetched lie, till one of them replied to "Why do you not have it on?" by saying, "Colonel, I find that if I have it on I get lousy."

"You mean to say you are not lousy?"

"Yes, sir."

The colonel turned to his orderly. "Arrest this man. Charge him with insubordination and insolence to a superior officer. *I* am lousy. Lord Roberts is lousy. And *he* dares to say he isn't."

Bell had been on vacation in Australia for several months and it was necessary for him to make frequent trips of inspection. This was a godsend to me, because going with him I reached many places that otherwise would have been impossible, and in each village Sergeant Alec recited his formula about me, which always resulted in specimens of one kind or another being brought in.

At one place we would be greeted vociferously, at another completely ignored; natives squatting or sitting on a palm log would stare past us, as a caged lion will stare past a zoo visitor. Some of the islanders had been carried away years before as blackbirds to what was practically slave labor in Australia and other islands in the Pacific. But this was eventually stopped by law, and they were returned home, where they immediately resumed their old way of life. We found one curious thing. Those who had been in Australia talked, of course, *bêche-la-mer;* those who had been in Fiji had learned some Fijian. When I shouted a Fijian greeting, there would often be an elderly man who would immediately jump up to talk, proud of his knowledge of another language. I was actually able on one or two occasions to introduce Bell to a chief who had hitherto ignored him.

Usually before any government business could be undertaken the chief was presented with his quid of betel nut. Not many orders were given, but Bell did try to get them to keep the villages reasonably clean, and he frowned heavily on their feuds with each other.

Most of the excursions we made were strictly official on Bell's part, though we made a treaty by which we could stop and collect on the outward journey until it was time to return, when Bell would take charge. One of his boys was exceedingly religious and annoyed Bell no end, for when Bell scolded him — which was necessary from time to time — he would always look benevolently at the Commissioner and say, "Me pray along you, Mr. Bell." The boy talked to me about my soul, also. On one occasion, when I was about to become leader, Bell quoted, "Lay on, Macduff, And damn'd be him that first cries, 'Hold, enough.' " I asked the boy if he knew who had said that in the Bible, and was informed: "I forget who say him, but plenty time I hear missionary tell him."

Ten years before all but one of the Reef Islanders had been converted and joined the church. This one held out steadfastly for his ancestral beliefs. When the visiting missionary had left, the natives met in council and drove the unbeliever out onto the reef and filled him full of arrows, making the island unanimously Christian.

One trip we made out of interest and for pleasure. Less than a mile away from the station was a lake of brackish water in an uninhabited district. We had read about it in the book of the English surgeon and naturalist, Guppy, who had done the first and almost the only intensive collecting in the islands; but Bell had never seen it. In a native canoe, paddled by four boys, we went down the coast, outside the reef for about a mile, and at the place nearest the lake shot the reef in thirty seconds of speed and thrill. Then the canoe had to be carried or towed a couple of hundred yards through a swamp filled with roots and swamp vegetation, the boys remarking, as they tugged, "This fellow place belong alligator."

Had I known what I now know about the salt-marsh crocodile I would have been more apprehensive on this trip.

When we reached clear water and got into the boat we saw two of them, about twelve feet long. One of them was swimming toward us — but apparently thought better of it, for he dived when he saw us. The other was floating, and Bell fired at it and hit it on a second shot. After a lot of thrashing about, it finally sank. The noise of the rifle attracted a solitary native who was standing on shore. In one hand he held a bow and in the other a treasure, Guppy's bullfrog, the world's second largest species of frog — rare in collections and one that I particularly wanted. We paddled over and I asked Alec to see if he would sell it to me. Alec replied, "Of course he sell'm along you. He catch'm along you."

In his village he had heard of the strange big fellow master who paid good tobacco for such things, and he had come down apparently to get some of these frogs before the market was spoiled. Intermediate in size between the American bullfrog and the Goliath of West Africa, it had been known before from the Solomons, but not from Malaita, where we later collected three more specimens.

The lake was afterwards "discovered" by the well-known American moving-picture photographer, Martin Johnson, who, accompanied by his delightful wife, Osa, came to the Solomons some months after I had left. As I told Martin later, I should be famous for having collected a frog on the shore of a lake four months before the lake was discovered.

In the lagoon in front of Auki was an artificial island made on the reef out of coral stone. This, as well as a number of others, was built in the lagoon by the shore people for safety. Until the government came in, the natives were afraid to go ashore except on certain days when there was a truce with the bush people who would bring down vegetables grown in the hills and exchange them for fish and other seafood. Even this was risky, because it was so easy for a bush native to spear a coast dweller and then escape into the hills where the others did not dare follow. Nowadays, the natives do their bartering on the grounds of the government station. Their arms must be deposited in the forest or on the beach before entering the clearing.

From a distance the island looked charming, but on approaching, the charm decreased geometrically; ashore there was none at all. The little shacks were close together, the streets were teaming with natives and crowded with pigs.

A group of three were making shell money. This is made of a shell obtained by diving, and then cut into disks. A hole is bored in the center of each disk by means of a bow drill. The drill, attached to the string, is rotated by the motion of the bow being moved up and down. One old woman was using the drill and two men were baking the disks on a heated rock. Afterwards these disks were strung on palm fiber and had a fixed value as legal tender of five shillings to the fathom.

The canoe house, which was also the men's club and the tabu house, was by far the largest building in the village. Its thatched roof was held by a center and two side poles, and there were three longitudinal beams, each decorated at the end with an old alarm clock — ornamental but not useful. Inside was the official canoe of the village, with a long, high-curving prow and stern, decorated with cockatoo feathers and cowrie shells. On the ceiling hung upward of a hundred baskets, each containing a human skull. These were not trophies, but relics of former inhabitants of the village. There were numerous small canoes on the beach and we saw one man carving the front part of a nearly finished one. I traded some tobacco for a few fishhooks, the lure of shiny mother-of-pearl shell and the hook of tortoise shell, bound together with coconut fiber. Each group of natives has its own design of fish-hook, some of them very elaborate. They are used mostly by the women to catch bonita as well as smaller fish. I presented a couple of European fishhooks, which the recipient put in his hair for safekeeping.

A number of mission societies were working in the islands — Catholic, Church of England, Wesleyan, Seventh Day Adventists, and an organization called the South Sea Evangelical Mission. This last had been founded by a Miss Young many years before in Australia, and when the various natives had been returned to their home islands, missionaries came with them. I remember one man questioning me on America and asking, "Catholic he stop?"

"Yes."

"Weseli he stop?"

"Yes."

"Seven Day he stop?"

"Yes."

"Miss Young he stop?"

Down the lagoon was a mission with a neat church and a native teacher in charge. There were rows of benches. Someone with a memory of old days in Australia, where he had seen cushions in the pews, had reproduced them here by carving them out of the wood. The schoolmaster discoursed to us on religion and took much personal satisfaction in the fact that the bush people near by were in for a lot of future punishment because they paid no attention when he told them "Jesus Saviour belong you."

Religious subjects discussed in *bêche-la-mer* have an odd twist. Catholic priests usually learn the native dialects; the Church of England has a school on San Cristoval where native boys from all parts of the islands are brought and taught one simple native language, Motu of the New Hebrides, which becomes a lingua franca among them. But there are tales of sermons in pidgin English like the following:

"Long time before, Jesus, him pickaninny belong big fellow master along top, walk about another fellow place. One fellow man belong here, plenty debil-debil stop along belly belong him. Jesus him say, 'What name you stop along belly belong this fellow man? Clear out.' Debil-debil him clear out. Plenty fellow piggy-piggy kai-kai along hillside. Debil-debil go along belly belong piggy-piggy. He sing out too much. He go along salt water. He die finish."

Another classic is the story of the Creation. This has been written before, and any South Sea trader could reel it off. I remember it somewhat as follows:

"Long time before, altogether place no man he stop. Him big fellow master along top he look'm no fellow man. He say, 'My word.' He take'm little bit mud, he make'm one fellow man. Name belong him Adam. Adam him stop along one good fellow garden. Plenty kai-kai he stop. Plenty fissi along salt water. But Adam he no sing out along good fellow. Him big fellow master he say, 'Me savvy too much. You want'm one fellow mary.' Close up, Adam him sleep. Big fellow master take bone along belly belong him, make'm one fellow mary, name belong him Eve. Alla time stop along garden one fellow fruit, name belong him apple. Him big fellow master he tell'm Adam 'You no savvy kai-kai him fellow apple.' Mary him look'm apple, tell'm Adam, 'This fellow apple him make'm good fellow kai-kai.' Adam say, 'No. Me got'm fright along kai-kai him.' But mary him talk, him talk, him talk. Adam he fed up, he tell'm, 'Bring'm he come, me kai-kai him.' Then he get'm fright like hell; he hide along scrub. Him big fellow master him walk about garden, he no look'm Adam, he say, 'My word, me savvy too much. You kai-kai him fruit name belong him apple. You take'm bokkis [the native keeps his valuable belongings in a box or chest] belong you, you take'm mary, you clear out.' Adam him clear out. Him big fellow master put'm one stone fence along garden, he put one fellow constabulary, he give'm one Snyder, plenty ammunition. He say, 'Suppose Adam he come back, you shoot him too much.' "

Even official court procedure is conducted in *bêche-la-mer*. In fact, we had a trial on our veranda. A group of natives arrived one day and the spokesman told Mr. Bell:

"Filia him kill'm one fellow Ramafuna belong my village. You take plenty constabulary go along shoot him."

BELL: What name Ramafuna do to Filia?
NATIVE: He no do something.
BELL: You gammon along me. Why he shoot him? He cross with him?
NATIVE: He cross along row.
BELL: What row?
NATIVE: Mara he kill Ramagooa. Ramagooa and Muskoa he relation of Ramafuna.
BELL: Why he shoot him?
NATIVE: Along row. Muskoa he shoot Gambata.
BELL: Why he shoot him?
NATIVE: Mara he poison father belong Filia. [Poison in this case means witchcraft, the suspicion of which had started this feud.]

Bell told them to go back to their village, and return in two days.

Meanwhile, we went into the interior, across the first coast range and up the crest of the next, a steep climb, part of the way along a rocky stream bed. The top of the hill had been used by generations of natives for gardens and there was little big timber left, but plenty of small trees and bamboo thickets. There were two women working in the garden, one dressed in a short apron and the other in a pair of shell armbands. They knew one of our soldiers and chatted from a discreet distance. When I opened my camera they disappeared into the bush. The last time this village had been visited was when Dr. Deck of the mission called; the inhabitants flourished spears and spat upon him — betel nut spittle, too. But with our dozen soldiers with loaded rifles nothing like this happened to us.

On the way back we had lunch in a delightful cool nook near the road, alongside a bamboo in which water was piped down from a near-by spring. It was here that I saw my first "lace-trimmed" frog (Ceratobatrachus), almost putting my hand on it at the base of a tree. It was rich vermilion and black, with a sharp pointed head, and skin developments looking like fine lace along the edge of the body and the legs. This frog is interesting because it is the only member of its family, and the only frog that has teeth present in both jaws of its large mouth. I tapped the mouth with a straw which it grabbed so firmly that I was able to swing the frog back and forth. At different times I had more than a hundred of this species in the collection, no two ever the same in color or pattern; they were green, orange, brown, black, and yellow.

When the day for the trial came, I sat crosslegged near Bell and listened to the evidence from Filia, who had shot Ramafuna, and to about fifty natives representing both factions.

The story was substantially the same as the one that had been given by the accusers on the first day. I wondered how Bell could decide it. There definitely had been a murder, but it had been occasioned by another, and that by still another, and it all went back to a witchcraft case. It seemed hardly fair to hang the latest of a series of murderers when the others had gone un-harmed.

Shaking his fist at the accused, Bell demanded that he and his village give four pigs and six fathoms of shell money to the other group; then, still shaking his fist, and raising his voice, he promised both sides that the next time there was a killing he would bring his soldiers in and shoot the murderer.

Both parties seemed satisfied with Bell's judgment, but before leaving, one native suggested, "Me like hear'm sing-sing," so I played a half-dozen raucous records on Bell's gramophone, and a nice time was had by all.

We heard later that the pigs were duly turned over, and that both groups had a big feast together, evidently terminating what had been a long feud.

Each evening after dinner I had a stock remark to make to Bell, "Tomorrow, sir, I am going to take you across Malaita."

Previously, a missionary had crossed the island at one end, a very narrow place, but nobody had ever been in the interior of the main part. One evening, as I repeated my invitation, Bell tired of the joke and said, "All right. If you can get transportation for us and twelve police boys, to the other side of the island, we will walk across from there."

Exhilarated, I dashed to the chief of the near-by island, which had the largest war canoe, and arranged for the trip. But Bell said, "Not *that* kind of transportation! If we are to walk across the island, you must get me to the other side in luxury." This put an end to my hopes.

Leacock, a trader and planter who had been recruiting on the north coast of Malaita, came into the harbor. He had a dozen natives aboard, boys mostly from the wilder part of the island. Coast natives, who find that they can just let coconuts grow, and later pick them up and sell them to the traders, do not care about going as labor to plantations on other islands; but bush boys, having no coconuts and few ways to raise funds for tobacco, send individuals away for the two years of indentured labor.

The procedure of recruiting was as follows: The schooner anchored in the harbor, and a saluting cannon was fired. The recruiter scanned the mountains and the forest for smoke, which was a signal that the cannon had been heard, and that some recruits would be available. When they came to the beach, always accompanied by the chief and the fighting men of the village, the recruiter would go ashore in his whaleboat, sometimes being covered by a companion in another boat carrying a rifle. The usual bargain was made, and for each recruit there was given "a case, a knife, an ax, and a parcel." The case was stick tobacco, and the parcel a red bandana handkerchief wrapped around some clay pipes, a box of matches, small hand mirrors, and hand lenses (used for lighting fires). The boys going away got none of this, which was immediately divided among their fellow citizens.

The pay was sixpence a day and food, and the law prohibited the planter — who was invariably also a storekeeper — from paying more than half the wages during the period of work. That was so that just before a boy returned he could invest the other half in a sandalwood chest, some calico, pipes, and other desirable consumer goods. This again was immediately divided among his fellow townsmen, he getting only a share of it, and the chief usually being given the chest. Next time, when the cannon signal was heard, he was very happy to vote "Aye" to having somebody else sent away.

One planter, Mr. Clift of Isabel Island, showed up on the north coast of Malaita and immediately picked up six of what he termed the finest and huskiest laborers he had ever seen. At Tulagi, he bragged about them; in fact, he exhibited them to other envious planters as proof of his prowess in getting fine employees, and hurried them to his plantation. They worked diligently for a few days and then grabbed him, tied him up in some smelly copra bags, took what they thought would be useful from his house and stores, and then, in his best whaleboat, sailed merrily back to their home.

Later it was found that he had recruited the most notorious gang of professional head-hunters on Malaita. The chief, Suinau, as Bell explained to me, had a record of one hundred and fifteen heads (no whites) from various tribes of the island. Head-hunting was a commercial enterprise; the chief of one tribe, angry at another tribe, would offer money for a head, and Suinau was one of several who made a profession of collecting heads at so much each. Rates varied, but the price of a white man's head was usually around ten pounds sterling. Suinau was well-to-do, and held in great respect by other natives.

The news of this *coup* spread around the islands, and soon a group of boys on Guadalcanal tried it with their employer, but with no luck and considerable damage done to them by the constabulary. Those that were not killed were jailed. This news also spread, and one day, when Bell and I were sitting on the veranda, there came up the coast a big war canoe. There are few of these left in the islands, as the government usually seizes them to discourage raids. This was the largest that Bell had ever seen, and he did not know what to make of it. It beached below us; the group got out, depositing as usual spears, axes and other weapons in charge of one of our constabulary, while they came up to the building and greeted Mr. Bell. The spokesman almost floored him when he said:

"Me Suinau. Me good fellow now."

He handed Bell a sack containing ten golden sovereigns and fathoms of red shell money. He was leaving his profession, and depositing these valuables as a bond that he had taken his last head.

He was an imposing, dignified, and perfectly composed man, dressed in a singlet, a *sulu* that had once belonged to the post office department of Fiji, and bangles and bracelets from different parts of the islands, showing that he had had connections everywhere.

Thinking he would not know what I was doing I took a couple of surreptitious snapshots of him, to be greeted with a broad grin and the query: "What name you take'm likeness along me?"

He admired my specimens, which by this time were really an excellent collection of the island's fauna — insects dried and in alcohol, preserved frogs, lizards, toads, and snakes, and mountains of land shells, some kept in fluid to preserve the animal itself, others cleaned and dried.

He even invited me to come back with him to his village. In reply to my joke — "Suppose I come along place belong you, boy belong village kai-kai me close up?" — he said very seriously: "No more. You friend belong Suinau. Boy belong my place he got'm fright along kai-kai you."

While Bell admitted this might be so, he put His Britannic Majesty's foot down on the question of my going. My plans of crossing the island, and of being Suinau's guest, were thus crippled, and I took advantage of Leacock being there to get back to Tulagi.

While I was in Tulagi, news came in through the government wireless station that Charles Evans Hughes had been elected president of the United States. It was a premature election report, before the California votes had been counted, and was sent over the wires both at home and abroad. It was soon corrected in the United States, but the wireless in Tulagi broke down; I left the following day, and traveled for three months full of allegiance to the wrong man.

CHAPTER XIII

Tree Ants

The *Kobiloko*, a little steamer belonging to Lever Brothers, was about to start for the eastern islands, and the supercargo, J. Selmes, got permission from Mr. Symmington, the manager of the firm, for me to travel on her. I signed on as second engineer (because she was not allowed to take passengers) even though I didn't know the difference between an oil rag and a piston shaft. She was a small, 63-net-ton shallow draft boat, with a crew of four Europeans, including the supercargo (but not the second engineer), and sailors from the Santa Cruz Archipelago. The passengers consisted entirely of Santa Cruz natives being returned from plantations to their homes. They sat silently on deck, with the goods they had bought from their accumulated pay — trade chests, and cases of tobacco. One had a miniature satchel, five inches long, tied to his neck by a leather belt. Their ears and noses were pierced, and one had a piece of blue ribbon tied through his nostrils. Several had cheap cowboy-style hats with bands of brilliant red ribbon.

Going along the coast of Guadalcanal, we stopped at each plantation, where I had opportunity to prowl around and collect. Eastward the character of the coast changes; the mountains, instead of being far back from the shore and precipitous, slope gently down to within a mile of the sea. We anchored each night and plantation people would come aboard to enjoy a steamer dinner.

Sometimes we fished from the deck with handlines, usually with luck, while the native crew played cards by the light of a hurricane lamp. They played in *bêche-la-mer* — I heard one of them call the other with "Me look'm king belong you."

On the shore we would see groups of natives, the coast boys wearing short trousers, the bush people without. They always stayed separate from each other.

The Three Sisters are known to the natives as "the Islands of the Dead." As we sailed past we could see great patches of forest that had been killed by some insect pest, and this, to the natives, was the work of ghosts clearing the forest to plant their gardens.

The two hundred and fifty miles of open sea between the Solomons and the Santa Cruz Archipelago were rough, and the trade winds ahead caused the *Kobiloko* to bounce continually. Some of our passengers got sick; one of them, sitting outside my cabin door, had a bad sore on his leg, which he was curing by wearing on his left wrist a string with two pieces of magic wood tied to it.

In a rain and heavy fog, we plugged along at about five knots an hour, and shortly after dark, when the weather was even worse, the captain put the boat into Graciosa Bay, through a narrow entrance but fortunately one free of reefs. There were lights on the shore, and the local white resident, Jack Matthews, who represented Lever Brothers, came out and signaled to us with a torch, showing us the proper place to anchor.

The weather cleared by morning and a dozen little outrigger canoes came out to the ship. They were very narrow, with the central cavity barely wide enough to let a man stand, and were whitened with lime on the inside. On the platform of each were bows and arrows. The men were different from those we had seen before, dressed in short aprons and decorated with armlets of shell and anklets of shell money. Some wore large disks of shell six or seven inches in diameter on their chests, and each man had an ornament of tortoise shell suspended from his nose and covering most of his mouth. With their brown bodies and their bushy, lime-reddened hair, they were a ferocious-looking crowd.

The shore, where not planted in coconuts, was densely wooded, and Matthews's house was on a promontory. He was the only white man ever able to live on the island of Santa Cruz. The natives seemed to have specialized in killing the great, or near great. As we have said, Mendaña, who discovered and attempted to colonize the place, sickened and died there; Commodore Goodenough of the British Navy, and John Coleridge Patteson, the first Anglican bishop of Melanesia, were both killed there.

It was arranged that I should stay at the station for a week and collect, while the ship went up to Duff and Reef Islands to load copra, so I moved into the house with Matthews.

There was forest near by; I went in about a hundred yards, and was busily breaking up a decayed log and bottling its contents when I looked up to find a group of five men beside me, watching me, each one holding a bow and a cluster of arrows. I grinned pleasantly but there was no facial expression on any of them. If they had grinned at me, I could not have seen it anyway because of the large tortoise shell ornaments over their mouths. Finally I got up and walked slowly back to the house, in a dilemma as to whether to walk in front of them (the proper way, showing my superiority) or to walk behind them so they couldn't jab me in the back. Jack told me this group was all right; he explained to them through an interpreter what I was there for, and asked them if I could go to their village. They promised to bring a canoe for me in the morning.

That evening Jack told me some of his experiences on the island. He had had very little trouble himself with the natives, but sometimes two factions would meet on his front lawn and shoot arrows at each other. I asked what he did at times like that, and he replied simply, "I just stay in the house till they stop."

He said they would not bother me unless I offended them, but when I asked what would offend them, he thought a moment and then said, "I'll be blasted if I know."

He told me they had never been cannibals or head-hunters, but regarded the custom with horror. After they got accustomed to Jack, they bothered him very little, though when he first went there they had attempted to blackmail him for cases of tobacco and had once or twice attacked the house, but he and his Solomon boys had driven them off.

In the morning an outrigger canoe came for me, and George, a native of the village, who had been bos'n on the *Kobiloko,* came along with me as guide and interpreter. Along the shore were scattered villages, each walled with stone. The houses were of hewn wooden slabs with roofs of thatch. We landed at one village, and the chief invited us into his house. The door was so low that we could get in only by crawling on our hands and knees. The walls had been blackened by smoke, and it was gloomy inside, but a fire was burning in a square pit in the center of the room, and as my eyes became accustomed to the darkness I noticed four carved poles stuck upright in the ground, holding two shelves on which were a pile of trade pots and native gourds. Arrows were stuck in the thatch for safekeeping, and hanging from the thatch were some highly decorated human heads.

When a notable dies, his head is removed and dried; the orifices are plugged to keep the spirit from escaping, and then the features are remodeled with native gum. The eyes and tattoo marks are replaced with pearl shell. The body itself is buried in a swamp, but exhumed after a couple of weeks, when the shinbones are broken into needlelike pieces with which to point the natives' arrows. The result of a wound from one of these arrows is usually tetanus and death; in fact, Jack had told me that he never had heard of a recovery.

We returned to Jack's place by canoe and in the rain; in fact, during my week's stay there it rained or drizzled practically all the time. The sound of the conch shell, being blown by the native witch doctor to drive away the rain, never ceased. Collecting in a drizzle is not pleasant, and I found myself strongly on the side of the sorcerer, though he and his people were more interested in suitable weather for fishing. Jack had a rain meter of sorts, and had measured four hundred inches of rain the preceding year.

The chief want of the people was tobacco, and day after day they came in small groups to exchange copra — dried half-coconuts, tied eight nuts to a string. A stick of tobacco bought each lot of copra, but one man purchased a kerosene lamp to the tune of two hundred and forty nuts.

The *Kobiloko* returned, and again I packed a sizable collection and took it aboard. I had found nothing strikingly distinctive from the specimens collected in the Solomons, and the fauna was notably smaller, but as in many isolated areas like this, the species were mostly different from those on the larger islands. Nearly all the ants from the forest proved to be new species.

The captain of the *Kobiloko* was an agreeable fellow, with a mildly amused and friendly attitude toward my endeavors. He decided to make an unauthorized stop at the Stewart Islands (Sikaiana). There would be some copra there for him, because there was a white agent living there, but he wondered if I could find anything worth while on these "pancakes."

The sun came out brilliantly and we sailed through silver-topped waves till evening and sighted Sikaiana by moonlight. The four islands that composed the group showed up as low, dark patches. There is no anchorage there, so we lay to until morning, and then the supercargo and I went ashore. The steamer was to sail slowly back and forth for the day, and pick us up again at night.

The island group is surrounded by a reef. The tide was coming out and water from the lagoon surged through a pass about thirty feet wide and tumbled in a broad cascade over part of the reef. We could not get our whaleboat over this torrent, so we beached farther down, where the resident trader, Mr. Skovböye, met us on the inside of the reef in a little dinghy fitted with an outboard motor. He took us to the village while our native crew, with the whaleboat heavily loaded with trade goods, waited for the tide to change so that they could get in.

Sikaiana is one of the last holdouts of Polynesians who have had little or no contact with the outside world. There were about three hundred of them living on the island, most of whom were on the beach to greet us, and followed us to the chief's house. They were comely and well-built, with no malformations visible, with clean skins, straight hair, and few ornaments except tortoise shell rings. They wore two of these, one on each side of a ring made of English shillings skillfully flattened and bent to fit the finger. The men were tattooed in an elongate pattern from the shoulders down the arms, and the women down the thorax and abdomen and on the thighs. Some of the men looked slightly Mongolian, an appearance accentuated by mustaches and by conical hats made of straw.

I was told that after the birth of a baby, a council was held and it was decided whether or not they would let it live. As there is little on the island except a few trees, a large population could not be supported. They showed me a baby with a sore nose and asked me frankly if they should let it live. I said I thought it would get well.

After a short conference in which I explained that I wanted all the insects and lizards they could find, I started collecting, holding my insect net in one hand, while the other was full of children's hands. They tried to put their arms around me, and others hung onto my coattails — the most affectionate group of strangers one could imagine. They were friendly with each other, too, and walked hand in hand or arm in arm. One tiny tot, evidently realizing that I had other uses for my hand, drove some of the children away and completely adopted me. Her name was Kai-ipi, and I was told that she was the daughter of a recently dead chief, and as such had considerable authority over the other children.

A couple of times she disengaged herself from me and danced

— evidently a war dance, putting out her tongue and making grimaces as horrible as her pretty face would permit. She advanced, stamping the ground and holding her arms out in a threatening attitude, sometimes pretending a picked-up stick was a spear.

The day was more of a visit than a collecting trip, but the children did bring in numbers of lizards and a few small weevils, which, added to the ones I picked up when I had a hand free, made a reasonable showing for such a short time.

Kai-ipi was dressed only in two tattoo lines around the base of each finger. I gave her a large bright red silk handkerchief, one of those I carried to wipe my eyeglasses; she tried it around her neck, around her knees, tied to her wrist, and even put it, temporarily, around her waist.

The natives live mostly on coconut and pandanus nuts, taro grown in a swamp on an adjacent island, and fish. They made toddy, and also a sort of molasses, quite palatable, from the seedling coconut.

No missionary had ever been permitted to live on the island and the devil-devils and their tabus were the law. Apparently everything, except a few personal ornaments, belonged to everybody, and I saw one most unselfish and generous act. A boy in his early teens brought in half a dozen lizards; after pickling them I pointed to my little stock of trade goods — tobacco, some beads, and a bolt of white calico. He pointed to the calico, and when I tore off enough for a *sulu*, he took it with a smile of gratitude and without looking behind him passed it back to his little sister. She took it, tied it on, and the two walked away together.

As we sat on a coconut log, the natives admired my pipe, one of those which Charlie Caldwell had given me; they wanted to exchange theirs for it. That bargain having fallen through, one of the men pulled it out of my mouth, took a puff on it, then passed it to the friend next to him, who repeated the process until finally it reached me again. When they showed signs of passing my pipe around again, I tapped its stem and said "Tabu," after which no-body would have thought of using it — except Kai-ipi, who had my special permission and took puffs prodigious for a nine-year-old, looking a little superior at the rest with their clay pipes. At home I give very little smoking material to nine-year-olds, but here, having seen a mother with a baby in arms give it a couple of puffs from her pipe, I had no reluctance in sharing mine with Kai-ipi.

It was a wonderful day, though there were a few awkward incidents. One of the natives turned his face up to me, and I, thinking he wanted to whisper, bent over and received a native kiss — that is, he rubbed my nose with his, the first time I had seen this done. His nose was very coconut-oily.

A couple of men had been on boats and learned a smattering of English, and had their names tattooed across their chests, some of the letters, as usual, upside down. One of them showed off by informing me: "Me savvy too much. Jesus him devil-devil place belong you."

In the morning we anchored at Pawa on the Island of Ugi, where Hall and Dickenson, two traders and planters, invited us into their large, three-roomed house, built of betel-palm wood, pleasantly situated on the beach in front of the broad and deep Selwyn Bay.

Behind the house a fine path through the forest led to the native village of Ete-ete, where we picked up an old hunter and guide, Daniel Butaro, who, when a small boy, had followed the British collector Guppy about, and remembered him. He stayed with me as long as I was on the island, and I found him a very good naturalist. He explained to me that the large apterous tiger beetle, generally considered an ant by the planters, was not an ant at all, but a cousin of some other tiger beetles that he pointed out. He also described a wasp with which he had recently had an en-counter: "Little bit needle stop along tail belong him."

Daniel was quite a historian. He gave me a detailed account, as his father had given it to him, of the first white men that came to Ugi. They were evidently on a whaling ship which tacked most of the day, with the natives following it along the coast, not even stopping to eat. As he said, "Him no kai-kai; him walk about." The boat finally anchored, and some of the braver Ugienses paddled out. "Man stop. Him white. People say devil-devil; him [the native] no savvy other place he stop. He look'm San Cristoval, Malaita and Guadalcanal. Him say 'All place him finish now.'"

A week after leaving Ugi I was on Malapaina, the largest of the Three Sisters Islands. Malapaina had no native population at all; the story is that they had been exterminated long ago by Malaita men. An Englishman, Mr. Ireland, was there with a group of Santa Cruz natives, felling the forest and planting coconuts.

They were cutting immense trees, some of them five or six feet in diameter, and again I had the good fortune of being able to collect arboreal creatures in the very tops of these trees as they were being felled. The tailor ants, Oecophylla, swarmed all over the place and on me, so that during the four days of work there was scarcely a moment that they were not biting me. I was kept busy picking them off my face and neck, squeezing them and throwing them away. Then once, glancing at one, I found that I had squeezed and destroyed another ant, one I had not seen before, a tree inhabitant named Podomyrma. It was a beautiful species that I afterward found nesting in small cavities high in the trees, but that necessitated my examining each ant picked off the back of my neck to see whether it was a desirable species or merely one of the pests.

The highest point in the island was one hundred and twenty-five feet in altitude. Wood lines cut across the island made excellent trails for collecting. We saw few birds, but among them were the red ones whose feathers are used as money in Santa Cruz, and some of the boys were doing a little business on the side by catching them with bird lime, which they made from the secretions of a land mollusk. This is smeared on branches where the birds habitually sit. The birds stick to the branch and the boys pull out some of the red feathers, and then let the birds go.

The so-called "coconut crab" was frequently picked up by the natives, and made good food, though rather rich. While this land crab is called a "coconut crab," I have never seen one eat the fruit. One that I kept alive for several days paid no attention when offered coconut meat.

Next was the little island of Bio where I was thrilled to hear frogs singing day and night. The natives named them from their calls. One was a plaintive *bwai-bwai*, one a shrill *tin-tin*, and a third a severe *kararow*. Back of my host's place there was a swamp, and with the aid of some of the natives we gathered fifty-seven specimens of Kreft's frog (*Rana kreftii*) — not so different in appearance from some of our common North American kinds. This frog ranges from the Santa Cruz Archipelago throughout the Solomons, and as far as New Britain. One wonders how this, as well as half a dozen other species, could have so wide a distribution on islands separated by salt water, which is supposedly deadly to the frog at any stage of its development. The eggs of some might possibly be carried on the feet of birds, but this could not explain how genera like Cornufer could get from the Solomons to Fiji. There were no new species among the eight different frogs collected on the trip, but a great many new locality records.

For a small island Bio was rich in its fauna, and yielded no less than three different species of boas, two of them abundant, and the third, Bibron's boa, rare.

Then back to Pawa where a few days in the forest resulted in a large collection. In one swampy area there were thousands of dragonflies, brilliant with blood-red wings.

Here, too, Polyrhachis was plentiful. These ants never ceased to be a delight to me. Of the one hundred and twenty-three different kinds I found in the islands, seventeen were Polyrhachis. In some places every tree sheltered colonies in nests made of carton or sometimes of pure silk. Carton is paper made by insects from vegetable matter which they chew up and mix with their saliva for the purpose of forming nests. One of them (*Polyrhachis wheeleri*) had a nest on the underside of an agave leaf, nearly all silk but with a few strands of vegetable matter through it, and resembling an inverted circus tent. A colony of a new species at Fulakora was in a triangular nest made of two leaves connected with a sheet of silk; partitions of silk divided the interior into three chambers. When I shook the bush on which this nest was situated, the workers rushed out and grouped themselves on top, each standing with thorax elevated and gaster shoved forward, as though it could sting — which it can't. They waved their antennae and their forelegs and made an appreciable amount of noise when they rushed about, the nest acting as a sounding box.

The fertilized female of these ants, when going out to establish a new home, chews a bit of bark and makes a tiny nest of carton, sometimes in the middle of a leaf, sometimes at the very tip. When the first larvae are hatched, the mother uses their spinning abilities to line the nest with silk, and as the colony develops in numbers, the workers chew up more bark and the nest grows until finally it may be five or six inches in length, and the leaf, which was the original site of the nest, is fastened around it with fine silk.

When a leaf with a nest on it is picked, the ants emerge and rush around. They can bite a little, but otherwise are inoffensive; and I found that when I put the nest on the ground they would soon enter it again, and after that remain in it even when I carried it back to camp. I examined numbers of these nests, preserving some specimens from each, and looking especially for beetle ant guests — without finding any.

A few ant-guests turned up with other kinds of hosts: several of the little beetles with clublike antennae; a fly (*Bardistopus papuanum*) a subgenus of Microdon, whose larvae and pupae, living in ant nests, look so much like mollusks or some of the scale insects, that they have actually, on two occasions, been described as new species of land shells by enthusiastic conchologists. There were three pupae in one nest. I put them in a bottle, and from them emerged the adult flies.

In the nest of the tailor ant was an amazing little moth (*Liphyra brassolis*). The caterpillar is encased with a hard substance, and looks like a miniature limpet, the edges of which adhere so closely to the leaf that the ants cannot pry them loose. The little caterpillar lives well-protected and feeds on the larvae of the ants; when it finally emerges as a full-fledged moth it is protected again, heavily covered with powderlike scales, so that the ants get their mouths uncomfortably full of them when trying to catch and eat the intruders.

Dickenson decided to cross to his place in San Cristoval, and offered to drop me at the mission station at Pamua, which we reached after a six-hour sail, landing through a heavy surf. He got very wet and proceeded to have a chill on the beach — malaria, no doubt. The Reverend H. J. Nind of the Church of England mission came to the beach to meet us, followed a few minutes later by one of the old-time missionaries, the Reverend C. R. Fox.

The settlement stood in a forty-acre clearing, some of which was planted in nuts. The missionaries' frame house had a lawn in front of it and a little church at the side. Beyond was a boathouse and the village of schoolchildren — three dormitories, a dining hall, a school, a storage house for vegetables, and a tool shed. There were forty boys there, brought from all parts of the islands, a mixture of Melanesians and Polynesians. These boys are collected at the age of ten or eleven, and taught at Pamua for four years, when some of them go to a higher grade school on Norfolk Island. When their education is finished, they are sent back to their own islands as teachers.

Fox, a naturalist as well as missionary, knew more about the islands and their natives than anyone I met, and he had introduced new methods in teaching and new ideas in social life. He had organized a secret society among the students, which had already reduced feuding in some of the islands, because the returned mission boys would not attack their society brethren.

He was a good geologist, knew a great deal about the shells, both land and water, and made many visits with me to near-by villages. At one of them, seven miles from the mission, he told me, "This is a particularly tough gang." They were very good collectors, however, and especially good at hunting wild boars, killing them with spears. Fox and I went with them on a hunt; although we could not keep up with them, they shared the meat with us that evening.

A few days later he asked me if I would like to walk to the village again. He was worried and disgusted. He had heard that a day or so after we left, some of them had gone up into the bush to another settlement and speared five women. They had brought back the body of one of them for a feast.

Fox wanted to give the chief a talking-to, but as we walked along the beach we heard conch shells being blown, and he guessed that they were signals, warning the natives of our coming. There was no one at the village except one ancient hag, who told us that everybody had gone into the forest to hunt.

Pamua was a pleasant place to stay; even the rain was not annoying because in the house there was an excellent library, including a good collection of books on the South Seas. Fox was always ready to answer my questions, and to tell yarns about some of his varied experiences. One story he told me was of an archdeacon who had given a sermon on the text: "He that hath two coats let him impart to him that hath none — " Afterwards he was approached by one of the congregation, clad in a loincloth, who pointed out that he had done the deacon's washing the day before, and had noticed that the deacon had two coats, whereas he, the washerman, had none.

The mission boys accompanied me on collecting trips in their off hours. Twenty pairs of eyes are better than one, and the boys considered an outing of any kind a picnic. Loud shouts and squeals announced the finding of a specimen, and Joe Dickenson, who went with us on one or two of these trips, made himself unusually popular with the boys by stumbling over a log and falling head-long into a stream.

These natives have learned to observe. Guppy, years ago, showed that their actual eyesight is no better than that of the white man, but better trained in certain ways. One of the boys pointed at a palm frond, on the underside of which was a fuzzy object a couple of inches across. "Tarantula" came into my mind, but there are no tarantulas in the Solomons. I shot into it, and down tumbled three of the smallest brown bats (*Emballonura nigrescens solomonis*), that I have ever seen. After the boys had pointed them out, I found a dozen more.

Fox and I visited a deserted village, Rafu-rafu, about a mile from the mission. He laid the desertion of the village to a bad epidemic of dysentery, but no one would go near it. The half-dozen houses were in bad repair, but the roofs were still decorated with hog's jaws and flying-fox skins, hog's jaws being considered more civilized than the human skulls formerly used.

The *Southern Cross*, the trim little steamer belonging to the mission, which kept the various stations supplied and also transported the young students and the older teachers to and from the islands, came into the harbor one evening.

Twenty new boys came ashore in the morning. They stood uncomfortably about, self-conscious, eying the older boys and being eyed by them, as happens with schoolboys all over the world. Each one was given his three loincloths, a blanket, towels, and mosquito net, and shown his quarters.

Bishop Wood, the Bishop of Melanesia, was aboard, making a tour of inspection of the missions. The next afternoon, Fox and

I boarded the *Southern Cross* with the twenty boys who were returning to their homes. He and I went ashore at Ete-ete on Ugi, and renewed our acquaintance with Daniel. Before we left, we saw two schooners coming into the harbor, one towing the other, and were told that one of them had aboard Campbell and his police. They were going to San Cristoval to look for the murderer of a white man. A trader named Leacock had been murdered the day I landed at Tulagi, but no one heard about it till a month later. He was unpacking some trade goods on the beach at Keri-keri, when suddenly one of the natives swung on him with an ax and killed him instantly. Leacock had been a good friend of the natives, and was liked by them, but this was a question of honor. Previously, the captain of a schooner had taken home two boys who had served their indenture on a plantation. The surf was bad, so the captain, instead of putting them ashore at the exact spot from which he had recruited them, landed at a better harbor half a mile down the coast. Then he sailed away, but the boys were speared and killed by another group before they reached their own village. Hence the usual money for the head of a white man was offered, and Leacock, who knew nothing of this occurrence, paid for it with his life. Campbell was going out to arrest the guilty ones.

A settee in the skipper's cabin on the *Southern Cross* made a comfortable bed for me, but we burned the light all night trying to keep the cockroaches away, or at least less active. They were robust creatures, and as they tramped across the newspaper on the desk they sounded like something bigger — and better.

I decided to stay ashore at Wanone Bay, where there was a Catholic mission. Fox went ashore with me. Father Moreau met us on the beach, and at the house Father Babineau welcomed us. He had been in Fiji for many years, and to our surprise there was a great bowl of *yanggona* ready for us to drink.

There was a square mile of clearing at the mission, with two good frame houses, one for the priests and another for two Sisters. The church stood between, and to the north was the boys' school. Though the mission was comparatively new, there were thirty boys of all ages, mostly from San Cristoval itself, and fifteen girls in the charge of the Sisters. I saw the girls only in the distance, because the two sexes were carefully segregated in school. The priests told me that one of the girls, only eleven years old, had been married twice.

The Fathers had built their house, the house for the Sisters, the store, the schools, and the church. Besides being carpenters, they had to be boatbuilders, planters, storekeepers, mechanics — in fact, almost everything as well as priests, teachers, and doctors.

The nuns paid a formal call the second afternoon we were there, and I used to see them working with the girls in the vegetable gardens, but the children would scamper into the forest at sight of me. The nuns cooked for themselves and also for the priests, and because of the care that the French always put into their cooking, the menu was varied and good. They lived almost entirely on the country. Each year they planted numerous coconuts, simply to use the hearts for salad, or boiled like cabbage. Dregs of the sacramental wine, which came from New Caledonia, were put into a large carboy and turned to vinegar. They knew how to make even the dry flesh of the bonita, eaten usually only by the natives, into a savory salad. Taro leaves made excellent greens, and even a little watercress had been planted. Fish were plentiful, and there were eggs from a small flock of chickens, maintained with difficulty on account of hawks. Wild pigs would sometimes come and root in the gardens, and occasionally pay for it by being shot and eaten. One reason for eating the local produce, instead of the customary tinned goods, was that the mission was desperately poor, the small income it had previously received from France cut off by war.

The priests preached and taught in the local dialect. Some of the boys spoke a little *bêche-la-mer*, and two of these, Donaciano and Emilio, were assigned to me as guides and helpers. When

Donaciano grabbed a lizard, and in the manner of lizards it snapped its tail loose leaving the boy holding it, he exclaimed, "Head belong him run away!"

Emilio had been purchased from his mother, actually before he was born. At that time she had another baby which, according to native custom, she was nursing although it was three years old, and she had resolved to kill Emilio, the second one, at birth. For a consideration, however, she turned him over to Father Babineau, who had raised him on tinned milk. He was now eleven years old and a very bright boy.

One tot, recently rescued from a feud in the bush where his parents had been killed, was very suspicious of me, but he brought me some lizards, and when I offered him his choice of blue or green beads it seemed impossible for him to decide which he wanted, his eyes wandering from one to the other, and a completely baffled look on his face. He got both strings, and afterward used them as necklaces, a belt, or armbands.

Father Babineau knew and understood the natives. He told me of taking in a small child to feed, clothe, nurse when sick, and educate. One day the boy disappeared, leaving no word. Three months before someone had taken one of his boiled bananas, and he had brooded about this silently, and then seized the first chance to get away, recruiting for a distant plantation.

The papers that occasionally drifted in from Australia sometimes carried articles about disputes between the different missions. The mission stations are usually so widely separated that there is little contact between them, but a mile from the Catholic mission at Wanone Bay there was another, the South Sea Evangelical. The boys would sometimes wander from one mission to the other, and I had read about some snatching of scapulars from the necks of the Catholic boys, and about priests burning the Protestant Bibles. But this I did not discuss with my hosts, nor did I see it done.

For early morning mass on Sunday came numerous natives from

the near-by bush, the men sitting on the floor on one side of the chapel, the women on the other, and I on a chair at the rear. The small, twice-married girl was there, her face marked with shallow burns which had been made with hot cuscus bones — intended to be ornamental. One woman, her skin a mass of ringworm marks, held a baby completely covered with sores. There were all stages of dress in the congregation, from scanty loincloths to a white coat and white lava-lava. The sermon was in native dialect. I was much impressed when at the Elevation of the Host everybody threw himself face down and flat on the floor.

After church some of the bush people came over to my room. One of them had brought in a frog, but I think the main object of their visit was to size up my supply of trade goods. I had made numerous offers, and they all knew that the supply at the mission itself had been badly depleted. In reply to a query as to how my tobacco was holding out, I showed them my "store" of tobacco, beads, hand mirrors, combs, and some elastic belts. One of them, clad only in a ragged and very dirty lava-lava, fixed his sad oxlike eyes on a belt and wistfully asked: "Is there anything in the bush worth that?"

There was indeed, for the next day he brought a large, chunky lizard, more than a foot long, with a thick, bluntly triangular head and a long tail much more slender than the body itself. It was greenish white above, with crossbars of dark brown spots. I did not know what it was at the time, but afterwards found that it lived in crevices high in trees and came out at night to feed on leaves. There was no common name for it that I could get, but it had been described (*Corusia zebrata*) from San Cristoval, and none had ever been found since the original specimen. The native got his pink web belt and so many sticks of tobacco that he went away actually looking pleased.

It is curious how one finds things, or one doesn't; it was many years before this lizard was collected again, but during World War II numbers were found on Bougainville and sent to various

Museums. I recently saw a dozen of them in one large container in the National Museum.

Then I found a delicate, slender, iridescent little sprite of a lizard (*Liolepismo noctua*). This ranges for thousands of miles up and down the islands — and yet I got only one specimen. Other people have found them by the dozens. Tom Barbour, however, when he went reptile collecting in Papua on his honeymoon, also found only one.

There are almost no land mammals in the islands. There are the opossumlike cuscus and a giant rat that occurs only on Guadalcanal. I had heard of this rat; it had been written up in scientific journals, but I could not get one. Later on I found that a specimen had been collected and sent to the British Museum. The Museum wanted more; they wrote to the planters, but despite the fact that Lever Brothers, Burns Philp and other planters and traders have made promises of substantial cash awards to natives to bring them in, none have come in. They may, like other animals, have a very restricted distribution, or it may be that they are on their way to extinction.

Of course, all through the South Seas there is an abundance of bats, the largest of which is the fruit bat or flying fox, which occurs throughout the islands of the Pacific, with different forms in different areas.

Father Moreau was fond of hiking and spent days with me in the bush, going from village to village, where he was always greeted in a friendly way. Donaciano also was a constant companion and became a good collector. Once, when I was making futile efforts with my insect net to gather some fish from a tide pool, he watched me and then went to a tree, returning with half a dozen fruits of the *wutu* (a pod from a tree of the genus Barringtonia). These were a little larger than a golf ball, and when he rubbed them on a bit of coral rock they wore away about as quickly as a bar of Sapolio, gave out a milky fluid that stained the water and irritated the fish — which soon showed signs of discomfort, some floating to the surface where I could catch them. We got a dozen species, of varied color and form, from one pool, but one little fellow, which looked especially interesting, I could not get. It would shoot out from one pool and then jump along the coral and enter another. We did not have enough *wutu* to poison all the pools, and finally a fierce rain drove us back to the house.

News came that Warepe, the chief at Boroto, a village a few miles down the coast, was to give a big feast, an invitation affair, with natives coming from other near-by islands. All day groups passed the mission, some walking on the beach, some in canoes. One large canoe, about twenty-five feet long with high prow and stern and painted red, black, and white, was laden with men and women. They had a pig with them, and one of the men, evidently the chief, sat grandly under an umbrella. We could see the rest of the cargo — spears, tomahawks with carved handles, and grass bags. The paddles, long and slender and curving at the tips, were used also as clubs and as shields. I could not believe this at first, but Father Babineau told me to throw some sticks at a boy standing near by who was holding one of these instruments. I threw a dozen at him in rapid succession — and each time he diverted them with his combination paddle-club-shield.

Next morning Father Babineau and I, accompanied by most of the mission boys and girls and a number of natives from near-by villages, started walking along single file through a cool forest, now and then getting a wetting as a gust of wind came through and shook the dew from the trees on us. There was a constant succession of small streams to wade through, and one sizable river, but this had conveniently disappeared near the beach, as do many of the San Cristoval streams, and we walked across the sand dry-shod.

Boroto was on top of a ridge that formed a peninsula, so that salt water was visible on three sides. To the seven houses in the village had been added another, built especially for this occasion. The ceiling was decorated with strips of red and white cotton cloth, and the food arranged in three dense rows with narrow passages between them. Piled up and hanging from the ceiling were hundreds of yams, taro, seedling coconuts, festoons of *nali* nuts on strings, bananas, and sugar cane, all to be divided and taken home by the guests, after they had been fed for two days here. There were big bowls of pudding made with the rich *nali* nuts. I had thought that the first such bowl I saw was a small canoe — it was made in the same manner as a dugout.

A group of men were strangling pigs; there was a rope around each animal's neck, with a stick in it which was twisted till the pig choked to death. After death, the pigs were put over a fire and turned and scraped for half an hour, and then cut up. The lower jaw was taken first as a souvenir of the feast, and the clotted blood put, with pieces of meat, in a bamboo tube to make a sort of blood sausage. One of my friends from the beach hurriedly shook hands with me when we arrived, and left a generous portion of pig's blood on my hand.

The guests included bush men and coast tribes from all about, and from as far away as Santa Ana, each decorated with his best ornaments: Shell money, cowries across the forehead, armlets made of the shell of the giant clam. There were necklaces of the teeth of cuscus, flying fox, and porpoise. I bought one with Donaciano as interpreter. He told me the terms: "He want'm ten fellow stick tobacco. Suppose ten fellow stick he no stop, he want'm six." One man had in his ear a key ring with a key dangling as a pendant, and another had a padlock in his nose.

Clothing varied from little or nothing to short trousers, vest and coat. None of the married women was completely naked, each wearing, besides her ornaments, a tiny coconut fiber skirt to indicate that she was married. I brought five of these skirts home with me in a letter-size envelope.

The chief stood at one side, a well-built man except for a deformed foot. He wore a hat, a belt of shell money, a cowrie shell beneath each knee, and plain grass anklets. He was holding his newest baby in his arms — the latter soiled with pig's blood from papa's hands — and looking proud but bored.

A new contingent of guests arrived, running up the hill, waving spears and a couple of Snyder rifles, shouting and weaving from side to side. When they reached the top, they executed a wild dance, finished by the hurling of their spears into the thatched side of the house. Father Babineau murmured to me: "Two or three years ago this would not have been funny."

Then he and I retired into a house, a long structure, gloomy and dirty, with rows of sleeping mats on the floor and the remains of fires between them — for the nights are sometimes cool, and most of the people sleep without cover. For dinner we had a tough pigeon which the Father had shot, and which had been roasted in the coals. This, with yams, bananas, and coconuts kept us from being hungry enough to eat the warmed-through pork.

In return for a coconut, I handed our hostess, an old woman, a stick of tobacco. She mentioned that she did not have a pipe, a broad hint; but when Father Babineau suggested that in that case she give the tobacco to him, she thought she might borrow a pipe after all.

We got back to the mission late in the evening, accompanied by natives carrying their share of the food that had been distributed, and lighting our way with torches made of *nali* nuts and grass, rolled in leaves.

I had told Dickenson that my own pipe tobacco, good old Australian Vice Regal, was about gone, and that I would soon need more trade tobacco. At the mission, I found to my delight that the captain of a cutter had come in the harbor during the day and had sent me ashore a supply of both. The trade tobacco is terrifically strong, and requires continual lighting in a pipe.

In fact, when traveling the natives carried a lighted firebrand which was passed from one to another repeatedly.

In my notes I wrote that the mission was ideally located. There were no mosquitoes, no sand flies, and a cooling breeze came every night. This was essentially correct, except that I had miscounted the mosquitoes, and on the twelfth day my malaria barometer (my right shoulder bone) developed an ache. That evening I came down with a heavy fever and severe chills. The floor of my bedroom had a distinct slope to it, so that when I was shaking violently the cot on which I was lying would slide on its castors across the floor. I told the alarmed priests that I was simply playing Buffalo Bill, and taught them the expression, "Ride 'em, cowboy!" But it was not very funny.

Next morning, I was too weak to get up. My worried hosts held a whispered conversation, and shortly afterward appeared with an opened and heated tin of lamb stew and cabbage, taken from their almost exhausted supply of such goods. Of course I could not eat that, but rather rejoiced at being the reason for the two of them having such a delicacy.

Captain Campbell had told me that he would come to San Cristoval and, when he had found the killer he was after, would pick me up for the return trip to Tulagi. When we heard, by grapevine, that he had landed with his police boys at Keri-keri, the priests sent a messenger with a note from me telling him where I was.

The return message from him read: "My boat is on the reef, completely smashed. Perhaps the government will eventually realize that something has happened and will send for me, and at that time I shall pick you up."

As it turned out, I was to rescue the captain and his soldiers myself, because Harry Jacobson, a planter and trader, came into the harbor at Wanone Bay in a small launch. He was on his way to his plantation near the eastern tip of the island and told me that he expected to go to Tulagi himself after a couple of weeks.

Father Babineau, who wanted to go to Santa Ana, came also on Jacobson's launch. This was equipped with a kerosene motor. Something was always the matter with it, and Jacobson would go below and work among the fumes, then emerge on deck looking most miserable, tears streaming from his eyes, muttering, "Who wouldn't sell the farm and go to sea?"

His partner, Henry Kuper, was at the plantation Bulimatarava, near Star Harbor. Both men had native wives. About one hundred and fifty acres along the shore were planted with coconuts. Each day natives brought dried coconut meats on a string — the price, a stick of tobacco for a dozen nuts. The great South Sea question was, "How many nuts make a dozen?" Traders thought fourteen was about right, but the natives preferred the idea of nine.

Kuper and Jacobson were Germans, and at the beginning of the war they had taken the launch and started out to sea, destination unknown even to them, but they had been seen by a British schooner and ordered back. They were provident, hard-working planters, and were let alone by the British during the following years.

A tremendous reef stretched out from the beach, and at low tide one could wander half a mile out. It was the finest reef I had ever seen and I spent days collecting marine objects — brittle starfish, blue stars, and sea urchins with needlelike spines. One common sea urchin was covered with the large spines sometimes used by the natives as nose or ear ornaments. I would try to pick them out of the water, but at the surface the spine which I was holding would loosen and the animal itself drop back. While carefully drawing one to the surface, I put my hand (I thought, very cleverly) underneath it. At the surface the thick spine dropped off as usual, and the animal settled on my hand, spreading the thick spines and bringing into play minute ones that pierced the palm in at least fifty places. I learned about sea urchins from that one, painfully; but a quick use of disinfectant prevented any bad results except a burning sensation that lasted some time.

Kuper's little dog adopted me, and liked to go collecting. It was the only dog I have ever seen that liked to ferret out snakes. Several times he darted into the bush off the trail and seized one I had not seen. One day on the reef I turned over a broad block of coral. There was a Moray eel under it that started crawling away. The dog grabbed it, as he had been grabbing snakes, and before I could get him free, it had ripped his face and ears very badly with its sharp teeth.

The privilege of walking on what had been the floor of the ocean a little time before did not lose its charm. There were giant clams, with their shells slightly ajar. When they closed them, with a loud sharp whistle, it would make me jump. There were Mantis shrimps, with forelegs like those of the praying mantis, heavily armored with sharp spines that clanged on my forceps when I picked them up. There were Holothurians — sea cucumbers or *bêche-la-mer,* which are dried into trepang and sold to the Chinese markets for food. Kuper and Jacobson did considerable trade in these, and told me that one had to know one's sea cucumbers to make anything out of them. There were several varieties; a black one called teetfish was hard and firm and five or six thousand of them made a ton, worth from ninety to two hundred and forty pounds; a white one, called snodfish, took so many to make a ton that it was of little commercial value.

Father Babineau had wanted to go to Santa Ana to talk to the natives, because some of his converts were not behaving themselves properly. We crossed over to what had been, in the past, one of the principal villages in this part of the world. Tom Butler, an old-time trader who had lived there for years, had built himself a house, mainly of ship's wreckage, with ship's doors, portholes, bunks, settees, and even a chest of drawers from some officer's quarters. He was old and feeble, but insisted on entertaining us till after midnight with an antique talking-machine and a few scratchy records whose defects he made up for by playing each one several times.

In the village there were five canoe houses, one of them about fifty by thirty by twenty feet long, containing nine canoes, the largest, an unusually fine one, forty-five feet long and actually supplied with nine seats, all finely carved and decorated. There were trade chests, mostly filled with skulls, and more skulls were hung on the ceiling. Wooden carvings, chiefly of shark's jaws and men, were everywhere. In the street were a number of Tridacna shells as large as pig troughs, though not used for the pigs who lead their own lives with no help from the natives till time came for a big feast.

Santa Ana has been in contact with the outside world longer than most of the islands. Whaling ships were accustomed to stop there, and the natives were the most degenerate of any that I met. I gave a string of beads to a very small boy, and a few moments later his bleary-eyed father brought them back and demanded tobacco in exchange, — an experience new to me because in general natives were very fond of and good to their children. There was no morality at all among the younger set, who wore nothing but a string of porpoise teeth around the waist. The married women wore wisps of skirts, as in San Cristoval.

At Keri-keri we found Campbell with his soldiers. He had preserved for me some rare burrowing snakes; one of them proved to be a new species of Typhlops and the other the second specimen of its kind ever known. But he would let me collect only in the vicinity of the camp, for fear our head-hunting friends might like another one before their inevitable capture and punishment.

Campbell had had a fracas here before, and this time one of his visitors was an elderly man who stood in front of him, put his finger to his cheek, and guffawed, all the near-by natives joining in the heavy laughter. He had a joke on Campbell. A year or two before, the constabulary had surrounded a village on top of a hill and the captain had ordered that no one leave it. This fellow had gone running down the slope, and received a shot in the cheek. His mouth had evidently been wide open at the time, so the bullet went through without touching a tooth. This had to be explained through an interpreter; and again everybody laughed heartily at the native's joke on Campbell.

Campbell had been here a couple of weeks trying to catch the murderer of Leacock — rather, the murderers, because two had been concerned with the beheading — but they had fled into the bush. He had taken into custody the chief and his family, who were kept guarded and looked unhappy. Scouting parties into the interior had failed to come up with the fugitives, who had, by way of defense, dug some holes in the trail, put sharp spearheads in, and covered them with leaves, so that some of the pursuers had had their feet pierced. Each day the chief sent his men out two by two, admonishing them to bring in the criminals. Two nights later, they were brought in, two sullen blacks, and were taken aboard the cutter.

Next morning we sailed for Tulagi, along the southern coast of Guadalcanal. We anchored at night, sometimes staying aboard the boat, at other times going ashore. At one abandoned trading house, there were two rooms, one with a wooden floor, the other with a dirt floor. Campbell and I took the one with the wood floor, leaving the other for the rest, who started doing a lot of murmuring, I thought, about discrimination. Campbell looked in and found that the floor was covered with thousand-leggers, or millipedes. The natives are terrified of these, and Campbell told me that none of them would be able to sleep that night. I went with a pair of forceps, and tossed the pests one by one out of the room, to receive, next morning, the eulogy, "Big fellow master him no savvy fright."

CHAPTER XIV

Lace-trimmed Frogs

ABBOT, the head of the government Labor Department, was making a trip to New Georgia, inspecting plantations and looking into the labor question, as well as the treatment of native workmen. He invited me along, so again I signed on as a ship's officer, this time First Mate, taking regular watches, which consisted of sitting in the cockpit and watching the native sailor at the wheel.

The plantations in the Russell group were like those elsewhere, but the natives differed in dress, the women wearing grass skirts, as all proper cannibal maids are supposed to do, and the men large sunshades, made of plaited pandanus leaves, over their eyes. In earlier days, raiding parties from Santa Isabel would impress the men to fight against Guadalcanal villages, and when the Guadalcanal people made return raids, they would force the Russell people to accompany them, so there were scarcely a hundred Russell people left alive.

At Manning Straits there was a pearling station. The German manager sent us some oysters, large and tough and strong, and some very fine crabs to eat.

As usual I inquired if anyone there had been to Fiji, and one native told me that his brother had been sent there for seven years. I told him I had been sent there for eleven months. This made a bond between us. Fiji, to the Solomon native who knows anything about it, is either a gold mine or a place of punishment.

This one got me aside and complained about the rations they were receiving: "Belly empty, no can work."

I asked him what he expected me, a foreigner, to do about it. He said, "Tell somebody."

"Tell whom?" I asked.

And then he gave the finest tribute I have ever heard given to a people: "Tell any Englishman."

Up the Roviana Lagoon was Lambetti, the home and plantation of the Nestor of all Solomon traders and planters, Norman Wheatley, known as the King of New Georgia. He had come there from Yorkshire many years ago, in partnership with an Australian. The latter was murdered and his head taken. Wheatley bought it back and buried it with the body. When I was there, the two chiefs who had done the killing came in once a week, to visit Wheatley. They were all elderly then, and friends, and they would sit on the veranda and talk about the good old days.

In front of the house was a swampy area that had been reclaimed with coconut husks. There were mountains of these on the beach, and large warehouses filled with trochus shell, ivory nuts, and dried and smoked copra.

The interior of New Georgia is rugged with one mountain peak nearly four thousand feet high. There was good coconut land along the coast, spotted with a number of private plantations, as well as those of Lever Brothers and Burns Philp. A thriving Wesleyan mission station was near us, and Wheatley maintained the common attitude of traders toward mission boys, who would not work for him, and toward missionaries, who, he said, "trade with the natives without paying any government tax."

Daytimes I collected, and at night played poker. I was a guest at these plantations; to offer to pay for food would have been an insult, though, due to wartime conditions, some of the traders really could not afford to have guests for any length of time. But they all played poker, and I was able to contribute a little here and there indirectly.

Then Campbell showed up (he was always showing up at opportune times). It was time for me to return to the States. My

Norman Wheatley
With His Two Former Head-hunting Friends

Bell and Constabulary

stock pile of coins, kept in an empty tobacco tin — there being no bank in the Solomons — was getting shallower and shallower, so reluctantly saying good-by to my good host and his crowd — I had the same feeling of reluctance every time I left a station — I went with Campbell. He was going to stop at Fulakora on the island of Santa Isabel, where lived the Bignells — Mr., Mrs., the nurse, and a new baby — and they had invited me to stay with them. Both Campbell and I wondered how welcome a fellow would be, barging in and depositing himself with the family, but we decided to have a look, and do at least a day's collecting on an island new to me. Then I was to give Campbell a high-sign as to whether I would stay or leave.

As we anchored, and stepped onto the little dock, we could see Mrs. Bignell on the veranda, waving a welcome to us with a towel. Bignell hurried down and we walked up the hill to the house. They had seen the boat at sea, and tea was ready, with real cake — not out of a tin, but *homemade* — and Bignell ushered me into a comfortable-looking room, stating it was ready for me.

It was a nice reception; I decided to stay, as Campbell supposed that sometime a boat would be passing by and pick me up. He sailed next morning and I spent a week collecting along the trail through the forest that reached close to the back of the house.

The Bignells were planters from Australia, and they made me one of the family. One morning Bignell had a "row" with some natives he had hired from near-by villages, and after much talking and shouting, with some Australian profanity on Bignell's part, they took what gear they had and stalked angrily into the bush. Bignell saw that his gun was loaded, and stood it near the door in case of an attack. In the afternoon he accompanied me a short distance on the trail to watch me pick up things, which I was doing at a great rate, when suddenly we heard Mrs. Bignell shriek, "Charlie, Charlie, come!"

We both thought of natives and ran to the house, Charlie picking up a heavy branch to use as a club, and I with my insect net prepared for any eventuality. We were both alarmed, and there was Mrs. Bignell back of the house, still shouting for Charlie to come. She had just found that the baby had sprouted its first tooth.

The fauna of the Solomons is mostly Papuan in character, and in remote times probably spread eastward down the islands from New Guinea. For this reason, each island to the east lacked a few things that were found farther to the west. For instance, in San Cristoval the cockatoo was absent, though abundant on Guadalcanal only forty miles away. When I had first collected on San Cristoval, I had found life tremendously abundant compared to that in Fiji, but collecting grew better and better as I journeyed westward. Whereas in Fiji the last several months of collecting had yielded few species of ants that had not been collected early in the visit, on Isabel in the last week I turned up five distinct species that I had not seen before. It made me realize that I had just scratched the surface of a wonderful fauna.

Birds were abundant in the thick woods near by, cockatoos, king parrots, small lories, everywhere; and occasionally a big hornbill, called *kuri-kuri* from the noise it makes as it takes flight. I shot one as a specimen, and when I hefted it, it seemed like a lot of good meat to waste. Mrs. Bignell took the flesh, put it through a meat grinder, and made excellent rissoles, a great change from tinned goods. Whenever it was possible afterwards, I got another, and we had hornbill rissoles regularly on our diet. A year later, when at home, I read the statement that this hornbill is so dirty in its feeding habits that even the Malays do not eat it. Whether this is so or not, I do not know, but I hope that the Bignells have never come across that same natural history.

New to me also as food in the islands were eggs of the megapode. These birds, related to fowls, but with long legs and big feet, are found in Australia and through the islands to the Philippines and the Nicobar Islands in the Indian Ocean. They travel in small flocks and we could hear their cries continually in the woods. The eggs, about three inches long, enormous in proportion to the size of the bird, are laid in the hot sand along the seashore, and left there to hatch by the heat of the sun. Stejneger has described the megapode as "the first feathered inventor of an artificial incubator." When the young are hatched, they dig out and run away into the forest, where they are able to take care of themselves from the very start, unusual among birds in receiving no parental care. Near some of the villages the natives enclosed the nesting sites with long lines of coral stones, and woe betide any alien who dug them out! The eggs are good to eat when fresh, and we enjoyed many messes of them, hard-boiled or in omelets.

The little lace-trimmed frog was abundant and I gathered thirty of them, hoping to bring them back alive to the States, where live ones had never been seen and where there were only two preserved ones in American museums.

One morning a sail was sighted and a small launch came into the harbor. It had come through five days of open sea from Ontong Java, a Polynesian island to the north, and was carrying an ill Pitcairn Islander to the hospital in Tulagi. After packing quickly I left my good friends and got aboard. The sick man was lying on deck, occupying one side of it. The captain and I shared the other, so it was necessary to put the frogs below. At night the engine became too hot, and in the morning I found all the frogs deliquesced into one shapeless mass.

In Tulagi, Campbell one day informed me that I was to do something for the government in return for what the government and traders had done for me. This was to act as assessor at a trial. Instead of a jury, there are two assessors, one sitting on each side of the judge; and after the case has been tried, the judge graciously asks their opinion, and then goes ahead and does what he was going to do anyway. This time it was another murder trial. The prisoner was from Malaita, as was the grass-skirted woman witness. Campbell was prosecuting attorney. Three men had entered a taro patch and killed a woman. The witness had been there at the time and had seen the killing.

After the oath — "Me promise me speak true good fellow" — had been taken, Campbell questioned the witness in order to establish the fact of death. The interpreter put it into *bêche-la-mer*. She had been working in the garden, she said, when suddenly these men had appeared and swung on her companion with an ax.

CAMPBELL: What name him do?
WITNESS: Him fall along belly belong him. Him die finish.
CAMPBELL: What name you savvy him die finish?
WITNESS: Him no walk about no more.

The accused, clad in a G string, had little to say, but by questioning both the witness and the prisoner it was established that this murder was one of a series that had started with the poisoning or bewitching of a child. The judge asked one assessor (me) if I had an opinion on the case. I pointed out that it was a tribal custom, three men had been concerned with the murder, and only one captured; we had heard that one had died in the meantime and one had disappeared; and that some leniency might be shown. That had nothing to do with the case, according to Judge Bates, who sat there with his proper gown and wig on, and delivered the sentence:

"I find you guilty of murder in the first degree and sentence you to be hanged by the neck until you are dead, and may God have mercy on your soul."

The prisoner was led away and the court dismissed. As I walked out with Campbell I protested at the verdict, and Campbell explained the procedure that would be followed. The prisoner would be sent to Fiji with a sentence of death, but the same envelope that contained this would also contain a plea for clemency. Instead of being hanged, he would probably get some penal servitude, and eventually be restored to his village — a better man, they all hoped.

As I had wandered here and there in the islands I often came upon a little group of five Japanese fishing boats. They were gathering shell and other commodities for their home and foreign trade, and going into every nook and cranny of the coast. The officers came one day into the government house and bade farewell to Governor Barnett, telling him that the islands were delightful; they thanked him for the hospitality of the government, but stated that the climate was really too hot for Nipponese to stand. They sailed away, and I heard rumors of them later off the coast of New Guinea.

In World War II, the Japanese knew the coastal line, and especially the tides, so well that when they wanted to send supplies to their troops they could put them on rafts and calculate exactly when and where the rafts would drift ashore.

The Sydney-bound ship was due. My natural history booty was packed and I was feeling as glum as a man could who had journeyed halfway round the world and then had to leave when his work had hardly commenced. There were so many other islands! And there were also the highlands of those where I had collected only at lower altitudes. But the cash supply was getting lower and lower. Campbell noticed my moodiness and I told him how I felt. He said:

"But you wanted to cross Malaita, didn't you? Tomorrow I am going to Auki to take supplies to Bell, and then I am going around to the north side of the island to have a talk with some villagers there. Better come along."

Auki and the north side of Malaita . . . !

"Would you take Bell and a dozen constabulary and drop us all off at the north side so we could walk across?"

Campbell said he would, and two days later I bounced up the

steps of the government house at Auki and informed an astonished Bell, who presumed that I had left the islands long ago, that I had come to take him to the north coast in luxury, as he had once demanded, and from there would personally conduct him across the island.

He grinned and said, "Right."

It was too good to be true. Campbell took us around the western end of Malaita and dumped us off at the mouth of a small stream, in the early morning. He landed, too, but before he started giving a bit of his mind to the chief, we left. He told us he would round the tip of the island again and be waiting for us at a village on the south side, and cheerfully said that if we didn't show up in a few days he would bring his soldiers in and look for us.

So Bell and I with our twelve trusty (we hoped) constabulary started out, walking some miles on a trail along a stream to a big waterfall. The trail was beside this, and we climbed up the steep hill. In the morning Bell had soberly handed me a Webley revolver, making me feel very much like Dr. Watson — but the Doctor did not have to carry it twenty miles a day in hot weather.

It was necessary for us to make a hurried trip. Harisimi, one of the chiefs in the interior, had once sent a sinister message to Bell, that if he came into his country he would stay there, and Bell really had no official reason for going. When the island had been crossed once before, at the other end, where it was indented by a bay and thus a much shorter walk, the missionary who made the trip escaped being killed only because he had taken a different trail from one where the natives were waiting in ambush for him.

Our trail was uphill and down dale, but it seemed to me mostly uphill, in a straight line as the crow is supposed to fly. We passed one small cluster of huts after another, but nobody was home. Conch shells blowing showed that the natives were warning one another that a contingent of constabulary was on the way. However, in one village there was a man, standing by a hut. He was gaudily garbed and gazed past us with no expression on his face.

I stopped a moment and took a snapshot of him. When it was developed, the picture was recognized by some of the Malaita boys at Auki as that of Harisimi himself. At noon we stopped by a little stream for a quick lunch, where between bites I picked up a few ants with twisted gasters and tremendous spines on the back. They were black except for the mandibles, antennae and tarsi, which were bright yellow; they proved to be not only a new species but a new subgenus (*Crematogaster Rachiocrema wheeleri*).

We were tired at nightfall. The boys cleared a little space on a hilltop for camp. Sergeant Alec posted a sentry line a hundred feet below us, and we made a small fire. Bell then dealt out my rations, one tin from New Caledonia with the label washed off. He dealt out another to himself. Mine proved to be pâté of hog liver, highly nutritious but better served as an hors d'œuvre with drinks. Bell drew something else — I forget what — but I ate half of his and he ate half of mine. The boys brought in additional twigs for the fire, and on them were two workers and a female of another new subgenus (*Polyrhachis Dolichorhachis malaensis*), also with unusually large spines even for this group of spiny ants.

We slept on the ground, covering ourselves with a blanket of ferns that our boys gathered, and I proceeded to have my second malarial chill, shaking off the ferns as fast as they were put on. It was not a nice night and we were glad when morning came to start out again for the last twenty miles of the trip.

The villages nearer the coast that we passed in midafternoon were not deserted like the others in the interior; in fact some of the people came out to meet us. One buxom *mary*, in the altogether, stopped to pick a large leaf and tuck it under her belt, and one man actually grinned in a friendly way at me. He had an unusually fine nose stick, about six inches long and made of tridacna shell. As we smiled at each other I put my hand in my knapsack, drew out some stick tobacco, held it toward him and touched the nose piece, to be astonished by his remark, in excellent Australian, "No bloody fear."

The second day was an uncomfortable one; in addition to being weak from fever I had a blister on my right heel. Bell and I had had many arguments, on many subjects, one of them the superiority of British shoes over American shoes. I had defended the American ones so stoutly that I was not going to admit the blister, but hobbled along to the beach, which we reached at twilight, Bell a good thirty feet ahead of me, making him the first white man to walk across Malaita. I was the first to do it with a sore foot.

It was just a stunt, crossing the island; there was little time to collect, though the things I picked up here and there were nearly all new species. The altitude at our highest point, where we spent the night, was twenty-two hundred feet, and I am sure that the high mountains in the island will produce an almost never-ending number of new and interesting species.

Campbell was waiting for us, and after dinner we boarded his launch and proceeded to Auki.

Some years later Bell and a group of his constabulary were all killed by natives of a village where he had gone to collect a most unpopular hut tax that had been imposed by the government.

CHAPTER XV

And So to Work

At Tulagi nearly all the white population of the islands had assembled. Judge Bates was getting married, and everybody had come for the occasion. It was a grand wedding party the night before the steamer was due. There was a cake but most of the refreshments flowed. The following morning it was definitely necessary to pack, as the boat was leaving early in the evening. I dressed in the white ducks that I had worn at the party and then strolled down to the government bonded warehouse where was locked up all the booty collected in eight months. I had had the key to this building, but when I put my hand in the coat pocket to get it, there was no key, only a piece of wedding cake. This was embarrassing, because the government had trusted me with the key. When I told Campbell about it, he distinctly remembered lifting the key from my pocket and replacing it with a bit of wedding cake, but for the life of him he couldn't remember where he had hidden it. So we had to get a chisel and mallet, break in, and buy a new lock for the building.

Aboard ship there was one bit of unpleasantness: An Australian walked up to me on deck and told me what he thought of damyankee Americans, and me in particular. I did not remember having met him before, and couldn't understand it till one of his friends whispered, "That's Jack. When you arrived here he came aboard the boat that night and invited you to stay with him at his plantation. You did not, and he is very angry." Such was hospitality in the islands.

Never have I felt more disconsolate than that night; never have

I liked a country or a people better — and have liked few so well. At times — many times — the thought of being out on the open sea and away from hordes of insects biting and stinging, crawling over me, and buzzing at me, had seemed better than the thought of Paradise; yet there was always sadness at leaving any of the islands or the friends of different shades.

Australia had not changed much during eight months, and old friendships were continued. When I dropped unannounced into Tillyard's laboratory, full of stories of collecting in the islands, he was looking into his microscope and greeted me with, "Hello, Mann; do you know I have just found out that the venation in the wings of this neuropteron is quite different from the way Handlirsch described it."

Handlirsch, the great Austrian entomologist and paleontologist in Vienna, differed considerably with Tillyard, and one of the latter's ambitions was to meet the professor in Paradise and with him collect the gigantic fossil dragonflies, extinct on earth millions of years, but undoubtedly still living in Elysium, and show Handlirsch definitely where he had been wrong.

Some of my friends were down when my boat sailed; Gurney brought me a live echidna, or spiny anteater, as a pet. Then when we were talking, he on the dock and I on the main deck, a newspaper boy cried his wares at the other end of the dock, and Gurney ran down, bought a paper, folded it, and tossed it up to me on the boat. I was immediately confronted by two young Australian officers, who demanded to examine it. Unfolding it, they found that it was just the latest edition of the Sydney paper, but one of them was so flustered that he asked me if I "had any unwritten letters in my possession." I had none, so the boat was permitted to leave.

There were handshakes at Suva, some more in Honolulu, but the voyage in general was uneventful. As I was sitting in the smoking room one evening, guarding, as it were, my remaining dollar bill, and staying as far as possible from the ship's concert for the benefit of some worthy cause (having nothing to benefit it with), I was accosted by the usual affable girl passenger and asked to contribute.

"How much?"

"Well," she said, "the gentlemen below are giving five dollars each."

I had intended to break my dollar and contribute a quarter, but she made it impossible.

I needed what I had to telegraph for money on arrival. A return telegram came from my mother immediately, and I caught the next train for Helena.

It was wonderful to get home food again, such as only my mother could cook. She boiled and baked all the things that she knew I liked, and I concealed my lack of interest in the sweet potatoes which she served as a special delicacy.

It was a nice homecoming, but interrupted by a sharp attack of malaria. The doctors in Montana did not know much about it — I think less than I did, for I had had it several times and always found that a continued dosage of quinine would check and then cure it. In the Solomons five grains a day had been considered a prophylactic, and it was only due to carelessness that I had picked this up on San Cristoval.

In Boston, Mr. Henshaw had unpacked and arranged the Fiji collection. Some of the Solomon Island material I had checked from Vancouver, the rest I carried by hand. The return is quite as thrilling as any part of a trip, and I started immediately to sort out the ants, dashing into Dr. Wheeler's office every once in a while with one of the bottles marked with an X on the cork, that had appealed to me as unusually interesting in the field. He would look through his hand lens and either grunt approvingly, or simply grunt — the latter at commonplace things that I had not recognized.

The Brueses took me into their home to live, and day after day I prepared specimens to be mounted for study. Tom Barbour opened up the five-gallon kerosene tins and took out the reptiles and other plunder. He would tell me from time to time when something unusual turned up, and Henshaw wiggled his nose and beamed. With a twinkle in his eye he asked, "Weren't there any ants in the islands?" I would trust Henshaw with anything in the world, except my ants.

Then Dr. Wheeler suggested that I get a job, settle down, and go to work. The thought was awful; but all good things must come to an end, even student days. He had a list of positions, one of them instructor in a State University, but I did not have to say yes or no immediately.

One evening when Tommie had gone to the Lowell Institute to give a lecture, I was talking to Beirne Brues about the recent trip. When I plaintively started begging her to stop the natives sticking spears in my stomach, she realized something was wrong, ran to the telephone, called the family physician, and the two of them put me to bed completely delirious. The fever had come back, this time to stay for three long weeks. Dr. Sellard of the Harvard Medical School, an assistant to Richard P. Strong (father of the study of tropical medicine in the United States), one of our best men on malaria, came out, and made some contribution to science out of me. He took most of the blood out of my left ear, more drops from here and there, and these were made into slides for the students to study some of the finest examples of plasmodia (the malaria-causing organism) that even the Harvard Medical School had seen.

After a week I was able to sit up in bed; Tommie Brues brought me a board to balance on my knees, and I went on sorting the insects. The delay in being able to go over the specimens was quite as disgusting to me as was the liquid quinine that Sellard had prescribed. The taste of quinine is not good at any time, but when dissolved and served in tablespoons it is terrific. Tommie thought it could not really be as bad as I said, and Beirne suggested, "Try it out, Tommie. Lick the spoon." He did, and then made a record dash for the kitchen, and returned chewing viciously on a mouthful of dried raisins.

Once, too soon, I got up, not knowing that the non-striated muscles of my heart had been badly affected, and keeled over. After coming to, I crawled on hands and knees back to bed, where I remained for two more weeks, living strictly according to the doctor's instructions, and not telling even the Brueses about this episode. Tommie would have been angry at me and Beirne would have said I didn't know any better.

When I was able to get up and wobble around, and assort ants, life was pleasant again till Wheeler resurrected that idea about a job. The one I intended to take did not commence until October, and B. Preston Clark came temporarily to the rescue. He had heard of some rare and much-sought-after hummingbird moths that might or might not occur in the Bahamas. Would I run down for a month? I would. After registering for the draft I started for Miami.

Washington was on the way, a good place for a stopover to visit friends, and to look over the museum and the zoo. I had, of course, become acquainted with many entomologists and zoologists, and did a couple of days of intensive visiting. E. R. Sasscer, of the Federal Quarantine Board in Agriculture, took me to see his chief, Dr. Charles Marlatt. The conversation was about tropical collecting, and then Marlatt asked:

"Have you ever thought of working for the government?"

I had not; as a matter of fact, I remembered what Wheeler had told me when I said I wanted a research job: "Hundreds of graduates in science this year, just out of college, want research jobs. That will come later. I suggest you take the position offered you in teaching."

So I replied, "Like all recent graduates, I have been looking around for the ideal job."

337

"What do you call the ideal job?"

"Collecting in the tropics half my time and working on ants the other half."

"*H'mmm*. Do you know," said Marlatt, "ever since Pergande died we have been looking for somebody to take over the ant problems of the Department of Agriculture, and to take care of the collection in the National Museum? We are also starting a survey of insect pests in the American tropics in connection with our quarantine work. Would a combination of these jobs interest you?"

I just looked at him.

He said, "I think we might pay you sixteen hundred a year."

For one of the few times in my life I was speechless.

Sasscer broke in: "You know, he's just received his doctor of science degree in entomology."

Marlatt then said: "I think we might offer you eighteen hundred a year. What about it?"

The job and this salary were incredible. The only time I had ever really wallowed in wealth was when, as fly-catching assistant at the Harvard Medical School, I had been paid fifty dollars a month.

I gulped, and then managed, "Yessir."

It was agreed that after the Bahama trip I would return to Washington, take an examination, and commence the highly paid, carefree life of a government employee.

I could not resist telegraphing Wheeler: THE UNIVERSITY'S LOSS IS THE GOVERNMENT'S GAIN.

Then I started for the Bahamas to look for hummingbird moths.